PLAYS FOR
CHRISTIAN THEATRE

T. M. WILLIAMS

MERIWETHER PUBLISHING LTD.
Colorado Springs, Colorado

Meriwether Publishing Ltd., Publisher
Box 7710
Colorado Springs, CO 80933

Editor: Rhonda Wray
Typesetting: Sharon E. Garlock
Cover design and interior illustrations: T. M. Williams

Library of Congress Cataloging-in-Publication Data

Williams, T. M. (Thomas Myron), 1941-
    Divine comedies : plays for Christian theatre / written &
  illustrated by T. M. Williams. -- 1st ed.
      p.   cm.
    ISBN 1-56608-004-5
    1. Christian drama, American. 2. Bible plays, American.
  I. Title.
PS3573.I45562D58   1994
812'.54--dc20
                                         94-1891
                                          CIP

2   3   4   5   6   7   8   99   98   97

To Audra and Nathan Lewis

CONTENTS

NOTE: The numerals running vertically down the left margin of each page of dialog are for the convenience of the director. With these, he/she may easily direct attention to a specific passage.

INTRODUCTION

People sometimes ask me why I write plays. Perhaps the best way I can answer is to borrow a line from *Fiddler on the Roof* in which Tevye says, "I'll tell you; I don't know." I suppose I do know why I began writing plays: it was in response to the need of my church drama group for material that was both funny and Christian. And now that I think about it, I suppose I continue writing for a similar reason — because there is a growing demand for plays as more and more churches discover the compelling power of drama to present the Christian message.

As Jesus himself showed by his lavish and colorful use of parables, metaphors, similes, analogies, allusions, and even jokes, no message, however important (and what message was more important than his?), will reach the hearer's heart unless presented by means of artful communication. Christian drama follows this principle and drives home timeless truths in a frankly audience-pleasing artform.

All the plays in this collection have three things in common: drama, humor, and "the message." You may assume that because these are Christian dramas, the message came first, then I contrived a dramatic vehicle to carry the point and loaded it with all the jokes and humor I could shovel in. Not so. I hope you will not be too shocked to learn that my first purpose was to entertain. Entertainment is the essence of a play; audiences go elsewhere for their teaching and preaching. To do less than entertain the audience that comes to your performance is to violate both their trust and the nature of drama itself.

I am not at all denying the message or the legitimacy of drama as a mode of presenting it. All but one of these nine plays are Bible incidents retold, and the message is inherent in the very nature of the material. I saw my task as taking this material and developing it into entertaining drama for contemporary audiences, letting the message emerge naturally.

You will notice that the four historically set plays in this collection make blatant use of anachronisms. There are two reasons for this. The first and obvious reason is for the humor. I assume audiences will find it funny that a first century Roman soldier works crossword puzzles or a prisoner in an ancient Philippian jail dreams of luxurious room service in a four-star hotel. The second reason is more subtle. To have biblical characters working for newspapers, singing in the shower, discussing life insurance, and doing the kinds of everyday things you and I do seems to make them more accessible to us. We can identify with them better and thus enter more readily into their situation.

I owe thanks to John and Sherrinda Ketchersid for reviewing the manuscripts and giving me valuable feedback, and to Rhonda Wray, my excellent and congenial editor at Meriwether for her professional work on the manuscript; and to Executive Art Director Tom Myers for his help and cooperation in preparing the art for this book.

— Tom Williams

A NOTE ABOUT SET DESIGN

The plays in this collection are written in such a way that the audience can comprehend the setting quickly through the dialog, eliminating the need for many visual clues. Therefore, elaborate stage settings are not required. Most of these plays can be performed on a virtually bare stage without backdrops or other complexities. This simplicity makes the plays very adaptable. They will fit any staging area — a fellowship hall, the chancel area of your church, or a traditional stage complete with lighting and curtains.

The production notes preceding each play include a list of props, costumes, and set suggestions for each scene. In cases where a called-for prop or set piece might be difficult to acquire, simple suggestions are included — illustrated with how-to drawings — for making the item out of available materials.

The director who wants to stage something more elaborate than a bare stage production will find help in the suggested set designs that accompany most of these plays. Most of these set drawings can be inexpensively enlarged onto film at a copy shop, then projected to size by overhead projector and traced directly onto your set material.

But the important thing to remember is that very little of what is proposed in the production notes is mandatory to successful production. Feel free to adapt, replace, reject, and reformat to fit the needs of your space, cast, and budget.

POSTER AND PROGRAM ART

The title pages for the plays in this book are designed to double as program or poster art. Groups that produce these plays are free to copy the title pages to any size needed, adding the time, place, date, performing group, and other pertinent information to promote performances. The publisher would appreciate receiving a courtesy copy of any such use of this art, along with any comments you wish to convey concerning the outcome of your production. Mail to:

Public Relations Director
Meriwether Publishing Ltd.
Box 7710
Colorado Springs, Colorado 80933

A COMEDY IN ONE ACT
BY T. M. WILLIAMS

THE MAN WHO HAD IT MADE

Blake had outgrown
his warehouse,
his wife, and his God.

The Man Who Had It Made

THE MAN WHO HAD IT MADE

A modern-day retelling of Jesus' parable, "The Rich Fool."

(Luke 12:13-21)

Cast

J.P. Blake (A successful, ambitious businessman)

Millie (Blake's secretary)

Bob Butterup (A manager in Blake's company)

Margie Blake (J.P.'s wife)

Mr. Underhand (An attorney)

Mr. Celcius (A sales rep)

Death

Angel No. 1

Angel No. 2

Costumes:

Businessmen BLAKE and BUTTERUP — should wear conservative suits with vests and ties. BUTTERUP should wear glasses. Add a touch of gray to the temples of J.P. and MARGIE BLAKE. UNDERHAND — should dress like a sleazy lawyer with rumpled pin-striped suit, loose tie and cigar. CELCIUS — should look like an undertaker, e.g., black suit, black tie, white shirt with stiff collar. MILLIE — should dress in bright, fashionable clothes that emphasize her feminine charms somewhat, but stay within the bounds of decency for a church play. MARGIE — should dress neatly but simply. DEATH — should wear a black robe that drags on the floor and has draping sleeves and a hooded cowl. The two ANGELS — should wear white robes and halos.

Props:

A pen set, papers, and telephone on J.P. Blake's desk; a gold-colored pen in his pocket. A fingernail file for Millie. A half-full grocery bag for Margie. A file folder full of papers for Bob Butterup. A two-part contract for Celcius. A revolver for Death. (Do not use a real revolver loaded with blanks. No need to risk a tragic accident or make cast and director nervous. Use a toy pistol that makes a realistic firing sound.)

7

Sound Effects:

Telephone rings.

Setting:

A well-furnished executive office with desk, credenza, chair, divan with decorative pillow, bar, home entertainment center with a TV, a side table with an oriental vase on it, a tapestry or large painting, an "original Picasso" painting, a company growth chart. (See sketches below.)

SUGGESTED SET DESIGN

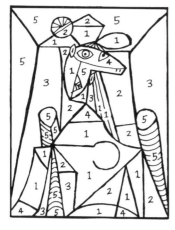

PICASSO PAINTING

Make enlarged film copy of sketch at left. Using overhead projector, project to frame size on poster board. Trace lines boldly and roughly with a black, broad-tipped marker. Then color spaces with poster paint, matching numbers on sketch to colors below.

1. Purple
2. Brown
3. Tan
4. Light Flesh
5. Rust

1 *(The play opens with J.P. BLAKE sitting alone at his desk,*
2 *looking through papers. He picks up his telephone . . .)*
3 **J.P. BLAKE: Millie, could you come in here a moment,**
4 **please?** *(Enter MILLIE, filing her fingernails.)*
5 **MILLIE: Yes, Mr. Blake?**
6 **BLAKE: Well, Millie, how was your first day on the job?**
7 **MILLIE: Oh, I just, you know, loved it! All the guys were, you**
8 **know, sooo nice.**
9 **BLAKE: I'll bet they were. I was just going over the letters**
10 **you typed today and noticed a few mistakes.**
11 **MILLIE: Oh, reeely? But I was sooo, you know, careful. What**
12 **was wrong, sir?**
13 **BLAKE: Well, just minor things, actually. For example, this**
14 **letter to General Motors really should not begin, "Dear**
15 **General."**
16 **MILLIE: But I thought, you know, all military men liked to**
17 **use, you know, their titles.**
18 **BLAKE: You've got a point, there; but General Motors is not**
19 **actually a person. It's a —**
20 **MILLIE: Oh, I get it! He's like in this movie I, you know, saw**
21 **on TV one time about a, you know, spy with like a, you**
22 **know, fake identity, but he didn't really exist so they**
23 **could, you know, fool the Russians and all.**
24 **BLAKE: Oh, no, it's nothing like that at all. General Motors**
25 **is a corporate entity — a company.** *(MILLIE looks blank.)*
26 **Never mind. Too much typing would probably break your**
27 **fingernails anyway. I'll just send these letters over to the**
28 **secretarial pool.**
29 **MILLIE: You mean you've got a pool here just for secretaries?**
30 **Cool! Tomorrow I'll bring my swimsuit.**
31 **BLAKE: No, no. I mean I'll have some other secretary type**
32 **this for you.**
33 **MILLIE: Oh, think yew, Mr. Blake. You're a real, you know,**
34 **doll of a boss.**
35 **BLAKE: Well, thanks, Millie. But there's no need to keep**

1	calling me Mr. Blake. All my friends just call me J.P. By
2	the way, have you had the grand tour of my office?
3	MILLIE: I don't think so, J.P.
4	BLAKE: Well, I manage my vast holdings from this five
5	thousand dollar leather chair and this sixteen thousand
6	dollar solid mahogany desk. That wall hanging is a rare
7	imported tapestry that cost me more than twenty-eight
8	thousand dollars. And on the table there is a Ming vase
9	that cost me seventeen thousand dollars.
10	MILLIE: Oh, I just love mink!
11	BLAKE: Uh, no. I said *Ming*. The vase is from the Chinese
12	Ming Dynasty period. And right there I have an original
13	Picasso that cost me six hundred thousand dollars. It's
14	worth over twice that now. Since I work late quite a bit,
15	I've set up a few things to make the office more homey —
16	like this twenty-five thousand dollar stereo/TV/VCR
17	entertainment center, this bar stocked with over ten
18	thousand dollars worth of the finest liquors, and this
19	eighteen thousand dollar couch. How do you like it?
20	MILLIE: Oh, everything is sooo wonderful, and, you know,
21	sooo expensive.
22	BLAKE: I knew when I first saw you that you were the type
23	who appreciates fine things. Uh, by the way, I need a
24	little favor. It's almost five o'clock and I'm expecting a
25	couple of late calls. Do you think you could stay a little
26	while tonight to help me? I'll pay double overtime.
27	MILLIE: Oh, I'd love to, Mr. Blake — I mean, you know, J.P.
28	But I already have something else, you know, planned
29	for tonight.
30	BLAKE: Really? What's that?
31	MILLIE: I need to wash out a pair of, you know, stockings
32	for, you know, tomorrow.
33	BLAKE: Oh, well, of course. By all means, you need to take
34	care of things like that. You just run along and I will get
35	someone else to stay tonight.

1   MILLIE: You're sooo sweet, J.P. I just, you know, looovι
2   working here. It's awesome. Well, good night.
3   BLAKE: Good night, Millie. *(Exit MILLIE. BLAKE picks up*
4   *telephone.)* **Butterup, I need you in here right away.** *(Hangs*
5   *up telephone. Enter BUTTERUP.)*
6   BUTTERUP: Yes, J.P. *(He sits familiarly on BLAKE's desk.)*
7   BLAKE: *(Coldly)* **Mere middle managers don't call corporate**
8   **presidents by their first names. This is a professional**
9   **corporation. And get off my sixteen thousand dollar desk!**
10   BUTTERUP: *(Jumps up and stands, nervously.)* **Yes, J.P. — I**
11   **mean, Mr. Blake. I just thought —**
12   BLAKE: Well, no more of that! When thinking is needed
13   around here, I hire it done.
14   BUTTERUP: And you hire it very well, sir.
15   BLAKE: Quit interrupting me! When I want your opinion,
16   I'll give it to you. Until then, all I want from you is peace
17   and quiet, and very little of that.
18   BUTTERUP: Right, sir. My thinking exactly, sir.
19   BLAKE: Now, let's get down to business. Do you have today's
20   stock reports on my companies?
21   BUTTERUP: Sure do, J.P. — I mean, Mr. Blake. Got them
22   right here. *(There is a short pause in which nothing happens.)*
23   BLAKE: Well, read them to me!
24   BUTTERUP: Oh, of course, sir. *(He nervously opens file folder*
25   *and reads.)* **Let's see, here ... Blake Elevators are up,**
26   **Goodblake Tires are down, Babyblake Diapers are**
27   **unchanged, Oceanblake Swimwear is taking a plunge,**
28   **Blake Aircraft is soaring, and Blakerite Yeast is rising.**
29   **An overall excellent performance for all your holdings,**
30   **sir. You really know how to rake in a dividend.**
31   BLAKE: And what about our takeover attempt against
32   Kitchen Korner Kontainers? Any news on that yet?
33   BUTTERUP: Not a word, sir. But I wouldn't worry. You are
34   already a major stockholder, you've got your proxies all
35   lined up, and with the best attorney in the business

1   representing you at the stockholder's meeting, how can
2   you miss? You haven't heard anything because the
3   meeting is still going on. Smither will call you with the
4   good news the moment it's over. Just think, J.P. — I
5   mean, Mr. Blake — when this deal goes through, you will
6   be one of the nation's biggest names in garbage pails.
7   BLAKE: *The* biggest, Butterup. I'd bet my fourteen hundred
8   dollar suit on it.
9   BUTTERUP: Oh, yes, of course: I meant *the* biggest. The *very*
10   biggest, sir. Uh, by the way, I've heard rumors that old
11   Bronson in sales is about to retire. You'll be needing a
12   new vice president to replace him, and I just wanted to
13   point out that I have considerable experience in sales —
14   used to sell newspaper subscriptions door-to-door when
15   I was a kid. I just wanted to say that I'm available should
16   you —
17   BLAKE: You? A VP in my company? Frankly, the idea had
18   never occurred to me. But I can assure you that if it ever
19   does, I'll be sure to give it all the attention it deserves.
20   BUTTERUP: *(Effusively)* Oh, thank you, sir! *(He grabs BLAKE's*
21   *hands and starts pumping energetically.)* I really appreciate
22   it.
23   BLAKE: *(Pulls his hand away from BUTTERUP's grasp.)* Now
24   cut that out! I didn't promise you anything, so just get
25   control of yourself. Come to think of it, I'm needing
26   someone to stay for a couple of hours tonight to help me
27   take care of a couple of late appointments. If you could
28   stay, it would give me a chance to see you in action and
29   sort of look you over.
30   BUTTERUP: Oh, I'd love to, sir. But I did have something else
31   planned for tonight.
32   BLAKE: Really? What's that?
33   BUTTERUP: My daughter's wedding. She is getting married
34   at the University Avenue Church just an hour and a half
35   from now. We have over three hundred guests coming and

1   a big reception planned afterward.

2 BLAKE: Really, now, Butterup; if you expect to make a big-

3   time vice president, you can't let your family life interfere

4   with your career. You've got to get your priorities right.

5 BUTTERUP: Oh, right, sir, right. I don't know what I was

6   thinking. I'll call my wife right away and tell her to go

7   on without me. I'm sure they can get Uncle Harry to give

8   the bride away.

9 BLAKE: That's more like it. I'll call you when I need you.

10 BUTTERUP: Glad to help out, Mr. Blake. *(Exit BUTTERUP.)*

11 BLAKE: *(Sits at desk.)* Just think. One ring of that four hundred

12   dollar phone, and I could become one of the richest men

13   in the nation. *(Phone rings. BLAKE dives for it excitedly.)*

14   Hello, Smither? What's the word? *(Deflatedly)* Oh, it's you,

15   dear. What? You're here? Oh, no! I hope you came up the

16   back stairway instead of parading through the office. Oh,

17   good. Well, since you're here you may as well come in.

18   *(He hangs up phone. Enter MARGIE.)*

19 MARGIE: Hello, dear.

20 BLAKE: Margie, what are you doing here? Haven't I told you

21   a thousand times not to come to the office any more

22   until —

23 MARGIE: I know, dear. You are ashamed of me and don't

24   want the vice presidents and managers to see me.

25 BLAKE: It's not that I'm ashamed of you — exactly. You

26   know what the problem is; we've been over it a million

27   dollars — I mean, a million times. You refuse to act or

28   dress the way a rich man's wife should. I have told you

29   and told you that we've got to impress people with our

30   wealth and make them envy us so we can manipulate

31   and intimidate them for our own purposes. Is that too

32   much to ask?

33 MARGIE: I thought I dressed neatly enough. Do I really look

34   that bad? You used to tell me I was cute as a corporate

35   sales curve.

1   BLAKE: It's not you, Margie; it's your clothes. And it's not
2   that they are what you would call bad by ordinary
3   standards; it's just that they are so — well, middle class.
4   I want my wife to flash and dazzle and sparkle with gold,
5   pearls, rubies, and furs. I want marble-sized diamonds
6   on every finger and hanging from your ears. I want you
7   wearing fingernails like tiger claws, reeking with
8   thousand-dollar perfume, and slinking around in two-
9   thousand-dollar dresses. Look at you! Anyone with any
10   taste could tell that dress you are wearing couldn't have
11   cost more than a hundred dollars. The whole problem is
12   that we've got it but you won't flaunt it. And I'm
13   embarrassed to have you around my friends.
14   MARGIE: Actually, this dress cost less than fifteen dollars. I
15   made it myself. Got the material on sale.
16   BLAKE: You *made* it?! Oh, no! How humiliating. How could I
17   ever hold up my head in board meetings if the directors
18   knew you make your own clothes? Margie, please:
19   Promise me you will never breathe a word of this to
20   anyone.
21   MARGIE: You used to be proud of me for making my own
22   clothes. You have changed since we first married.
23   BLAKE: I have simply adjusted myself to the changes in our
24   condition, Margie, which is what you have stubbornly
25   refused to do. And if you don't start facing up to the new
26   realities of our status, there is going to be real trouble
27   between us. Now, I don't have time to keep arguing with
28   you; I've got work to do. So just tell my why you came
29   and then get on with whatever little affairs you're
30   involved in.
31   MARGIE: I was on my way to the ladies' prayer meeting and
32   I figured you would work late, as usual, then stay to watch
33   Monday Night Football. So I brought you a little snack.
34   I thought it might remind you of home a little. *(She hands*
35   *BLAKE a bag.)*

1 BLAKE: What's in there?
2 MARGIE: Oh, just a few little things I threw together: a
3   couple of smoked turkey sandwiches, a bowl of tossed
4   salad, a batch of homemade cookies, a box of popcorn, a
5   bottle of cola, and a few pieces of your favorite candy —
6   million dollar fudge.
7 BLAKE: There you go again! You spent hours making that
8   stuff and drove miles to bring it down here, and I don't
9   want it. I'm a big-time executive; I don't eat that lunchbox
10   stuff anymore. When I want a snack, I have a secretary
11   order up caviar, shrimp cocktails, and hors d'oeuvres from
12   the deli. Margie, we can afford the best, and we can afford
13   to have others make it for us and deliver it to us. That
14   is what I'm trying to get through your head. Why won't
15   you hire cooks, maids, butlers, gardeners, and chauffeurs
16   to do your work so you can join bridge clubs, take
17   aerobics, and see psychiatrists like the other corporate
18   wives?
19 MARGIE: But I like to cook and sew and do things for my
20   family. Being a wife and homemaker has been my only
21   ambition ever since I was a little girl. These are the skills
22   I have cultivated and developed. Take them away and
23   I'm not sure I would know who I am. You have become
24   so rich you don't really need me anymore. I'm beginning
25   to wonder if you still love me.
26 BLAKE: Don't be silly. You're my favorite tax deduction.
27 MARGIE: And you are so caught up in your work that you are
28   never home on nights or weekends. You never see our
29   children and never talk to them.
30 BLAKE: Now, that's not true. I write to Jeff every year.
31 MARGIE: *(Brightening)* Really? I didn't know that. What do
32   you write?
33 BLAKE: A check. I send him his annual tuition for his
34   medical studies at State University.
35 MARGIE: But Jeff is not studying medicine; he is studying

1   architecture. And he doesn't go to State University; he

2   goes to Central College.

3   BLAKE: He does? Well, well. That explains why the checks

4   are never cashed. Anyway, I have my secretary send two

5   hundred dollars worth of birthday flowers every year to

6   uh — ah — oh, what is her name?

7   MARGIE: What is whose name?

8   BLAKE: Our daughter. Now, don't tell me; I know it. Just

9   give me a moment and it will come to me . . .

10   MARGIE: Cindy.

11   BLAKE: Of course — Cindy! I knew that. Anyway, you see, I

12   don't neglect our children.

13   MARGIE: And what about Joey?

14   BLAKE: Who?

15   MARGIE: Joey — our oldest son.

16   BLAKE: Joey? Oh, of course — Joey! Hmmm, let's see, just

17   jog my memory a little. Where does he go to school?

18   MARGIE: He doesn't go to school. He graduated last spring.

19   He works in your widget manufacturing company in

20   Omaha.

21   BLAKE: Uh, sure; I knew that. My mind is just a little tired

22   right now. Heh, heh.

23   MARGIE: Things are much worse than I thought, J.P. We

24   need to see a counselor.

25   BLAKE: *(Bristling)* Me, see a shrink? Not on your Freudian

26   slip. I believe in being man enough to handle my own

27   problems. People who let themselves get so unraveled

28   that they need to cry on someone else's shoulder are

29   nothing but a bunch of stupid, spineless, lazy, wimpy

30   nerds. *(Enter BUTTERUP.)*

31   BUTTERUP: Did you call, sir? Oh, excuse me. I didn't know

32   you had a lady with you.

33   BLAKE: Oh, this is no lady, this is my — uh — cleaning

34   woman. I — uh — was just about to show her a few things

35   that need attention here. *(To MARGIE)* Uh, look, madam,

1   see this floor and these walls? They are a mess. You've
2   got to do better if you want to keep working here. *(To*
3   *BUTTERUP)* What is it, Butterup? Have you heard from
4   Smither about the takeover?
5   BUTTERUP: No, sir, but Mr. Underhand, your attorney
6   working on the Amalgamated Hardware deal, is here and
7   needs to talk to you.
8   BLAKE: Send him in.
9   BUTTERUP: Quicker than a ticker tape, sir. *(Exit BUTTERUP.)*
10   BLAKE: Quick, Margie — get behind that divan. I don't
11   want to have to explain you to Underhand.
12   MARGIE: But I —
13   BLAKE: No buts. Just get back there — quickly. *(He guides*
14   *her by the arm to the divan. She crouches behind it. Enter*
15   *UNDERHAND. BLAKE sits at desk.)* What's the problem
16   with Amalgamated, Underhand? Don't they want the
17   contract to wholesale our hammers?
18   UNDERHAND: Of course they want it, J.P. They've already
19   signed it. Our problem is that this snooty little district
20   judge is about to block the deal. Something about
21   monopolies or antitrust laws or some such nonsense. I
22   never could understand all that legal gobbledeygook.
23   BLAKE: What? You're my lawyer! I'm paying you through
24   the nose to know all about that tangled legal stuff so you
25   can get my deals through.
26   UNDERHAND: Oh, come on, Blake; you know by now that we
27   lawyers don't understand our contracts any better than
28   our victims. But it doesn't matter. We understand what
29   the bottom line is: if you've got money, you can't lose,
30   and if you don't have it, you can't win. But don't worry,
31   I've got things under control. I don't do my stuff in the
32   courtroom; I do it in the back room, or sometimes in the
33   alley. Now, listen; I have a friend in Chicago who owes
34   me a favor. He was charged with embezzling a few years
35   ago, and he was as guilty as sin. But I got him off on a

1   technicality. Now, he knows this judge on your case, you

2   see, and he has told me that the old bench warmer fancies

3   himself something of a sailor. The trouble is, on his salary

4   he can't afford the kind of yacht he thinks he ought to

5   have. But he has let us know that if we could see our way

6   clear to —

7   BLAKE: I get the picture, Underhand. What does the yacht

8   cost?

9   UNDERHAND: About two hundred fifty thousand dollars.

10   BLAKE: Is that all? That's chicken feed. We stand to make

11   millions on this deal. Buy the old man the yacht and

12   throw in a couple of dinghies. *(BLAKE begins to do paper*

13   *work on his desk.)*

14   UNDERHAND: Consider it done. Nothing can stand in the

15   way of your hammers now. They're about to hit it big.

16   I'll see you around, J.P. *(Exit UNDERHAND. MARGIE*

17   *slowly raises up and looks out.)*

18   MARGIE: Is he gone?

19   BLAKE: *(Jumps.)* Oh! You scared me. I forgot you were back

20   there.

21   MARGIE: J.P., I heard the whole thing. You just authorized

22   a bribe. That is illegal and immoral. I can't believe you

23   would do that.

24   BLAKE: Margie, please get your old-fashioned morality off

25   my back. You just don't understand how business works

26   these days. It's done all the time. It doesn't hurt anyone,

27   and it keeps the wheels of commerce greased. Besides, I

28   stand to make millions on this deal.

29   MARGIE: You never think of anything but money.

30   BLAKE: *(Still working at desk)* Now that's not true and you

31   know it. I think about other things sometimes — mutual

32   funds, tax shelters, preferred stocks ...

33   MARGIE: But don't you worry about your future?

34   BLAKE: Absolutely not. It's all taken care of — investments,

35   insurance policies, maturing bonds, pensions, interest-

1   bearing accounts . . .
2 MARGIE: I don't mean retirement; I mean eternity. What
3   will happen to you when you die?
4 BLAKE: It's much too early to worry about that. I've got half
5   my life ahead of me.
6 MARGIE: Not necessarily. It can happen at any moment.
7   Remember your friend Alex —
8 BLAKE: No need to be morbid, Margie. Actually, since you
9   mention it, I am taking care of my eternity.
10 MARGIE: *(Brightening)* Really? You mean you are becoming a
11   Christian?
12 BLAKE: Don't be ridiculous. None of that faith and fancy
13   hope and hokum stuff for me. No one who uses his brain
14   believes all that Bible prattle anymore.
15 MARGIE: Oh, but that isn't so, J.P. Some of the best thinkers —
16 BLAKE: Margie, sometimes I think it was a mistake for us to
17   get married. You don't want a real man who thinks for
18   himself. You need to find yourself a brainwashed jellyfish
19   who doesn't know his head from a bowling ball. *(Enter*
20   *BUTTERUP.)*
21 BUTTERUP: Sorry to bother you again, J.P. — I mean, Mr.
22   Blake. Oh, I see the cleaning woman is still here. Ma'am,
23   when you finish in here, I've got a window in my office
24   that needs —
25 BLAKE: Never mind, Butterup. What is it now? Do you have
26   news from Smither?
27 BUTTERUP: Not yet, sir. But there is a man out here to see
28   you. His name's Celcius. Says he represents a company
29   called Frigid Infinity, Incorporated. He claims he has an
30   appointment.
31 BLAKE: Well, speak of the devil. This is the eternity deal I
32   was just about to explain to you, Margie. Send him in,
33   Butterup.
34 BUTTERUP: Quicker than a ticker tape, sir. And lady,
35   there's a little spot on my carpet —

1   **BLAKE: Butterup!**

2   **BUTTERUP: Sorry, sir.** *(Exit BUTTERUP.)*

3   **BLAKE: Quick, Margie, behind the divan.** *(Enter CELCIUS.)* **Uh**

4   **oh, too late. We'll just have to make the best of it.**

5   **CELCIUS: Good evening, Mr. Blake.** *(He speaks with the*

6   *exaggerated courtliness of a stereotypical undertaker; somewhat*

7   *like Boris Karloff or Vincent Price.)*

8   **BLAKE: Hello, Celcius. Uh, this is my — uh — wife, Margie.**

9   **Uh, she's having to sort of slum it today. Her — uh —**

10   **vast wardrobe of furs, jewels, and dresses were — ah —**

11   **stolen last night, and she hasn't had a chance to get over**

12   **to Neiman-Markup yet.**

13   **MARGIE: Why, J.P., you know I didn't —**

14   **BLAKE: Now, let's not bother Mr. Celcius with our personal**

15   **losses, dear. He's a busy man and has other appointments,**

16   **I'm sure. Let's let him get on with it.**

17   **CELCIUS: Thank you, Mr. Blake. How do you do, Mrs. Blake?**

18   **I'm so very sorry to hear of your tragic loss, my dear. But**

19   **I deeply appreciate this opportunity to address the two**

20   **of you simultaneously. It is imperative that pre-need**

21   **counseling include both husband and wife.**

22   **MARGIE: Pre-need counseling? Do you sell funeral plots?**

23   **CELCIUS: Oh, no, no, no, Mrs. Blake. I offer a permanent,**

24   **living alternative to funeral plots. Our company has**

25   **disarmed the grim reaper, rendering funerals and graves**

26   **obsolete for those fortunate personages possessing the**

27   **monetary capability to utilize our services.**

28   **MARGIE: What in the world are you talking about?**

29   **CELCIUS: I am offering you a way to remain forever on this**

30   **side of that dread river of death. As you must be aware,**

31   **there is presently no remedy for those insidious diseases**

32   **that precipitate the untimely demise of most of us.**

33   **However, the continuous and relentless advance of**

34   **modern medicine assures us of the inevitable eradication**

35   **of these diseases. Smallpox, polio, diphtheria, tetanus,**

1   and other potentially terminal maladies have already
2   succumbed to the remedial sword of medical research.
3   Tomorrow it will overcome heart disease, cancer,
4   diabetes, and perhaps even the sniffles.
5   MARGIE: What?
6   BLAKE: He says science is going to cure all the killer diseases.
7   CELCIUS: Precisely, Mr. Blake. But, alas, the march of
8   modern medicine, while incredibly effective, is
9   exceedingly ponderous. Many years, even decades may
10   elapse before these conquests come to fruition.
11   Meanwhile, our own mortality ruthlessly approaches —
12   BLAKE: In other words, most of us will die before these cures
13   are found.
14   CELCIUS: Succinctly put, Mr. Blake. I envy your unparalleled
15   penchant for penetrating brevity. But I fear I am afflicted
16   with intransigent sesquipedalianism. *(Ses-kuip-ih-daý-lee-*
17   *un-ism)*
18   BLAKE: What?
19   MARGIE: He says he can't help talking too much and using
20   big words.
21   CELCIUS: Please forgive me and allow me to simplify. Let us
22   say that your physician informs you that you have
23   incurable heart disease. You put your earthly affairs in
24   order and come immediately to us. Then, utilizing a
25   carefully developed, highly sophisticated scientific
26   technique, we gradually reduce the temperature of your
27   body to achieve a state of suspended animation, which
28   we can sustain indefinitely. Actually, it is merely a form
29   of what is termed hibernation in animals, but
30   technologically rather than naturally induced in
31   humans. Then we store you in a temperature-controlled
32   vault where your vital signs are carefully monitored at
33   all times. And when medical researchers announce a cure
34   for your disease, we re-animate your body, cure the
35   disease, and to appropriate a biblical metaphor, we

1   breathe into your nostrils the breath of life, and you walk

2   out healthy and whole.

3   BLAKE: *(Excitedly)* **Isn't that great, Margie? They can freeze**

4   us for years — even centuries — until a cure is found for

5   what ails us, then thaw us out and patch us up like new.

6   All the advantages of heaven with none of the liabilities

7   of religion. And no uncertainty about the hereafter. With

8   the Frigid Infinity plan, we get to live forever right here

9   on earth in the paradise I've made for us myself.

10   MARGIE: I won't have any part of your freeze-dried future.

11   BLAKE: Why not, Margie? Think of it: no fuzzy promises

12   from a maybe God who won't speak out loud or show his

13   face to prove he is there, and no more kowtowing to a

14   churchy morality. No boring eternity sitting on a cloud

15   in a dull heaven where everybody wears nightgowns and

16   plays harps. This plan will give us an eternity we can

17   relate to — one made of what we have worked for all our

18   lives. What do you say, Margie? Let's do it. Celcius, where

19   do we sign?

20   MARGIE: I won't sign it, J.P. Surely you can't believe we can

21   turn this world into a paradise. You can't really want to

22   live here forever in the middle of all the war, suffering,

23   murder, hunger, hate, lust, greed, and — and bribery.

24   And in spite of what those humanistic dreamers tell you,

25   it's not going to get better, it's going to get worse. For

26   Christians, death is not the end. It is the door out of a

27   hopelessly messed-up world into a real paradise of true

28   perfection.

29   BLAKE: But you have no proof of that. It's all faith and fancy.

30   I prefer to hang on to what I know is real. Where do I

31   sign, Celcius?

32   CELCIUS: Right here, if you please, Mr. Blake. Here is a pen.

33   BLAKE: I prefer to use my own. It's gold plated. Cost me two

34   hundred fifty dollars. *(He signs.)*

35   CELCIUS: Thank you very much, Mr. Blake. You have just

1   purchased your immortality. The required deposit for
2   this service is $175,000.
3   BLAKE: The cost is no object. Just leave me a copy of the
4   contract and send me an invoice.
5   CELCIUS: Very well, sir. And good evening to you, and to
6   you as well, madam. Should you have a change of heart . . .
7   MARGIE: Don't hold your freon. *(CELCIUS bows and exits.)*
8   BLAKE: You just made a foolish choice, Margie. You gambled
9   away a sure thing for an imagined castle in the air. What
10   if you are wrong? What if you die and there turns out to
11   be no heaven?
12   MARGIE: I would rather live a short life full of the joy that
13   comes from believing than to live forever on this
14   hopeless, degenerating planet.
15   BLAKE: I cannot imagine anything more inane and stupid.
16   *(Enter BUTTERUP.)*
17   BUTTERUP: Let me be the first to congratulate you, you
18   brilliant boardroom bandit. You did it! You are now the
19   controlling stockholder and chairman of the board of
20   Kitchen Korner Kontainers.
21   BLAKE: Well, bless my profit motive; I pulled it off! I have
22   cornered the national garbage pail market.
23   BUTTERUP: Just think, your name will become a household
24   word. When people think of garbage, they will think of
25   J.P. Blake. Why, your name might even become a generic
26   word for kitchen trash. I can just see housewives all over
27   the country saying, "Honey, would you please carry out
28   the Blake?"
29   BLAKE: *(Obviously pleased)* Do you really think so?
30   BUTTERUP: I really do. Why, you will be to trash what the
31   Colonel is to fried chicken.
32   BLAKE: What Hilton is to hotels.
33   BUTTERUP: *(Gets very dramatic.)* Sir, you will be to garbage
34   what the Statue of Liberty is to the homeless.
35   BLAKE: *(Strikes a noble pose.)* Oh, bring me your table scraps,

1   your melon rinds, your coffee grounds longing to be free.

2   **BLAKE and BUTTERUP:** *(They break into a song and dance*

3   *routine, sung to the tune of "For He's a Jolly Good Fellow.")*

4   Your apple peel, onion, and fish tail,

5   Those things that offend when you inhale,

6   Will have a good home in our trash pail,

7   For nine-ninety-five retail.

8   **MARGIE:**   My goodness! The way you men are carrying on,

9   you would think that selling garbage pails is on a par

10   with discovering a cure for cancer.

11   **BLAKE:**   *(Straightens coat and tie, regains dignified composure.)* **Is**

12   that all, Butterup?

13   **BUTTERUP:**   We do have one little problem to take care of.

14   **BLAKE:**   What's that?

15   **BUTTERUP:**   Warehouse   space.   When   Kitchen   Korner

16   Kontainers started having financial trouble, they lost the

17   leases on most of their warehouses. We've got to come

18   up with storage space for several hundred thousand

19   garbage pails.

20   **BLAKE:**   Oh, that's no problem. You know our warehouses

21   on Industrial Avenue? We'll tear them down and build

22   them three times as big. Go call our architects and get

23   them right on it.

24   **BUTTERUP:**   Absolutely brilliant, sir. I'll get on it quicker

25   than a ticker tape. *(Exit BUTTERUP.)*

26   **BLAKE:**   Honey, this garbage pail deal will make us filthy

27   rich. I'm talking Rockefeller rich, J. Paul Getty rich,

28   H. Ross Perot rich, Scrooge McDuck rich! We can relax

29   and take it easy now, and you can have anything in the

30   world you want.

31   **MARGIE:**   There is only one thing I want.

32   **BLAKE:**   The Hope Diamond? No problem. I'll get it for you.

33   **MARGIE:**   No, J.P., I'm not talking about —

34   **BLAKE:**   The Mona Lisa? I'll call the Louvre.

35   **MARGIE:**   No, J.P., I —

1   BLAKE: The Taj Mahal? The Eiffel Tower? The Statue of
2   Liberty? You name it and it's yours.
3   MARGIE: No, no, no! Nothing like that. I would gladly give
4   up our fortune and go back to being poor again if you
5   would just become a Christian.
6   BLAKE: Margie, we've been over this time and again. I've
7   told you, I don't need God. I make my own morality; I
8   have my own eternity, and God has nothing to offer that
9   I can't get for myself. I built my business empire by myself
10   without God's help. I will leave him alone and I want him
11   to leave me alone.
12   MARGIE: I'm really worried about you, J.P.
13   BLAKE: I'll tell you what, Margie. Let's make a deal. I'll meet
14   you halfway. Give up going to that dinky little
15   neighborhood Bible church and join the First United
16   Uptown Church and I will go with you at least once a
17   month when I'm in town. What do you say?
18   MARGIE: The First United Uptown Church? Why them?
19   BLAKE: Because they've got class. Their buildings cover
20   more than two city blocks. They have a five-story, million-
21   dollar bell tower, twenty-eight two-hundred-thousand-
22   dollar stained-glass windows, imported arched beams
23   that cost one hundred twenty thousand dollars each, and
24   carpet up to your ankles. And the most influential
25   businessmen and government leaders in the state go
26   there — even the governor, when he goes. Think of all
27   the business contacts I could make in a church like that.
28   MARGIE: I'm sorry, J.P., I can't do it.
29   BLAKE: Why not? What does it matter where you go? A church
30   is a church is a church.
31   MARGIE: Not really. I can't go to a church that does not
32   honor Christ.
33   BLAKE: And I won't go unless they honor the governor.
34   Margie, your Christ has come between us long enough.
35   I'm tired of him always pulling you in the opposite direction

1   from me. It's time for you to make a choice: Him or me.

2   MARGIE: J.P., this is not necessary. My love for Christ does

3   not compete with my love for you.

4   BLAKE: Hurry up, Margie, choose. I haven't got all night.

5   The football game is about to come on.

6   MARGIE: Please, J.P., don't make me do this. We can't end

7   twenty-five years of marriage just like that.

8   BLAKE: *(Looks at his watch.)* Make your choice, Margie.

9   MARGIE: Good-bye, J.P.

10   BLAKE: Good-bye, Margie. It's been nice, generally. We had

11   some great times together, like at the Sink and Pipe

12   Sellers Convention. See you around sometime. Tell the

13   kids good-bye for me — Jeff, Cindy, and uh . . .

14   MARGIE: Joey. *(Exit MARGIE.)*

15   BLAKE: Yeah, Joey. Whew! I'm glad that's over. That sort of

16   thing can almost ruin your whole day if you let it. But I

17   don't intend to let it. I'm just going to kick off my shoes

18   and watch the football game. *(He loosens his tie, turns on*

19   *the TV, stretches out on the divan and puts his feet up.)*

20   Ahhh . . . this is just what I need — a relaxing evening

21   with no more stupid, nitpicky, bothersome, niggling little

22   people interrupting me. *(Enter BUTTERUP.)*

23   BUTTERUP: Uh, J.P. — I mean, Mr. Blake . . .

24   BLAKE: *(Crossly)* What is it now, Butterup?

25   BUTTERUP: I was just wondering if you needed anything

26   else, sir. I thought if I could leave now I might at least

27   make the reception.

28   BLAKE: Uh, yes. Just one thing before you go. Call the

29   Golden Peacock Restaurant and order me their finest

30   lobster dinner with all the trimmings. Just have them

31   deliver it here.

32   BUTTERUP: Glad to, Mr. Blake. I'll have it done quicker than

33   a ticker tape. In fact, I could just go ahead and order for

34   two and join you so you won't have to eat alone. There

35   probably won't be much food left at the reception anyway.

1   **BLAKE:** I can't think of anything I would like less.

2   **BUTTERUP:** Great! Oh — uh — I mean, I understand, sir. I'm

3   sure you have lots to think about and really need a little

4   executive solitude. Good night, Mr. Blake. *(Exit*

5   *BUTTERUP.)*

6   **BLAKE:** *(Settles onto the divan.)* **Man, this is the life. I've**

7   **really got it made.** *(He watches TV for a moment, then drifts*

8   *off to sleep and begins snoring. Enter DEATH.)*

9   **DEATH:** *(Speaking in a "spooky" voice with extended vowels and*

10   *hissing S's)* **Blake. Blake.**

11   **BLAKE:** *(Stirs, sputters, mumbles.)* **Huh?**

12   **DEATH:** **J.P. Blake. The game is over, Blake.**

13   **BLAKE:** *(Not fully awake)* **Um, OK, just turn off the TV.**

14   **DEATH:** **No, Blake.** *Your* **game is over. The final gun has**

15   **sounded.** *(DEATH draws a pistol and fires it in the air.)*

16   **BLAKE:** *(Sits bolt upright at sound of gunshot, sees DEATH,*

17   *screams in terror.)* **Who are you?**

18   **DEATH:** **I am the official timekeeper, Blake. It's all over. You**

19   **must leave the field of play.**

20   **BLAKE:** **But — but — where are we going?**

21   **DEATH:** *(With evil laugh)* **Guess.**

22   **BLAKE:** **No! Wait! Don't I get a two-minute warning? Time**

23   **out!** *(He frantically makes the official referee's signal for time*

24   *out.)*

25   **DEATH:** **No warnings, no time outs. Come.**

26   **BLAKE:** **But — but — wait! You can't do this. It's not legal.**

27   **I have this contract, see?** *(He shows DEATH the Frigid*

28   *Infinity contract.)* **I'm supposed to be frozen.**

29   **DEATH:** **I honor no contracts. And where you're going,**

30   **freezing is out of the question.**

31   **BLAKE:** **But it's not fair, I tell you. I didn't expect you for**

32   **years.**

33   **DEATH:** **Fair? The word means nothing to me.**

34   **BLAKE:** **Well, let me get my dictionary and I'll —**

35   **DEATH:** **Quiet, Blake. Your stalling is doing no good. I don't**

1   play by any man's rules. I am sneaky and unscrupulous,

2   but certain and final. Now, come. *(Enter two ANGELS.)*

3   BLAKE: *(To ANGELS)* Man, am I glad to see you guys. You

4   know my wife, Margie? She's a great fan of yours. Tell

5   this creep to unhand me and I'll make a deal with you.

6   FIRST ANGEL: Sorry, Mr. Blake. We would love to help you,

7   but we are carefully instructed to honor your final

8   wishes.

9   BLAKE: My final wishes?

10   SECOND ANGEL: Yes. Remember? "I don't need God. I built

11   this vast financial empire by myself, without his help. I

12   will leave God alone and I want him to leave me alone."

13   FIRST ANGEL: You see, Mr. Blake, you chose to be independent

14   of us and we must honor that choice.

15   BLAKE: But do you know where this bag of bones is taking

16   me? Right straight to —

17   SECOND ANGEL: Please, Mr. Blake. No need to be profane.

18   We would appreciate it if you would not mention that

19   word in our presence. *(Stage lights dim to darkness or curtain*

20   *closes, with ANGELS standing in front of it as DEATH drags*

21   *BLAKE Off-stage, screaming.)*

22   FIRST ANGEL: *(From out of darkness or in front of curtain)* Too

23   bad about Mr. Blake. He had such a nice set-up. I know

24   he hated to leave it.

25   SECOND ANGEL: Yes, but it was nothing compared to what

26   he would have had if he had thrown in with us. I wonder

27   who will get all his things now? *(Exit ANGELS. Lights come*

28   *up, or curtain opens, revealing BUTTERUP sitting at BLAKE's*

29   *desk. He picks up the telephone.)*

30   BUTTERUP: Millie, would you come in here a moment?

31   *(Enter MILLIE, chewing gum and filing nails.)*

32   MILLIE: Yes, Mr. Butterup?

33   BUTTERUP: I was just going over the letters you typed

34   yesterday and noticed a few things that need fixing.

35   MILLIE: Reeely? And I was sooo, you know, careful. What

1   was, you know, wrong, sir?

2   BUTTERUP: Well, on this letter to our coffee service company

3   — do you know how to spell *coffee?*

4   MILLIE: Sure. You know, K-A-U-P-H-Y.

5   BUTTERUP: Well, that's not quite accurate. In fact, you

6   didn't even get one letter right.

7   MILLIE: But that's, you know, a big word, sir. It has two

8   cylinders.

9   BUTTERUP: Heh, heh. I think you mean syllables. But the

10   point is —

11   MILLIE: *(Huffily)* Well, if K-A-U-P-H-Y doesn't spell, you

12   know, coffee, just what does it spell?

13   BUTTERUP: Well, it spells — uh — heh, heh. You've got me

14   there. Anyway, I think it's about the cutest spelling of

15   coffee I've ever seen.

16   MILLIE: Think yew.

17   BUTTERUP: By the way, have you had the grand tour of my

18   office?

19   MILLIE: I don't think so.

20   BUTTERUP: I'll show it to you. Over here I have my six

21   hundred thousand dollar Picasso, and there is my twenty-

22   five thousand dollar stereo/TV/VCR combination, and on

23   the table there is a Ming vase, and —

24   MILLIE: Oh, I just love mink!

25   *(Blackout)*

26

27

28

29

30

31

32

33

34

35

Props:

A plastic punch bowl, a tray of glasses (plastic cups will do), napkins, a plate of snacks, a military medal attached to a neck chain or ribbon, eight copies of Naaman's portrait (reproduce a photo of the actor who plays Naaman on a copy machine), a bandage for Naaman's hand, a road map, two suitcases, two letters of introduction, a piece of paper for a prescription, a broom or feather duster, a magazine.

Settings:

Scene 1 — General and Dorie Naaman's ballroom (see sketch on page 35). Furnish with various pieces of furniture as oriental in styling as possible. Include at least one large chair, a side table, possibly a reclining couch, one or more potted plants, and decorative pottery as available. Curtains, if available, will add a touch of elegance. A household Baal idol is at Stage Left (see sketch on page 35). Early in Scene 1, the servants bring in a serving table, which can be an ordinary folding table skirted to hide the legs.

Scene 2 — A rustic, Middle Eastern shack with an open door in front. If a backdrop is available, it should be of an empty countryside (see sketch on page 35).

Scene 3 — Same as Scene 1, but without the serving table.

SCENES 1 AND 3

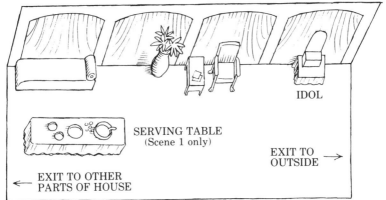

IDOL

SERVING TABLE
(Scene 1 only)

EXIT TO
OUTSIDE →

← EXIT TO OTHER
PARTS OF HOUSE

SCENE 2

ELISHA'S SHACK

Made of cardboard and supported on back with
1" x 2" framing as needed. Door frames and window
frames painted on. Door opening to be cut out.
Windows painted black to hide actor inside.

BAAL IDOL

Construct base and back panel of cardboard, at
least 3 feet high. Paint a creamy color in a thin,
tempera wash to give surface a stonelike effect.
Then project enlarged film copy of sketch at left
onto panel and trace in black marker. Include heavy
shadow edge as shown to retain dimensional effect.

35

1   and call me in the morning." That's his standard

2   treatment for everything from heartburn to heart

3   attacks. But I'll talk to him about it. *(A knock at the door)*

4   Alfap, Hormish, Golda, get to your posts. *(Enter ALFAP,*

5   *HORMISH, and GOLDA. ALFAP goes to the door and lets in*

6   *the first guests. HORMISH stands at attention as a guard.*

7   *GOLDA takes her place at the table to serve the punch. NAAMAN*

8   *and DORIE stand at the right of the door to receive their guests.)*

9   **ALFAP:**   Announcing Senator and Mrs. Asa Lawson. *(They*

10   *enter.)*

11   **SENATOR:**   General Naaman, may I congratulate you on

12   behalf of the entire parliament? You certainly won a

13   great victory for the nation of Aram. *(Shakes hands with*

14   *NAAMAN.)*

15   **NAAMAN:**   You certainly may, and I certainly did.

16   **SENATOR:**   Uh, General, I have a little favor to ask of you.

17   As you may know, my re-election is coming right up. It

18   wouldn't hurt a thing for me to have your endorsement

19   and maybe a few pictures of you and I together to run

20   in my promotional campaign.

21   **NAAMAN:**   Sure, I'll do it. But you'll have to get on the waiting

22   list. You know how it is when your name is a household

23   word. People are always clamoring for your time and

24   attention. Ah, the price of fame.

25   **SENATOR:**   Thank you, General. I'll contact your office and

26   set up a time. *(SENATOR and MRS. LAWSON greet DORIE*

27   *and move to Stage Right.)*

28   **ALFAP:**   Announcing Chief Justice and Mrs. Cedric Gavel.

29   *(They enter.)*

30   **JUSTICE GAVEL:**   *(Shakes hands with NAAMAN.)* Well, General,

31   Aram is truly fortunate to have a great leader such as

32   you to direct our armies to victory after victory. In my

33   judgment, you rank right up there with the great military

34   geniuses in history.

35   **NAAMAN:**   No doubt judgments like that got you where you

1 **are today.** *(The JUSTICE and WIFE greet DORIE and move*
2 *to the right to chat quietly with the LAWSONS.)*
3 **ALFAP: Announcing Prime Minister Hosef Abadan and his**
4 **guest Miss Trixie Fullsome.** *(They enter.)*
5 **PRIME MINISTER:** *(Shakes hands with NAAMAN.)* **General, I**
6 **am happy to tell you that I have sent a resolution to**
7 **parliament recommending that a larger-than-life marble**
8 **statue of you be placed in front of the king's palace.**
9 **NAAMAN: The king will be honored, I'm sure.**
10 **PRIME MINISTER: The resolution comes up for vote**
11 **tomorrow. I'll let you know how it turns out.**
12 **NAAMAN: Don't bother. How could anyone vote against a**
13 **resolution like that? I am confident that you will get**
14 **unanimous approval. Just tell the sculptor that I am**
15 **ready when he is.** *(Puts hand to chest and strikes a noble pose.)*
16 **TRIXIE:** *(Slinks up to NAAMAN, touches star on his shoulder and*
17 *lets her finger trail down his arm.)* **Oh, I've never seen a real**
18 **general before.**
19 **NAAMAN: Well, believe me, lady, you are looking at one now.**
20 **TRIXIE: My, you look so strong. Tell me, what does a real**
21 **general do?**
22 **NAAMAN: Well, I command vast armies, I win brilliant**
23 **victories, I destroy powerful enemies, I leap tall buildings**
24 **with a single bound. But mainly, I protect our country**
25 **so that girls like you can feel safe and secure.**
26 **TRIXIE: Oh, I'm sure I would always feel safe and secure**
27 **with a big, strong, brave, handsome man like you around.**
28 **NAAMAN: Well, you should, lady.**
29 **TRIXIE:** *(Coyly)* **And what makes you think I'm a lady?**
30 **NAAMAN: Well, you certainly look like a —**
31 **DORIE:** *(Clears throat and interrupts sharply.)* **Uh, Miss Fullsome,**
32 **I think you must be ready for a little punch.** *(She takes the*
33 *reluctant TRIXIE by the arm and leads her to the punch bowl.)*
34 **Come right this way and I'll see that you get it.**
35 **ALFAP: Announcing Dr. Jonas Hackar.** *(HACKAR enters.)*

1   DR. HACKAR: *(Shakes hands with NAAMAN.)* **Congratulations,**
2   **General. You have done it again. You crushed those**
3   **Philistines like aluminum wineskins. You are one of the**
4   **world's great military strategists, General Naaman.**
5   NAAMAN: **Aw, you're just saying that because you know it's**
6   **true. By the way, I'm glad you're here. I've been having**
7   **this little problem with my —**
8   ALFAP: **Hear ye, hear ye. I now present his majesty the King**
9   **of Aram and his wife, the Queen.** *(Enter KING and QUEEN.)*
10   KING: **Well, well, well. How is my javorite feneral — I**
11   **mean — my favorite general?**
12   NAAMAN: **I'm great, of course. And how is my favorite king?**
13   QUEEN: **But he is your only king.**
14   KING: **Let's get right down to business, shall we, Naaman?**
15   *(Addresses the entire group.)* **I think we all know why we're**
16   **here tonight. We have come to honor a man who has**
17   **become a national zero in this hate — er — a national**
18   **hero in this state. This is a man to whom Aram owes its**
19   **very existence; a man who has led Aram's armies into**
20   **battle many times and has never suffered defeat. Ladies**
21   **and gentlemen, it pleases me very much to award to**
22   **General Naaman the coveted Golden Scimitar to**
23   **commemorate his valor, heroism, and success in battle.**
24   **General, please accept this little token of our glove and**
25   **latitude — uh — love and gratitude.** *(He drapes the medal*
26   *around NAAMAN's neck as GUESTS applaud.)*
27   JUSTICE GAVEL: *(Holds up glass.)* **I would like to propose a**
28   **toast: to General Naaman, the greatest general Aram has**
29   **ever known.**
30   NAAMAN: **I'll drink to that.**
31   GUESTS: **Hear, hear!** *(They drink.)*
32   PRIME MINISTER: **How about a little speech, General?**
33   GUESTS: *(Ad-lib)* **Yeah! Speech! Speech!**
34   NAAMAN: **As you know, I don't do much public speaking.**
35   **Generally there is no need to, because my mighty deeds**

1   speak so eloquently for themselves. However, I do thank
2   the king for giving me this honor, which I so richly
3   deserve. To celebrate this occasion, I have prepared a
4   little memento for each of you to take home and cherish.
5   Hormish, come here. *(HORMISH takes NAAMAN the stack*
6   *of portrait copies. NAAMAN takes one of them and holds it*
7   *toward the group.)* This is an eight-by-ten picture of me
8   taken from my best side — not that there is anything
9   wrong with the other side, of course. Inscribed beneath
10   the picture is a list of my ten greatest victories. I'm sorry
11   that there was not enough room to list them all. It is
12   suitable for framing and will look quite nice above your
13   mantle. And I will be glad to autograph your copy
14   personally while you are here. No, don't thank me. I know
15   that each of you will cherish the picture dearly, just as
16   I will cherish my own copy. *(He stares at the picture and*
17   *sighs lovingly as HORMISH hands them out to the guests.)*
18   KING: What can we say, Naaman? I am sure that speach of us
19   is eechless — ah — each of us is speechless.
20   JUSTICE GAVEL: I'll certainly put mine in an appropriate
21   place.
22   MRS. GAVEL: *(Sarcastically)* Yes, Henry, I already have a
23   perfect place in mind — right above the commo —
24   JUSTICE GAVEL: Yes, dear, I was thinking of the exact same
25   place: right above the comforter on our bed.
26   SENATOR: I feel I can safely say that I have never had a gift
27   quite like it.
28   PRIME MINISTER: You really shouldn't have done it,
29   General.
30   TRIXIE: *(Squeals.)* Oh, he's so cute!
31   DORIE: Well, now that the formalities are out of the way,
32   everyone help yourself to the punch and goodies. *(The*
33   *GUESTS start mingling and chatting with each other. DR.*
34   *HACKAR and MRS. LAWSON casually meet at Front Center.)*
35   MRS. LAWSON: Dr. Hackar, I wonder if you could give me a

1   **little professional advice. I did something this morning**
2   **that has me just a little concerned: I accidentally ate a**
3   **can of dog food thinking it was hash. Do you think I will**
4   **suffer any harmful effects?**
5   **DR. HACKAR: Well, I don't know. How did you feel after you**
6   **ate it?**
7   **MRS. LAWSON: I felt exhausted and hoarse.**
8   **DR. HACKAR: Exhausted? Hoarse? From eating dog food?**
9   **MRS. LAWSON: Sure. Exhausted from chasing the neighbor's**
10   **cat up a cedar tree, and hoarse from barking at him all**
11   **afternoon.**
12   **DR. HACKAR: Uh, I see. And how do you feel now?**
13   **MRS. LAWSON: Oh, just fine. Want to see me roll over?**
14   **DR. HACKAR: Oh, no, no . . .**
15   **MRS. LAWSON: Sit up? Beg? Shake hands? Fetch a stick?**
16   **DR. HACKAR: I don't think any of that will be necessary,**
17   **Mrs. Lawson. Just take a couple of aspirin and call me**
18   **in the morning. I can give you the number of a good**
19   **veterinarian.**
20   **MRS. LAWSON: Thank you, Doctor.** *(She tries to lick his hand*
21   *but he draws it back. She returns to the other guests as MRS.*
22   *GAVEL approaches HACKAR.)*
23   **MRS. GAVEL: Dr. Hackar, I wonder if you could help me with**
24   **a little problem we've been having in our family.**
25   **DR. HACKAR: I'll be glad to if I can. What's the problem?**
26   **MRS. GAVEL: It's my grandfather. He thinks he's a clock.**
27   **He stands in the corner all day, slowly rotating his hands**
28   **to show the time, and chimes every hour on the hour.**
29   **DR. HACKAR: And you want me to cure him of this delusion,**
30   **of course.**
31   **MRS. GAVEL: Oh, no. It's kind of nice having a grandfather**
32   **clock in the house. I was just wondering if you could**
33   **reset him. He's been running a bit slow lately.**
34   **DR. HACKAR: Just have him take a couple of aspirin with a**
35   **glass of WD-40, then call me in the morning. I can give**

1   you the name of a good clock repair shop.
2 MRS. GAVEL: Very well. Thank you, Doctor. *(She returns to*
3   *the other guests as the QUEEN approaches HACKAR.)*
4 QUEEN: Dr. Hackar, I've been having a problem lately with
5   my memory. It seems I can't remember anything for any
6   length of time at all. It's most distressing.
7 DR. HACKAR: Hmmm. How long have you had this problem?
8 QUEEN: What problem?
9 DR. HACKAR: Never mind. Just take a couple of aspirin and
10   call me in the morning. *(Aside to audience)* From now on,
11   I've got to remember always to collect my fee from her
12   in advance. *(The QUEEN returns to the other guests. NAAMAN*
13   *approaches DR. HACKAR.)*
14 NAAMAN: Say, Doctor, I thought you might give me a little
15   advice about this pesky rash and sort of numb feeling
16   I've been having in my hand lately.
17 DR. HACKAR: *(Looks at NAAMAN's hand.)* Hmmm . . . rash . . .
18   no feeling . . . Oh, I think you've just got a little touch of
19   leprosy there. Take a couple of aspirin and — *(His mouth*
20   *suddenly drops open and his eyes widen as he realizes what he*
21   *has just said. He drops NAAMAN's hand and begins wiping*
22   *his own hand on his robe.)* Leprosy! Leprosy — and I
23   touched you! Yuck! Gross! And you have probably
24   handled everything in this house. It's all contaminated.
25   I'm getting out of here! *(DR. HACKAR exits rapidly, holding*
26   *his hands up, surgeon-like, careful to touch nothing. The*
27   *GUESTS get deathly quiet when they hear the word "leprosy."*
28   *They drop their pictures, wipe hands on clothing, and stare at*
29   *NAAMAN.)*
30 NAAMAN: *(Shocked, staring at his own hand)* Leprosy! *(The*
31   *CROWD begins to back away from NAAMAN. They form a loose*
32   *semicircle behind him, facing the audience. Whispers and*
33   *murmurs of words, "leprosy, horrible, awful, tragic," are heard*
34   *from among them. After a moment, TRIXIE comes forward but*
35   *is careful to keep her distance from NAAMAN.)*

1   **TRIXIE:**   I hate to be a party pooper, General Naaman, but I
2   just remembered that I need to iron a handkerchief
3   before I go to work in the morning. You all go on with
4   your party and don't mind about little ol' me. Could you
5   take me home, Mr. Prime Minister?

6   **PRIME MINISTER:** *(Obviously delighted to have an excuse to*
7   *leave)* **Of course, my dear. Hate to run, General, but as
8   you can see, the lady has pressing matters to attend to.
9   Uh, about the statue; I'm sure you will understand if we
10   put that project on hold for a while — just until you get
11   this little medical problem cleared up. It just wouldn't
12   do to have a statue of a lep — well, you know how people
13   feel about leprosy. It wouldn't be appropriate. You do
14   understand, of course. Sorry, old fellow. Good evening,
15   all.** *(Exit PRIME MINISTER and TRIXIE.)*

16   **MRS. LAWSON:**   Oh my, Asa. I just remembered, I may have
17   forgotten to feed the goldfish. Poor little fellow, he may
18   not have eaten since noon. We must go see about him at
19   once, uh, as much as I hate to leave.

20   **SENATOR:**   You are absolutely right, my dear. It wouldn't do
21   to have the animal rights lobby on our backs, would it?
22   Please excuse us, General. It seems we may have a hungry
23   little mouth to feed at home. Good night, everyone. *(Exit*
24   *SENATOR and MRS. LAWSON.)*

25   **JUSTICE GAVEL:**   I just remembered, I've got to be on the
26   golf course at 11:00 in the morning. I had better get home
27   and get a little shuteye. No, don't bother to show me to
28   the door. We'll just slip out quietly and be on our way.
29   Nice party, General, Mrs. Naaman. Good night. *(Exit*
30   *JUSTICE and MRS. GAVEL.)*

31   **KING:**   Blast it all, Naaman! Why did you have to go and get a
32   confounded disease like that without checking with me
33   first? You are ruining everything. I had big plans and I
34   was counting on your help. First we were going to inveed
35   Grace — I mean — invade Greece, and turn that country

1 into a vassal state. Then after your triumphal march back
2 to Aram, I was planning to appoint you chairman of the
3 chief staff of joints — uh — joint chiefs of staff. Then I
4 was hoping we could expand the Aramean Empire to the
5 east — all the way to China. And as a reward for that, I
6 would have made you my secretary of state. But now I
7 suppose it's early retirement for you, and I will have to
8 promote General Hashembarker to commander-in-chief
9 of my farmed horses — er — armed forces.
10 NAAMAN: *(Exploding)* Hashembarker! Why, that strutting
11 little banty rooster doesn't know a broadsword from a
12 butter knife. He couldn't fight his way out of a closet full
13 of petticoats. This country needs *me*.
14 KING: I understand how you feel, Naaman. But look at it this
15 way: you have earned a rest. You've had a magnificent
16 career, so why not go out on top? Your pilitary mension —
17 uh, military pension — will get you and Dorie a nice place
18 in the country where you will be isolated — I mean —
19 where you will have all the privacy you could want.
20 NAAMAN: But I'm not ready to retire. I'm at the peak of my
21 powers.
22 KING: Yes, but when you're on a peak, the only way you can
23 go is down. Just think, Naaman; you can settle down
24 while you're still on top and just wade afay — I mean
25 fade away — like old soldiers do. Now, don't get me
26 wrong. I'm not trying to pressure you. You do whatever
27 you think best, and take all the time you want to mull it
28 over — the rest of the night if you need it. And whatever
29 you decide will be fine with me . . . as long as you turn in
30 your resignation in the morning. Uh, no need to come to
31 the palace anymore. Save your strength; send a
32 messenger. Well, sorry about all this, old fellow. We've
33 had some fun times together — great wars and lovely
34 invasions. But all good ends must come to a thing, and
35 into every rain a little life must fall. *(He starts to pat NAAMAN*

45

1   *on the shoulder but thinks better of it as his hand hovers*
2   *momentarily over NAAMAN's shoulder, then drops to his side.)*
3   **Good night, all. Great party. We enjoyed it, didn't we, dear?**
4 **QUEEN:**   **What party?** *(Exit KING and QUEEN.)*
5 **NAAMAN:**   *(Dazed and stunned)* **Leprosy!** *(He slowly sits and*
6   *stares into space.)* **My career is over — just like that! I am**
7   **suddenly an outcast. My friends are afraid to be around**
8   **me.** *(Angrily)* **And my commission goes to that pansy**
9   **Hashembarker! It's too much. This can't be happening to**
10   **me. To ordinary people, yes. To privates, corporals, and a**
11   **few second lieutenants now and then, but not to *me*, a**
12   **world-class general. It's not fair. It's not fair!** *(Bangs fist*
13   *against chair arm, walks over to idol, kneels and prays.)* **Oh, great**
14   **Baal, I call on you to heal my hand. Make it pure and whole**
15   **again. Let me keep my commission. Let parliament approve**
16   **the statue, and let General Hashembarker be trampled**
17   **under his own horse. In Ashtaroth's name, Amen.** *(He rises.)*
18   **This is all just a bad dream. I am going to bed, and when**
19   **I wake up, none of this will have happened, except the**
20   **medal, of course.** *(Exit NAAMAN.)*
21 **DORIE:**   **Oh, dear, this is just too awful. What are we going to**
22   **do?** *(Sits with head in hands.)*
23 **GOLDA:**   **Don't worry, Mrs. Naaman. I know a way to help**
24   **your husband.**
25 **DORIE:**   **If you want to help, clean up this mess.** *(She gestures*
26   *to the room.)*
27 **GOLDA:**   **I'll be glad to, but that isn't what I meant. I know**
28   **how General Naaman can be cured.**
29 **DORIE:**   **Don't talk nonsense, Golda. There is no cure for**
30   **leprosy. Now, leave me alone. I have a lot on my mind.**
31 **GOLDA:**   **Please listen, Mrs. Naaman. I know of a prophet in**
32   **Israel who can cure all kinds of diseases.**
33 **DORIE:**   **And I suppose he also reads palms, tells fortunes,**
34   **and casts horoscopes. We've got plenty of charlatans of**
35   **that sort right here in Aram.**

1 GOLDA: Oh, no, he isn't like that. He works real miracles by
2 the power of the God of Israel.
3 DORIE: Gods are of no help whatsoever. *(Gestures toward idol.)*
4 We've got plenty of them here in Aram, too, and all of
5 them put together can't cure a hangnail.
6 GOLDA: But the God of Israel can cure anything. By his
7 power the prophet even raised a boy from the dead not
8 very long ago.
9 DORIE: I wish I could believe that.
10 GOLDA: I'm telling you the truth. Everyone in Israel knows
11 about him. Try to get General Naaman to go see him,
12 please, Mrs. Naaman. *(Enter NAAMAN.)*
13 DORIE: What are you doing up? I thought you went to bed.
14 NAAMAN: *(Grumpily)* I can't find my teddy bear.
15 DORIE: Listen, Naaman. Golda has an idea that may be
16 worth trying. She says there is a prophet in Israel who
17 raised a boy from the dead. I know it sounds wild, but
18 what if it is true? A man who could do a thing like that
19 could certainly cure leprosy.
20 NAAMAN: What is this prophet's name, girl?
21 GOLDA: Elisha.
22 NAAMAN: Elisha? I've heard of him. Isn't he the one who
23 called fire down from heaven back when Ahab was your
24 king?
25 GOLDA: No, that was another prophet named Elijah. Elisha
26 took Elijah's place. But it is said that Elisha has twice
27 the power that Elijah had.
28 DORIE: Naaman, what have we got to lose? Anything is worth
29 a try.
30 NAAMAN: Hmmm. If Elisha has twice the power of old Elijah,
31 he must be some humdinger of a prophet. Dorie, I say,
32 what have we got to lose? Anything is worth a try.
33 DORIE: A brilliant idea, dear.
34 NAAMAN: Of course, honey. That's the only kind of idea I
35 ever have. Well, if I'm going off to Israel, there's no use

1   **pussyfooting around about it. I will leave immediately.**
2   *(To SERVANTS)* **Hormish, Alfap, go pack some rations**
3   **and supplies. We are heading for Israel.**
4 **HORMISH and ALFAP:** *(In unison)* **Yes, sir.** *(They salute, collide,*
5   *and exit.)*
6 **NAAMAN:** **If we hurry, we can get to the palace before the**
7   **king goes to bed. I'll stop by and get him to write a letter**
8   **of introduction, then we will be on our way.**
9 **DORIE:** **Do be careful, Naaman.**
10 **NAAMAN:** **Aw, don't always tell me that. You sound like my**
11   **mother.** *(He strides to the door, stops, and strikes a heroic pose.)*
12   **I shall return.** *(Exit NAAMAN as lights fade on Scene 1.)*
13
14   **Scene 2**
15
16   *(Lights rise on a rustic, run-down shack with an open door in*
17   *front. Enter NAAMAN with HORMISH and ALFAP, both of*
18   *whom carry a suitcase. HORMISH is also carrying an unfolded*
19   *road map. NAAMAN's left hand is bandaged. They stop in front*
20   *of the shack.)*
21 **ALFAP:** **This must be the place.**
22 **NAAMAN:** **This little shack? It couldn't be.**
23 **HORMISH:** *(Looking at map)* **According to the map, this has**
24   **got to be it.**
25 **NAAMAN:** **A great prophet wouldn't live in a shack like this.**
26   **Either the map is wrong, or you misread it. Let's go a**
27   **little farther.**
28 **ALFAP:** **Why don't we just knock and get directions?** *(ALFAP*
29   *and HORMISH collide as both start toward the door. ALFAP*
30   *goes to the door and knocks.)*
31 **GEHAZI:** *(From inside the house)* **Come on in, it's open.**
32 **ALFAP:** *(Looks inside.)* **Hello. We're looking for the prophet**
33   **Elisha.**
34 **GEHAZI:** *(Emerges from shack door.)* **Well, you-all have come to**
35   **the right place. This here's Elisha's cabin and I'm his**

1   **number-one servant Gehazi. What can I do for you fellers?**

2   **HORMISH:** Our master, General Naaman, has a little

3   medical problem, and he would like for Elisha to take a

4   look at it.

5   **GEHAZI:** Howdy, Mr. Naaman. Mighty pleased to meetcha.

6   *(Offers NAAMAN his hand in greeting. NAAMAN remains aloof*

7   *with arms folded.)*

8   **HORMISH:** *(Stiffly)* It's *General* Naaman to you, buster.

9   *General* Naaman, Commander-in-Chief of the Armed

10   Forces of Aram. He does not shake hands with common

11   servants.

12   **GEHAZI:** Well, ex-*cuuuse* me!

13   **ALFAP:** Let's get on with our business here. I have letters of

14   introduction from the kings of Aram and Israel. Take

15   them to your prophet and tell him that General Naaman

16   is here.

17   **GEHAZI:** Wellll, I don't know. Colonel Naaman here —

18   **HORMISH:** *General* Naaman!

19   **GEHAZI:** Oh, yeah. Anyway, he don't have no appointment,

20   you know. But tell me, what is this here problem he's

21   got? If it's serious enough, I reckon I might go and see if

22   Mr. Elisha has a hankerin' to break into his busy schedule

23   and take a look at him.

24   **ALFAP:** He has leprosy.

25   **GEHAZI:** That oughta do it. Man, you're talkin' big time

26   serious now. That stuff will eat you up like —

27   **HORMISH:** Cut the gab, Hazy. Get in there and get your

28   prophet.

29   **GEHAZI:** OK, OK. You fellers just hang loose a bit and I'll be

30   back quicker'n you can say "sixty thrifty thistle sifters."

31   *(GEHAZI must articulate this phrase effortlessly, clearly, and*

32   *without a bobble. Exit GEHAZI.)*

33   **ALFAP:** Sixty thrifty sissel fifters.

34   **HORMISH:** Sixty srifty fissel sisters. *(They alternately make two*

35   *or three attempts at the tongue twister.)*

1　NAAMAN:　You clowns cut out the malarky and stand at
2　attention. When that two-bit prophet learns who is here,
3　he'll be out here faster than a lawyer at an accident.
4　Then after bowing, scraping, and apologizing, he will
5　begin the healing ceremony. I can just see it; he will recite
6　an elaborate incantation, then he will wave a wand over
7　my hand a few times. Then he will lift up his arms and
8　call for the power of his god in a mighty voice. The wind
9　will start blowing and the sky will get dark. There will
10　be thunder and lightning and — *(Enter GEHAZI.)*
11　GEHAZI:　Well, Major —
12　HORMISH:　General!
13　GEHAZI:　Whatever. I spoke to Mr. Elisha about your little
14　problem and he said he ain't got time to see you right
15　now, but he wrote out this here pre-scription for you.
16　*(GEHAZI hands paper toward NAAMAN, who keeps his arms*
17　*folded and makes no move to take it.)*
18　ALFAP:　*(Grabs paper from GEHAZI and looks at it, puzzled.)* I
19　can't read this. What miserable handwriting! Why can't
20　these doctor types write?
21　GEHAZI:　Here, I'll try to make it out. Hmmm, it is a mite
22　scrawly, ain't it? Kinda looks like the scratchin's of a
23　double-jointed snake sufferin' from chigger bites. Let's
24　see, it says, "Go . . . jump . . . in . . . the . . . river . . ."
25　HORMISH:　*(Draws sword, grabs GEHAZI by the collar and shouts.)*
26　I'll have your hide for that, you cockroach! What do you
27　mean, telling the General to jump in the river?
28　GEHAZI:　Now, don't go gettin' all riled up. Just simmer down,
29　put up your little tater slicer and let me finish. My, you
30　gents are touchy. *(He straightens himself, clears his throat,*
31　*and continues reading.)* It says, go jump in the River
32　Jordan . . . let's see, uh . . . seven times . . . and you will
33　be . . . crude — er, cured. That's *cured.* Sorry about that.
34　Heh, heh.
35　ALFAP:　Well, go on.

50

1   GEHAZI: Go where?

2   ALFAP: Read the rest of it! Go on!

3   GEHAZI: Nowhere else to go. That's it. I done read the whole

4   kit and kaboodle. Don't I get no tip? *(Holds out hand.)*

5   HORMISH: *(Hand on sword, steps threateningly toward GEHAZI.)*

6   I'll slice off the tip of your nose and shove it down your

7   throat if you don't get out of our sight.

8   GEHAZI: No problem. I got plenty of chores to get at. Hope

9   you have a good swim, Captain. Uh, if I was you, I'd get

10   out of that there tin can before I dived in. *(Exit GEHAZI*

11   *into house.)*

12   NAAMAN: Well, I never! Here I am, one of the great military

13   figures in history. I come hundreds of miles on a mission

14   of importance to two nations, and this flea-bitten country

15   prophet treats me like a buck private. No red carpet, no

16   orchestra to play a fanfare, no twenty-one arrow salute,

17   no adoring crowds of thousands to greet me, no gifts of

18   camels, donkeys, and maidservants, no fourteen-course

19   banquet in my honor — whatever happened to good, old-

20   fashioned, simple hospitality?

21   ALFAP: Oh, well, let's blow it off and get on with our business.

22   *(Looks at map.)* Let's see, where is this Jordan River?

23   NAAMAN: Forget it. I'll be jiggered if I'm going to contaminate

24   myself in that slimy Jordan River. I wouldn't wash a hog

25   in that Yiddish sewer. If I thought a swim could cure

26   leprosy, I would have stayed home and gone to one of

27   our own unpolluted rivers like the Pharpar or the Abana.

28   A curse on all desert prophets! Let's get out of here.

29   *(NAAMAN strides toward exit.)*

30   ALFAP: Wait, General. According to the map, the Jordan is

31   just up the road a little way. We're already here, so why

32   not give it a try? What have you got to lose?

33   NAAMAN: Don't be ridiculous. Do you expect me to humiliate

34   myself going through that stupid routine while that boor

35   of a prophet and his hick servant laugh up their sleeves?

1   And what if someone saw me? Do you realize how silly I

2   would look — jumping in the river, crawling back out,

3   jumping in again, crawling out again, jumping back in . . .

4   ALFAP: I know, I know, General. But what if it worked?

5   Wouldn't you be willing to crawl, grovel, jump through

6   hoops, stand on your head, or beg on your knees to get

7   rid of that awful disease? *(NAAMAN turns away and stands*

8   *silently thinking with fingers to chin.)* **Well, wouldn't you?**

9   NAAMAN: *(Testily)* I'm thinking about it.

10   HORMISH: General, if that prophet had asked you to do some

11   brave and dangerous thing like fighting a den full of lions,

12   you would have grabbed your sword and jumped in. If

13   he had asked you to do some treacherous and difficult

14   thing like climb to the top of the tallest mountain in Tibet,

15   you would have grabbed a pickaxe and headed up. If he

16   had asked you to do some expensive thing that cost you

17   your entire fortune, you would have signed the check

18   without a second thought. Just think how much easier

19   it is to do this simple, cheap, easy, and safe little thing

20   he is asking of you. And there's a chance it might save

21   your life. You may whip me for this, but I'm going to tell

22   you what I think, General. You are acting like a fool.

23   You're like a starving man who won't eat cornbread and

24   red beans because it's not the steak dinner with all the

25   trimmings he was hoping for. You'd better take what's

26   offered, General, and be grateful for it.

27   NAAMAN: *(Bristling with anger)* **Why, you little twerp . . .**

28   *(Reaches for sword, takes a threatening step toward HORMISH,*

29   *then stops and relaxes.)* **You are absolutely right. I am acting**

30   **like a fool. Take me to the Jordan.** *(HORMISH and ALFAP*

31   *cheer excitedly. They hug NAAMAN, pat him on the back, gather*

32   *up their things, collide, and exit with NAAMAN as lights dim*

33   *on Scene 2.)*

34

35

1   **Scene 3**
2
3   *(The setting is the same as Scene 1 — NAAMAN's living room.*
4   *As the lights come up, DORIE is anxiously pacing back and*
5   *forth. GOLDA is dusting furniture or sweeping the floor.)*
6   **DORIE: I do wish we would hear something from Naaman. I**
7   **really expected a message today.**
8   **GOLDA: Please don't worry, Mrs. Naaman. Elisha is the very**
9   **hand of God. Your husband will be cured. Please try to**
10   **relax.**
11   **DORIE: I will try.** *(She sits, fidgets, picks up a magazine and*
12   *thumbs through it, puts it down, drums fingers on the chair arm,*
13   *gets up and paces again.)* **You really have faith in that God**
14   **of yours. I wish I could believe as you do, but I doubt**
15   **that your God or any god can cure leprosy. I'm afraid it's**
16   **hopeless.** *(She sits, head in hands, and begins to sob. GOLDA*
17   *puts her arm around DORIE.)*
18   **GOLDA: You're right. Not just any god can cure leprosy,**
19   **because not just any god is really God. But Elisha's God**
20   **is the one, true, and only God — the God who made the**
21   **world and everything in it. All things are possible with**
22   **him.**
23   **DORIE: It sounds wonderful. If only it were true.**
24   **GOLDA: Listen, I think I hear something.** *(Singing is heard*
25   *Off-stage as NAAMAN, ALFAP, and HORMISH return. They*
26   *are singing a military song, with gusto but without precision.*
27   *Much laughter is heard between musical phrases. GOLDA*
28   *alarmed)* **I think there are wounded bears out there!**
29   **DORIE:** *(Stands and listens.)* **No, it's Naaman with Hormish**
30   **and Alfap.** *(She sighs.)* **It's just as I thought; he couldn't**
31   **be cured, so they went and got drunk.** *(Enter NAAMAN,*
32   *ALFAP, and HORMISH, boisterously. NAAMAN's left hand is*
33   *hidden in his cape.)*
34   **NAAMAN:** *(Grinning from ear to ear)* **Hello, darling Dorie.**
35   **DORIE: He couldn't help you, could he? You're drunk.**

1   **NAAMAN:**   No, I'm not drunk, and yes, he did help me.
2   **DORIE:**   *(Hopefully)* **He did?**
3   **NAAMAN:**   Yes. He cured me of that most hideous of diseases.
4   That grim and devastating disease that every man should
5   fear with dread and loathing. That ghastly disease that
6   makes a man's friends and loved ones shun him and
7   makes his life a hell on earth. Yes, Dorie, the prophet
8   cured me of that worst disease a man can have — my
9   rotten, stinking pride. I've been such a pompous peacock,
10   strutting around thinking I was the center of the
11   universe. How could you stand me, Dorie?
12   **DORIE:**   Why, I loved you, Naaman. But the leprosy —
13   **NAAMAN:**   You loved me. That we had in common. I loved me,
14   too. I thought I was the greatest thing since the battering
15   ram. But now I have found the real way to be great, which
16   is simply to be a servant. The truly great persons are
17   those who unselfishly help others — like these three
18   magnificent people who grace our household. *(He gestures*
19   *toward the three SERVANTS.)* **Dorie, if it hadn't been for**
20   these three, pointing the way, keeping me on track, and
21   even slapping me in the face when I needed it most, I
22   would have been a goner, eaten alive by my own bloated
23   ego. How can I ever thank you three truly great and
24   wonderful servants?
25   **GOLDA, HORMISH and ALFAP:**   *(In unison, looking at the floor*
26   *and smiling shyly)* **Aw, shucks, 'tweren't nothing.**
27   **NAAMAN:**   To me, it was everything, and I will see that each
28   of you is well rewarded.
29   **DORIE:**   This is all very wonderful, but what about the leprosy?
30   **NAAMAN:**   The what? Oh, yes, the leprosy. *(Holds up unband-*
31   *aged hand.)* **Ta-daaa.**
32   **DORIE:**   *(Squeals with delight and jumps up and down.)* **Ohhh!**
33   **He did it! He did it! He did it!** *(DORIE and NAAMAN embrace*
34   *happily.)*
35   **NAAMAN:**   Now I have one more thing to do. *(He picks up the*

1   *idol and throws it Off-stage.)* **There is no god but the God**
2   **of Israel. And from this day forward, this household will**
3   **worship only him.**
4   **DORIE, GOLDA, ALFAP and HORMISH:**   *(In unison)* **Amen.**
5   *(Blackout)*
6
7
8
9
10
11
12
13
14
15
16
17
18
19
20
21
22
23
24
25
26
27
28
29
30
31
32
33
34
35

GOOD OL' SAM

Do you
ever have
the feeling
you're being
watched?

A COMEDY IN ONE ACT BY T. M. WILLIAMS

Good Ol' Sam

GOOD OL' SAM

A contemporary version of "The Good Samaritan"
(Luke 10:30-36; Hebrews 13:2; Matthew 25:34-36)

Cast

Victim (A seriously injured man)

Crumley (An insurance salesman)

Ralph
Debbie — (A young yuppie couple)

Henry
Myrtle — (A middle-aged couple)

Deacon

Preacher

Sam (A "good ol' boy")

Stranded Motorist

Lost Child

Elderly Shopper — (Optional walk-on characters)

Blind Man

Poor Widow

Costumes:

VICTIM — a suit and tie. SAM — ordinary street clothes with a T-shirt beneath his outer shirt. CRUMLEY, RALPH, DEBBIE, HENRY, MYRTLE, DEACON and PREACHER — they should all be wearing their Sunday best. WALK-ON CHARACTERS — ordinary clothes appropriate to their individual activity.

Music:

All the songs are sung to the tune of "This Is the Way We Go to School."

Props:

A badge, a pocket tape player, and a pocket telephone for Victim. A business card for Crumley. A soft drink in a can for Sam. A Bible for Preacher. A gasoline can for Motorist. A lollipop for Lost Child. Two full grocery bags for Elderly Shopper. A tapping cane and dark glasses for Blind Man. A hand-held fan for Poor Widow.

Sound Effects:

Telephone rings.

Note:

On page 73 the voice of Preacher is heard on audio cassette. If your staging area is equipped with a sophisticated sound system, Preacher's lines can be pre-recorded and played back over the system by the audio engineer. The visual cue to start playback will be when Victim punches the "play" button of his tape recorder. If you do not have a sound system, Preacher must repeat these lines backstage, taking his cue aurally from Victim.

Setting:

A church yard (see sketch on page 61).

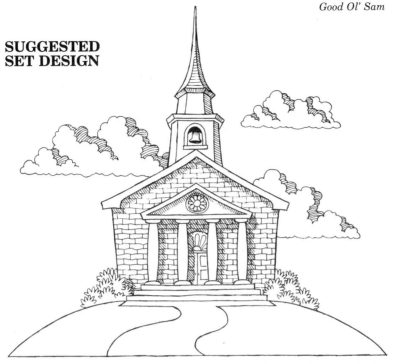

SUGGESTED SET DESIGN

THREE DIMENSIONAL OPTION

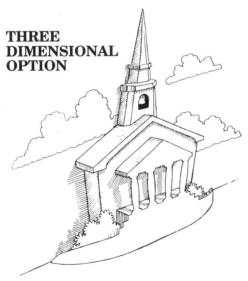

Make enlarged film copy of building drawing above, trace lines with heavy black marker or black poster paint. Building should be as large as your staging area allows. It can be drawn, painted, and cut out of flat cardboard, and mounted on back wall of stage, or it can be constructed three dimensionally as in sketch at left. Suggested colors are as follows:

Bricks — red
Steps, sidewalk, shadows on bell tower — light gray
Steeple — dark gray
Shadows on bricks — dark red (red used for bricks mixed with black)
Pillars and all "wooden" areas of building — white
Grass and shrubs — green
Clouds — white with light blue shadows

Notes: If you construct the building three-dimensionally, do not paint any shadows that will be cast naturally by construction. Black outlines of bricks and leaves on shrubbery will need to be projected and painted *after* the colors have been applied.

1   *(The play opens with VICTIM lying on his back at Center Stage.*
2   *He moans with pain. Enter CRUMLEY.)*
3   CRUMLEY: *(Singing)* **On Sunday morning I go to church.**
4   **I smile and chat and do good works,**
5   **So God will bless me in my search,**
6   **For sales, and profits and cash flow.**
7   *(He sees VICTIM lying by the curb.)* **Say, what have we here?**
8   VICTIM: **Ohhh ... help me ... please, help me.**
9   CRUMLEY: **What's wrong, man; are you sick or something?**
10 VICTIM: **Yes ... my head ... my chest ... ohhh ... please,**
11   **help me.**
12 CRUMLEY: **I'll do what I can. First I'll try to see to your**
13   **immediate needs, then I'll go call an ambulance. What's**
14   **wrong with you, anyway?**
15 VICTIM: **Beaten ... robbed ... tried to kill me ... ohhh, my**
16   **head!**
17 CRUMLEY: **Oh, uh — I didn't realize you had been involved**
18   **in foul play. I thought you might have had a seizure or**
19   **heart attack or something more respectable. Were you**
20   **able to identify your attackers?**
21 VICTIM: **Yes ... got a good look ... license number of car ...**
22   **ohhh, my ribs!**
23 CRUMLEY: **Hmmm. Sounds like this could turn into a messy**
24   **deal. I don't much like getting involved in things like**
25   **this. Lots of hassle, you know. If I help you, I'll have to**
26   **wait for the police to come. I'll have to give them a**
27   **statement, and probably get called to be a witness at the**
28   **trial. I really can't afford to get mixed up in all that. I'm**
29   **a businessman, you see — got a thriving insurance**
30   **agency downtown — Crumley Insurance Company. If**
31   **you've seen our ads on TV, you probably know our motto:**
32   **"When you make a claim, we feel the pain." We were the**
33   **top agency in the state association last month. If I had**
34   **to be away from the office for the kind of time all this**
35   **will take, we would risk slipping into second place. I'm**

1   sure you understand.

2   VICTIM: Please ... I need help.

3   CRUMLEY: I'm really sorry, fella. I sort of hate to leave you
4   here, but you are right in front of the city's number-one
5   church, and it's getting close to meeting time. Someone
6   is sure to be along soon who will be glad to help you —
7   someone with a little more leisure time than I have. But
8   hang in there. Remember, tough times don't last, but
9   tough people do. Every cloud has a silver lining. There's
10   a light at the end of the tunnel. When the night seems
11   darkest, morning is on the way.

12   VICTIM: Aaauuugh!

13   CRUMLEY: That's the spirit. Oh, by the way, when you get
14   back on your feet, you might like to take a look at one of
15   our insurance programs. We have some just tailored for
16   incidents like this — you know, theft, accident, injury,
17   and even life — just in case you don't survive. Here, I'll
18   leave you my card. *(He extends his card toward VICTIM, who*
19   *is unable to reach for it.)* I'll just put it in your pocket here.

20   VICTIM: Aaauuugh!

21   CRUMLEY: You're welcome. Call me when you feel better
22   and we can set up an appointment. Well, have a nice day.
23   *(Exit CRUMLEY.)*

24   VICTIM: Ohhh, nooo ... please ... don't leave me ... help
25   me ... *(Enter RALPH and DEBBIE.)*

26   RALPH and DEBBIE: *(Singing)* On Sunday morn to church
27   we go,

28   But ask for more and we'll say no,

29   To teach or visit or save a soul,

30   Would interfere with our lifestyle.

31   DEBBIE: Oh, look, Ralph, there's a man lying there. Do you
32   suppose he's hurt or sick or something?

33   VICTIM: Owww ... ohhh ...

34   RALPH: Uh, sir, do you need help?

35   VICTIM: Ohhh ... Aauurrgh ...

1   DEBBIE: I think that means yes.

2   RALPH: I suppose so. I guess we ought to do something,

3   Debbie. But I don't know what. Do you have any ideas?

4   DEBBIE: No, I never took any of those first aid classes at

5   the fitness club. And I've heard that if you do the wrong

6   thing, you can hurt the victim more than you help him.

7   RALPH: Well, we could at least try to move him to a shadier

8   place on the grass to make him more comfortable.

9   DEBBIE: No, Ralph, we'd better not do that. What if he has a

10   spinal injury? Moving him the wrong way could paralyze

11   him for life. Besides, I'm wearing my new Bill Blass dress,

12   and you remember what that cost. I'd hate to get it dirty.

13   RALPH: Yeah, I suppose you're right. Oh, look, he seems to

14   be bleeding from the back of his head — see? Right there

15   behind his ear.

16   DEBBIE: Yuck! Gross!

17   RALPH: I guess we could at least try to bandage that wound

18   with a handkerchief or something.

19   DEBBIE: No, you'd better not do that, either. You're wearing

20   your new Calvin Klein suit, and bloodstains are sure hard

21   to get out. Besides, what if he got an infection from your

22   handkerchief? He could hold us responsible, you know.

23   RALPH: He could also hold us responsible if we just let him

24   lie there and bleed, couldn't he?

25   DEBBIE: Not if he bleeds to death.

26   RALPH: I'm not sure we'll be that lucky. But it does look like

27   he may have lost quite a bit of blood. Maybe he's getting

28   dehydrated or something. Why don't we at least get him

29   a drink of water?

30   DEBBIE: No, Ralph. You don't know if that is really what he

31   needs in his condition. For all we know, water may be

32   the last thing you should give a bleeding man. If it caused

33   some sort of shock to his system, we'd be in big trouble.

34   I've heard of people getting sued for millions because

35   they tried to help accident victims and did the wrong

1   thing. We'd better just go on our way and leave him to
2   someone who knows more about first aid.
3   RALPH: But our insurance company would probably cover
4   a lawsuit. Maybe we should take the risk for once.
5   DEBBIE: Don't be silly, Ralph. Our insurance doubled when
6   we added the pool and hot tub. If we got sued, it would
7   quadruple. And we'd have to give up our plans to buy
8   your sailboat and my tanning machine.
9   RALPH: I suppose you're right. But I kind of hate to just
10   leave him here without doing anything. Why don't you
11   drive the car around and we can take him to the medical
12   center?
13   DEBBIE: What?! And risk getting blood on the seats of our
14   BMW?
15   RALPH: But we've got to do something.
16   DEBBIE: Well, I suppose you could call him an ambulance.
17   RALPH: Do what?
18   DEBBIE: Call him an ambulance.
19   RALPH: *(Shrugs.)* Well, OK. Uh, sir, you're an ambulance. I
20   don't see what good it does, but if you think it helps —
21   DEBBIE: No, no, stupid. I meant call an ambulance *for* him.
22   But on second thought, we can do something even better.
23   We can pray for him. Come on, let's go. Church will start
24   in a few minutes, and we've got to hurry if we want to
25   get a back seat. *(Exit RALPH and DEBBIE; enter HENRY*
26   *and MYRTLE.)*
27   MYRTLE: . . . and so I said to Helen, "Now if I tell you what
28   Gertrude said Lizzie told her about Jenny, you've got to
29   promise never to let on that you know. You see, Gertrude
30   made me swear never to breathe this to a soul, and so I
31   don't want it getting back to her. Of course, I mentioned
32   it to Nellie, but I know she won't tell because she knows
33   I know what she told Lizzie she wouldn't tell Florence.
34   And — are you listening to me, Henry?
35   HENRY: Hmmm? Oh, yes, dear.

1   **MYRTLE:**   As I was saying, Retta told Carole that Judy said
2   — oh my goodness, Henry, will you look at that!
3   **HENRY:**   What's that, dear?
4   **MYRTLE:**   *(Points to VICTIM.)* That! Some shameless drunk
5   has passed out right here on our church sidewalk. Have
6   they no decency? You'd think they would do their
7   drinking somewhere else. That's the trouble with the
8   world nowadays — no respect for religion. They do their
9   drinking on Sunday when they've got six perfectly good
10   weekdays for that sort of thing; then they go and
11   desecrate the Lord's property by passing out on his
12   sidewalk. It's disgusting, I say. Don't you agree, Henry?
13   **HENRY:**   Of course, dear.
14   **VICTIM:**   Ohhh ... help me ... please ...
15   **HENRY:**   *(As he reaches into his pocket)* Well, I guess we could
16   give him a —
17   **MYRTLE:**   Absolutely not! He doesn't get a penny from us.
18   He'd just go and spend it on more whiskey. You just put
19   that money right back in your pocket where it belongs.
20   **HENRY:**   Yes, dear.
21   **MYRTLE:**   Our dollar goes into the church collection plate
22   where it will be well-spent on spiritual things like pews,
23   carpets, church bulletins, and choir robes. We're not
24   about to squander it to finance debauchery and
25   dissipation in some sleazy street corner tavern.
26   **HENRY:**   But Myrtle, dear, maybe he's not dr —
27   **MYRTLE:**   Hush, Henry; you don't know how to deal with this
28   sort of thing. I'll handle it. *(She sings.)*
29   For one whose sins are few as mine,
30   Must watch those who are less divine,
31   And prod them till they toe the line,
32   And point it out when they don't.
33   **HENRY:**   *(Singing)* Perhaps he's not —
34   **MYRTLE:**   *(Completes musical phrase.)* Don't be a fool,
35   He's drunk enough to souse a mule,

1   HENRY: But maybe he —
2   MYRTLE: Shut up or you'll
3   Be lying right there beside him.
4   VICTIM: Owww ... my head ... my head!
5   MYRTLE: Well, I should think so! A hangover is the natural
6   fruit that grows from the seed of indulgence. Do you know
7   what you need, young man? Do you know what would
8   put a stop to the pain of overindulgence? Tell him, Henry.
9   HENRY: Well, maybe a good cup of coffee after each —
10   MYRTLE: Don't be ridiculous, Henry! The man needs to
11   repent. He needs to turn away from the folly of the bottle
12   to a life of discipline and self-control. And to teach him
13   that lesson, we shall let him just lie there and receive the
14   full impact of the suffering he has brought on himself.
15   That will make him think twice before hitting the bottle
16   again.
17   HENRY: But Myrtle, dear, don't you think we should —
18   MYRTLE: Hush, Henry. Young man, you may think we are
19   being hard on you by leaving you here to teach you a
20   lesson. But when you've learned it, you will thank us for
21   it. And one more thing: should you happen to slip back
22   into this drunken habit of yours again, in the name of
23   decency, please find another place to pass out. There's a
24   Methodist church *(Or other denomination)* about four
25   blocks down the street. Come, Henry; it's time for us to
26   go worship God.
27   HENRY: Yes, dear. *(Exit HENRY and MYRTLE; enter DEACON.)*
28   DEACON: *(Singing)* I always had a strong ambition,
29   To gain respect and recognition,
30   Not by my deeds, but by position,
31   And that's why I am a deacon.
32   VICTIM: Ohhh ... help me, please ... help me.
33   DEACON: What's your problem, man? And please be quick.
34   *(He looks at his watch.)* I'm a deacon in the church here
35   and I've got lots to do before the service starts.

1   VICTIM: Robbed ... beaten ... tried to kill me ... can't get

2   up ... please, help me.

3   DEACON: Sorry, my ministry is building and grounds. I

4   don't do benevolence; that's Bob Johnson. You need to

5   see Bob and let him fix you up. *(Starts to walk on.)* Well, I

6   gotta hurry. Gotta get in there and see that the air

7   conditioner is set just right to handle the crowd. Mrs.

8   Ferguson always complains if it's a little cool, and Mr.

9   Harrington complains if it's a little warm. The Lord only

10   knows how much unappreciated behind-the-scenes work

11   I put in every Sunday adjusting that thermostat. Being

12   a deacon is no piece of cake.

13   VICTIM: No, please ... don't go ... please ... send Bob ...

14   DEACON: Send Bob? You think he's not busy too? I'm sure

15   he's in there right now, just like every Sunday morning,

16   making out the agenda for Tuesday night's benevolence

17   committee meeting. It's gotta be done before church

18   starts so he can distribute it to the committee members.

19   He can't just drop everything and treat you as if you were

20   the only person in the world with a problem.

21   VICTIM: But ... I need help ... now ... please.

22   DEACON: Oh, all right! I'll risk Mrs. Ferguson's glare and try

23   to help you.

24   VICTIM: Oh, thank you ... thank you ... was beginning to

25   think ... no one cared.

26   DEACON: Of course we care. It's just that we try to do things

27   as the Bible says, "decently and in order," not hapazardly

28   and without planning. Your little problem is not on our

29   schedule. Now, here's what I'm going to do. I'm going to

30   go find Bob — even though it means I'll be late manning

31   my post at the thermostat — and tell him you're out here.

32   And I feel sure that he will add your case to the

33   benevolent committee meeting agenda, if it isn't already

34   too long. Then it will surely be first on the list for the

35   following week. He will contact you when the committee

1 decides what action to take on your case. So, hang in
2 there, keep the faith, be of good cheer. I gotta hurry along.
3 *(Exit DEACON; enter PREACHER, carrying Bible.)*
4 PREACHER: *(Singing)* God, help me preach your love and care,
5 To searching sinners everywhere,
6 And send me out wherever there,
7 Is no reduction in salary.
8 *(He looks up, praying as he walks.)* God, please take my
9 tongue, my body, and my life, and make them instruments
10 of yours to accomplish your will on earth. Guide my feet
11 to the task you would have me do — *(He trips on the body*
12 *of VICTIM, but does not fall.)* Say, what have we here?
13 VICTIM: Owww . . . please . . . help me.
14 PREACHER: Oh my, oh my! Uh, sir, are you sick or hurt?
15 VICTIM: Hurt . . . bad . . . thank God you've come . . . need
16 help.
17 PREACHER: *(Looks at his watch.)* Why do these things always
18 seem to happen at such inopportune times? *(He kneels beside*
19 *VICTIM, careful to keep his knees from touching the ground.)* Uh,
20 sir, I want to help you — I intend to help you. It is my duty
21 as a Christian. But, you see, I am the pulpit minister of
22 this church with a responsibility to my assembled flock. It
23 is most unfortunate that your present need conflicts with
24 theirs, but I am certain you will understand that their need
25 is a deeply spiritual one, while yours is merely physical.
26 In spite of your present discomfort, I'm certain you can
27 see that we must put the Lord first. His flock is waiting,
28 and worship will begin in a few minutes. Can you imagine
29 the awkward silence, the gap in continuity, the jarring
30 shock to their carefully cultivated worshipful mood if I am
31 not in there to mount the pulpit and impart spiritual
32 sustenance at the appointed time?
33 VICTIM: Ohhh . . .
34 PREACHER: I knew you would understand. But remember
35 as you lie here that you are not alone. Jesus is with you at

1   all times, and you can draw strength and comfort from
2   that glorious surety. Now, after the service, I will send
3   an assistant out to check on you. And if you are still here,
4   I will be more than happy to attend to your needs.
5   Meanwhile, should assistance present itself from some
6   other source, please do not hesitate on my account to
7   accept it. I assure you that I will not be offended.
8 VICTIM: Ohhh ...
9 PREACHER: No, I really mean it. I'll get another opportunity
10   to be of Christian service to someone else at another time,
11   I'm sure. So don't feel obliged to wait for me to return.
12   Well, I must depart for now, but take heart from the
13   knowledge that I wish you well and love you with God's
14   own love. *(He rises.)* Why do these things always seem to
15   happen at such inopportune times? I really would like
16   to help the poor fellow. It would have made a wonderful
17   sermon illustration. *(Exit PREACHER.)*
18 VICTIM: Ohhh ... *(Enter SAM, carrying a soft drink.)*
19 SAM: *(Singing)* These Sunday Christians sing and pray,
20   Don't lie or cheat or talk risqué,
21   But signs of schizophreni-ā,
22   Will show on Monday morning.
23
24   Their halo will evaporate,
25   They'll lie and steal and cheat and hate,
26   So why should I affiliate,
27   With hypocrites like them.
28
29   I don't need church to sing and pray,
30   I worship God as well as they,
31   In house or home or Chevrolet,
32   And even out on the lake.
33   *(He sees VICTIM.)* Hey, man, what are you doing lying
34   there? These churchgoing types aren't going to cotton to
35   your messing up their holy landscape.

1   **VICTIM:**   Ohhh . . . help me . . . please.

2   **SAM:**   You're in trouble, aren't you? *(He bends over to get a closer*

3   *look.)* **Hey, you're hurt.**

4   **VICTIM:**   Yes . . . I know . . .

5   **SAM:**   Well, why didn't you say so? Here, let me look at that

6   **head.** *(He gets on knees and examines VICTIM's head.)*

7   **VICTIM:**   Owww . . .

8   **SAM:**   Sorry, man. That's a really bad-looking gash you've got

9   **there. Just relax and I'll try to stop the bleeding, then**

10   **we're going to have to go get you some stitches.** *(As SAM*

11   *talks, he removes his shirt and converts it into a bandage, which*

12   *he ties around VICTIM's head.)* **I've heard they sometimes**

13   **use staples now instead of stitches. If I had a staple gun,**

14   **I would fix you up myself and save you some expense.**

15   **Just joking, just joking. But you're probably in no mood**

16   **for humor right now. There you go — all fixed up. I'm no**

17   **Florence Nightingale, but that ought to keep some of your**

18   **blood on the inside of your skin. Now, I'll bet you could**

19   **use a drink. Here, I've got over half a cola left.** *(He helps*

20   *VICTIM to sit and drink.)*

21   **VICTIM:**   Thanks, I needed that. I feel . . . a little better . . .

22   now . . . but I'm still . . . awfully weak.

23   **SAM:**   Do you think anything is broken?

24   **VICTIM:**   A commandment or two, I'd say.

25   **SAM:**   I mean anything like bones or teeth?

26   **VICTIM:**   *(Gingerly feeling rib cage)* I don't know. I could have

27   a couple of cracked ribs.

28   **SAM:**   I'd better call you an ambulance.

29   **VICTIM:**   No, please. Not that again.

30   **SAM:**   Well, if you think you could walk with me helping you,

31   I could get you to that emergency clinic a couple of blocks

32   from here. Then while they patch you up I can call my

33   girlfriend to bring her car and we'll take you home.

34   **VICTIM:**   Yes, let's try that. I think I can do it. It's awfully nice

35   of you to go to all this trouble. I was beginning to think no

1   one was going to help me at all, but then you came along
2   and gave me the shirt right off your back. You're a good
3   man, and I deeply appreciate it.
4   SAM: Aw, don't mention it. *(He carefully helps VICTIM to his*
5   *feet, puts VICTIM's arm around his neck, and they begin to walk*
6   *toward exit. After a few steps, VICTIM straightens fully, removes*
7   *his arm from SAM, and stands alone.)*
8   VICTIM: That's OK; I won't be needing your help anymore.
9   I'm just fine now.
10   SAM: Hey, man, don't you go trying to be macho. You've lost
11   too much blood to make it on your own. I'm going to help
12   you get to that clinic.
13   VICTIM: No, really, I'm fine. Believe me, there is nothing
14   wrong with me at all. This was all an act.
15   SAM: Don't give me that, man. You've got a three-inch, bone-
16   deep gash in your head and those lumps look like the
17   Rocky Mountains painted purple. I think you'd better
18   just sit down here and let me call that ambulance after
19   all. Those blows to your head have done something to
20   your brain.
21   VICTIM: *(Firmly)* No, I'm perfectly fine, really. You see, I'm
22   not what I appear to be. I can't go to the clinic; they
23   would want identification and I'd blow my cover.
24   SAM: What in heaven's name are you talking about?
25   VICTIM: *(Takes badge from coat and shows it to SAM.)* I'm Angel
26   seven-seventy-seven, Solar System Division, Department
27   Earth, Data Recording Detail.
28   SAM: Hey, man, you're delirious. Come on.
29   VICTIM: Not at all. Take the bandage from my head and tell
30   me what you find.
31   SAM: *(Unwraps VICTIM's head and stands stunned for a moment.)*
32   The — the cuts and bruises and lumps are gone! This is
33   crazy! I can't believe this! What's going on here? You —
34   you can't really be an angel. Whoever heard of such a
35   thing?

1   VICTIM: Adam, Abraham, Jacob, Balaam, Manoah, Mary,
2   and Peter, to name a few.
3   SAM: But that was back in Bible times. Angels don't roam
4   around down here anymore.
5   VICTIM: Are you sure about that? Then tell me how I know
6   your name, Sam.
7   SAM: Well, I — uh — that was a lucky guess.
8   VICTIM: Is it also a lucky guess that I know your full name
9   is Sampson P. Worthington of 1414 Maple Street; twenty-
10   seven years old, with a girlfriend named Kristy and a
11   mole right on your —
12   SAM: OK! OK! Wow! This is crazy! You really are an angel.
13   But — but, why did you . . . what are you trying
14   to . . . what's the deal here?
15   VICTIM: I'm on a special unaware assignment.
16   SAM: What? An underwear assignment?! You mean you want
17   my T-shirt, too?
18   VICTIM: No, Sam, not underwear, *un-aware*. I pose as a
19   person in trouble to give believers an opportunity to
20   render Christian service. They are unaware that I am an
21   angel and unaware that I am recording their reaction to
22   my apparent need.
23   SAM: You record their reaction? I didn't see you taking notes.
24   VICTIM: No, we've updated our system. We don't use the old
25   write and blot method anymore. My boss Gabriel got a
26   whole new quadraphonic sound system so we can put
27   everything on tape. He says the old way was inefficient,
28   but I think he did it so he could hear himself practice on
29   his trumpet. Here, I'll show you. *(He takes a cassette player*
30   *from his coat and turns it on. PREACHER's voice is heard saying:*
31   *"Why do these things always seem to happen at such inopportune*
32   *times? Uh, sir, I want to help you — I intend to help you. It is*
33   *my duty as a Christian. But you see, I am the pulpit minister of*
34   *this church with a —" VICTIM turns off the tape player.)*
35   SAM: Man, you got him good! What will you do with that

1   recording?
2   VICTIM: I send it to the Justice Department in heaven to be
3   placed on permanent file.
4   SAM: Permanent file? What for?
5   VICTIM: On the day of judgment, tapes such as this will be
6   used as evidence at each subject's final trial.
7   SAM: Uh, you got me on that tape, too, didn't you?
8   VICTIM: Sure did, Sam, in quadraphonic stereo.
9   SAM: Oh, well, I guess I don't have anything to worry about.
10   I did what I was supposed to do, didn't I?
11   VICTIM: You did very well on compassion, which is at the
12   very heart of Christianity. And I congratulate you. But
13   what about that little song you were singing as you
14   walked up? Let me find it here . . . *(He starts to play the tape.)*
15   SAM: No! Please, don't play that! Uh — I hate to hear myself
16   on tape.
17   VICTIM: I can understand that. How do you think it will
18   sound to God's ears? You pretty much wrote off the whole
19   church as nothing but a bunch of hypocrites and set
20   yourself up as being too good to worship with the likes
21   of them.
22   SAM: Man, why are you picking on me? I did better on your
23   little test than those stained-glass types, didn't I? Face
24   it; they are hypocrites. They talk like they're so goody-
25   goody, but they act just like everybody else. I don't do
26   that.
27   VICTIM: Oh, then you really are too good to worship with all
28   these sinners that attend church here. No hypocrisy
29   there, huh? Just the cold, hard facts, right?
30   SAM: Well, I —
31   VICTIM: What about the time you faked a limp so you could
32   use a "Handicapped only" parking place?
33   SAM: I was in a hurry. I needed —
34   VICTIM: Did you know you caused a disabled veteran to
35   wheel himself all the way across the parking lot to get a

1   **prescription filled?**

2   **SAM:**   **Oh, no! I never thought —**

3   **VICTIM:**   **And what about the time you brought twelve items**

4   **to the "Limit ten items" express checkout counter?**

5   **SAM:**   **But all the lines were so long —**

6   **VICTIM:**   **And you think those churchgoers who passed me**

7   **by didn't have similar excuses? What's the difference**

8   **between them and you?**

9   **SAM:**   **Well, I — uh — say, how do you know all this stuff about**

10   **me, anyway? You must really get around with that little**

11   **recorder of yours.**

12   **VICTIM:**   **Other agents have recorded you at various times.**

13   **We have an international network that covers the planet.**

14   **And we always get our man. Everyone encounters us at**

15   **one time or another. We're the stranded motorist**

16   **trudging down the road with an empty gasoline can.**

17   *(Enter STRANDED MOTORIST with gas can, hot, puffing, and*

18   *dragging. He crosses the stage and exits opposite.)* **We're the**

19   **lost child crying in the shopping mall.** *(Enter LOST CHILD*

20   *holding lollipop, crying loudly for his mother. He crosses the*

21   *stage and exits opposite.)* **We're the elderly shopper who**

22   **needs help with her bag of groceries.** *(Enter ELDERLY*

23   *SHOPPER juggling two full grocery bags, careening and*

24   *struggling for balance as she crosses the stage and exits opposite.*

25   *After her exit, the crash and spill of a dropped bag is heard,*

26   *followed by her loud moan, "Oh, no!")* **We're the blind man**

27   **needing help to cross the street.** *(Enter BLIND MAN*

28   *wearing dark glasses and tapping his stick, meandering around*

29   *the stage and almost colliding with SAM before exiting opposite.*

30   *After exit, the screeching of tires is heard Off-stage [via pre-*

31   *recorded tape].)* **We're the poor widow with a broken-down**

32   **air conditioner.** *(Enter POOR WIDOW fanning herself with a*

33   *hand-held fan as she crosses the stage and exits opposite.)* **We're**

34   **the —**

35   **SAM:**   **Enough already! I get the picture. I've seen almost all**

1   those angels, and I admit it — I just ignored most of them.

2   And you guys have all that on tape?

3   VICTIM: In quadraphonic stereo.

4   SAM: *(Worried)* **Oh boy, I'm in big-time trouble. I'm just as**

5   **hypocritical as those churchy types I've been putting**

6   **down. I fooled myself into thinking I was better than they**

7   **are. I can see now that I was wrong, but it's too late.**

8   **You've got it all on permanent record.**

9   VICTIM: In quadraphonic stereo.

10   SAM: *(Falls to his knees in anguish.)* **What am I going to do?**

11   VICTIM: There is a way you can get those tapes erased.

12   SAM: *(Brightening)* **Really? How?**

13   VICTIM: It's simple. You just apply for erasure.

14   SAM: Oh, that's great! I'll do it. Do you have any application

15   forms on you?

16   VICTIM: You don't have to fill out any forms. You apply for

17   erasure simply by repenting. When a Christian is

18   genuinely sorry for his sins and asks forgiveness, we

19   immediately pull his tape and erase it. And when we do

20   that, the record is gone forever — literally forever.

21   SAM: *(Still on knees, clings desperately to VICTIM's legs.)* **Oh, I'm**

22   **sorry, I'm sorry, I'm sorry! Please erase the tapes. I**

23   **promise to be good. I promise not to be hypocritical. I'll**

24   **do anything — only please get rid of those tapes. Just tell**

25   **me what I have to do.**

26   VICTIM: Well, you can start by letting go of my legs. *(SAM*

27   *lets go.)* Thanks. Now, here's what you need to do: just go

28   right in there. *(He points toward the church building.)* In a

29   few minutes the preacher will finish his sermon and you

30   can march right down to the front and tell the church

31   you have sinned against them and want to be forgiven.

32   Then all your tapes will be erased.

33   SAM: *(Looks where VICTIM is pointing, slowly stands, straightens*

34   *clothes.)* **There's got to be some other way.**

35   VICTIM: No. That is the only way.

1   SAM: But I always thought repentance was a matter of the
2   heart. I didn't think it had to be done in a church to be
3   official.
4   VICTIM: Technically, you're right, Sam. But in your case,
5   you need the exercise of public confession to tame your
6   pride. For your own sake, you need to humble yourself
7   before those you have wronged.
8   SAM: Man, I didn't think it would be this tough.
9   VICTIM: True repentance is never easy. It means turning
10   away from sins you can hardly resist and living a life by
11   God's standards.
12   SAM: I don't think I can do it.
13   VICTIM: Sam, have you ever heard of grace?
14   SAM: Sure. Everyone in town knows about her. But what
15   does she have to do with all this?
16   VICTIM: Not that Grace, Sam! I'm talking about the grace
17   of God. You know, Amazing Grace.
18   SAM: What did she do that was so amazing?
19   VICTIM: No, no, no! I'm saying you don't have to live a perfect
20   life for God to accept you. Having Jesus in your life makes
21   up for the shortfall. As long as you're trying to be like
22   Jesus, God accepts what you intend as the real thing.
23   You can do that, Sam.
24   SAM: Yes, I think I can, by George.
25   VICTIM: No, not by George; by Christ. You've got to remember
26   that at all times. *(Phone rings.)* Excuse me; I seem to have
27   a call coming in.
28   SAM: You mean angels get phone calls?
29   VICTIM: Sure. What did you expect — a burning bush?
30   SAM: No, not really. I'm just surprised. I knew AT&T was
31   big, but I had no idea . . .
32   VICTIM: This is not AT&T — it's Golden Bell. Now, get quiet.
33   It's probably headquarters calling in my new assignment.
34   *(He reaches into his coat and pulls out a telephone receiver.)*
35   Halo. Seven-seventy-seven here. Oh, that's OK; no problem.

1   **Good-bye.** *(Takes phone from ear.)* **Wrong number.** *(Returns*
2   *phone to coat. It rings again.)* **Excuse me again, Sam.** *(Into*
3   *phone)* **Halo. Seven-seventy-seven here.** *(Pause)* **Yes,**
4   **Harvey, Project Samaritan is completed.** *(Pause)* **Yes,**
5   **highly successful. Got a good tape, and you'll be getting**
6   **an erasure application within the hour.** *(Looks at SAM and*
7   *makes the OK sign with his fingers.)* **The name is Sampson**
8   **P. Worthington, eternal security number 861-23-5674. Yes,**
9   **I'm ready for another assignment.** *(Pause)* **Wow, that's a**
10   **tough one. What else have you got? OK, OK, I'll take it.**
11   *(Pause)* **Sure, I'll do you a favor. What do you need? Bring**
12   **you back a box of candy? Sure. What kind?** *(Pause)*
13   **Divinity — of course; I should have known. I'll do it. OK,**
14   **I'm signing off now. Amen to you, too.** *(Returns phone to*
15   *coat.)* **Well, Sam, I've got to go. My next unaware**
16   **assignment is set up for one-thirty this afternoon. I'm**
17   **scheduled to be a pregnant woman who faints while**
18   **shopping in a supermarket.**
19 SAM: **Really? How interesting. How far along will you be?**
20 VICTIM: **Oh, about to the frozen food section.**
21 SAM: **I mean, how far along in the pregnancy?**
22 VICTIM: **I'll be ready to deliver. In fact, I'll go into labor right**
23   **there by the TV dinners. Should get a great tape.**
24 SAM: **Hey, wait a minute! You're a man. How can you be a**
25   **pregnant woman?**
26 VICTIM: **We angels are extremely versatile. We can be**
27   **whatever the occasion requires. Once I was a skunk with**
28   **its head caught in a pickle jar. That was a real test of**
29   **humane compassion. But a twelve-year-old boy passed it**
30   **with flying odors — I mean, flying colors. They had to**
31   **bury his clothes, though. I just couldn't help myself. Well,**
32   **I must be off, and you've got to get in that church before**
33   **the sermon ends, which probably won't be anytime soon,**
34   **come to think of it. Good-bye, Sam.**
35 SAM: **Good-bye, Angel seven-seventy-seven. Have a nice —**

1   **uh — eternity.** *(They shake hands; VICTIM exits. SAM squares*
2   *himself, straightens his clothes, and marches resolutely toward*
3   *the church door as the lights fade to blackout.)*
4
5
6
7
8
9
10
11
12
13
14
15
16
17
18
19
20
21
22
23
24
25
26
27
28
29
30
31
32
33
34
35

A COMEDY IN ONE ACT
BY T. M. WILLIAMS

THE
CATFISH
AND THE
BOOKWORM

Opposites attract, but there are limits!

The Catfish and the Bookworm

THE CATFISH AND THE BOOKWORM

A comical look at a blind date that flounders until the couple realizes they hold the most important thing in common.

(Galatians 3:28)

Cast

Betty Jo (A country girl)

Rob (A city boy)

Costumes:

BETTY JO — jeans or western skirt, western boots, a western-style shirt, and a handkerchief. ROB — a conservative suit, dress shirt, and tie.

Props:

A magazine, a dozen roses (artificial ones will do), a dictionary, a newspaper.

Setting:

An average, middle-class living room, with chairs, a sofa, a coffee table, etc. It is decorated with touches of country charm.

Notes:

References to popular singers, movies, and clothing in this play need to be current. If the names, titles, and brands named in the dialog have become dated at the time of your performance, please substitute to keep the play relevant to your audience.

Much of the humor in the play is based on the contrast between Betty Jo and Rob. Betty Jo should speak with a pleasant country drawl while Rob should speak with academic precision. For Rob to be credible, he must say the names of the composers, music, and artists in the script accurately and effortlessly. Of course, we realize you probably already have them down pat, but just in case you might be a little rusty on one or two, here is a handy list.

Handy Pronunciation Key:

Dvorak (dvahr′ zshahk)

Borodin (boh′ roh deen)

Polovetsian (pah loh vet′ see an)

Grieg (greeg)
Renoir (ren wahr´)
Degas (day gah´)
Manet (mah nay´)
Toulouse-Lautrec (too´looz loh trek´)
Monet (maw nay´)
Cezanne (say zahn´)
Gerome (zshay rome´)
Bouguereau (boo´gur oh)
Ingres (ahn´gr)
Willie Nelson (wih´lee nel´sun)
Wagner (vahg´nur)
Tannhauser (tan´how zer)

1   *(The play opens with BETTY JO sitting nervously in a chair,*
2   *trying to read a magazine. She looks at her watch and places*
3   *the magazine on the coffee table.)*
4   **BETTY JO: Why did I have to go and let Mary talk me into**
5   **another blind date?** My last one had all the personality
6   **of a head of cauliflower — couldn't say more than two**
7   **words at a time all evening until he started talking about**
8   **his bottle cap collection. Then that's all I heard for the**
9   **next hour and a half. But stupid me — didn't learn a thing.**
10 **Here I am again, about to date another guy sight unseen.**
11 **But Mary seemed so certain that this fellow Rob and I**
12 **would hit it off. Maybe it'll work out this time. It's almost**
13 **seven; I hope he's not late.** *(Doorbell rings.)* **Oh, good —**
14 **right on time, just like a heifer at a feed trough.** *(She opens*
15 *the door revealing ROB holding a bouquet of roses.)*
16 **ROB: Hello, Betty Jo?**
17 **BETTY JO: That's me. You must be Rob. Come on in.** *(Enter*
18 *ROB.)*
19 **ROB: Thank you. You certainly have a fine place. Do you**
20 **enjoy living in the country?**
21 **BETTY JO: I sure do. Of course, since my daddy is a farmer,**
22 **I grew up out here with all the cattle and chickens, so**
23 **I'm kinda like a catfish in a horsetank: I can hardly**
24 **imagine anything different. How about you?**
25 **ROB: I'm an inveterate city boy. My father is a professor at**
26 **the university and it's likely that I will also pursue an**
27 **academic career. If I might venture a parallel to your**
28 **picturesque aquatic simile, I'm rather like a bookworm**
29 **in a dictionary — trying to ingest all the knowledge I can.**
30 **BETTY JO: Well, my daddy is no professor, but he sure is out**
31 **standing in his field.**
32 **ROB:** *(Laughs politely at the old joke.)* **Oh, here, I brought you**
33 **some flowers.** *(He hands them to her.)*
34 **BETTY JO:** *(As she takes them)* **Oh, no — roses! I'm allergic to —**
35 **ah — ah — ah — choo!** *(She sniffs, sneezes a few times, and*

1   *blows her nose until ROB takes the flowers and throws them*
2   *Off-stage.)*
3   ROB: I'm very sorry. I didn't know.
4   BETTY JO: That's OK. Dext tibe you cad breeg crysadthebubs.
5   I'b dot allergic to theb. *(She sniffs and snorts.)*
6   ROB: Do you think you will recover soon?
7   BETTY JO: Oh, yes, id just a beddit. Dese flareups dod't last
8   log. *(She blows her nose.)*
9   ROB: I'm thankful for that. Well, I hesitate to rush you,
10   Betty Jo, but you'd better hurry and get ready or we'll
11   be late for the concert.
12   BETTY JO: What do you mead? I ab ready. *(Sniff)*
13   ROB: You intend to go to the symphony dressed like that?
14   BETTY JO: The sybphody?
15   ROB: *(Excitedly)* Yes. Tonight they're playing Dvorak's* *Ninth*
16   *Symphony in E Minor* — you know, the *New World*
17   *Symphony* with the spectacular trumpets in the fourth
18   movement. Then they are doing Borodin's *Polovetsian*
19   *Dances,* and finishing with Grieg's *Piano Concerto in A*
20   *Minor.* Can you imagine all that in a single program? I
21   can hardly wait!
22   BETTY JO: I thought we were going to the Willie Nelson
23   concert.
24   ROB: I didn't even know there was a Willie Nelson concert.
25   BETTY JO: Well, there is, so when you called and said, "The
26   concert," I assumed . . .
27   ROB: You mean you like that kind of music?
28   BETTY JO: Oh, I just love it! Willie Nelson, Garth Brooks,
29   Wynona   Judd,   Reba   McIntyre,   Shenandoah,   The
30   Geezenslaw Brothers —
31   ROB: The who?
32   BETTY JO: No, I didn't like The Who. I never got into rock,
33   just C and W.
34   ROB: Well, I don't care for country music myself, but I
35   *See pronunciation key on pages 83 and 84.*

1   wouldn't want you to have to endure an evening of music
2   you wouldn't enjoy, so why don't we simply forgo the
3   concert and proceed directly to dinner? I have
4   reservations at the Hightower Restaurant after the
5   concert; I'll just call and reschedule them for eight
6   o'clock.
7   BETTY JO: The Hightower Restaurant? That's the fanciest
8   place in town. I can't go there dressed like this. How
9   about Rancho's Barbeque?
10 ROB: Rancho's? I can't go there dressed like this. But I have
11   an idea. We can cancel the reservations and just pick up
12   some fried chicken, and then go to the art museum. They
13   have assembled a superb exhibit featuring the most
14   notable examples of French Impressionism of the late
15   1800s — Renoir, Degas, Manet, Toulouse-Lautrec, Monet,
16   and Cezanne. You do like impressionism, don't you?
17 BETTY JO: Oh, sure. Rich Little is my favorite. He does a
18   great Humphrey Bogart and John Wayne. And his
19   Richard Nixon really cracks me up.
20 ROB: Uh, I said impression*ism*, not impression*ists*. Impres-
21   sionism is a genre of painting instigated by a group of
22   French artists rebelling against the rigid strictures of
23   traditional French academic painters such as Gerome,
24   Bouguereau, and Ingres. They were considered
25   innovators because they emphasized light refraction
26   rather than crisply delineated form.
27 BETTY JO: Oh, *that* impressionism. Of course. How silly of
28   me. Do you think there might be any pictures of horses
29   there?
30 ROB: Well, no, I hardly think so. But that's all right. We can
31   find something else to do. Say, do you like baseball? The
32   Sox are playing tonight.
33 BETTY JO: Not really. I never could keep up with what
34   quarter it is. But there's a good rodeo going on out at the
35   arena. I like rodeos, don't you?

1   ROB: Well, no, not really. They don't smell very good.

2   BETTY JO: How about a movie? *Star Trek XII* is showing at

3   the Majestic. I've been wanting to see that.

4   ROB: Sorry, I'm not a Trekkie. But there's a Shakespeare

5   play being staged at the university theater — *As You Like It.*

6   BETTY JO: No, I can't say that I do. Maybe we should look for

7   something to do instead of something to watch. Do you

8   square dance? *(She grabs ROB by the arm and tries to lead*

9   *him through the opening steps of the dance. Caught by surprise,*

10   *he follows clumsily, nearly falling.)*

11   ROB: *(After regaining composure)* I'm afraid I can't dance in

12   any geometric configuration. Do you bowl?

13   BETTY JO: In the low forties. Do you play miniature golf?

14   ROB: In the high nineties. We could take a stroll on the river

15   walk.

16   BETTY JO: Not in these boots. How about video games down

17   at the arcade?

18   ROB: No, those places are hangouts.

19   BETTY JO: Well, why don't we just stay here for the evening?

20   I'll pop some corn and we can watch that Tom Cruise

21   racing movie on channel eight. It's OK, my folks are home.

22   ROB: Or better yet, Wagner's opera *Tannhauser* is on PBS

23   tonight.

24   BETTY JO: Well, maybe we could play a game. Do you like

25   card games?

26   ROB: They bore me. Do you like chess?

27   BETTY JO: I fall asleep.

28   ROB: Well, maybe we could talk about poetry and literature.

29   Do you like Melville?

30   BETTY JO: I can't say. I've never been there.

31   ROB: What do you think of Kipling?

32   BETTY JO: I don't know. I've never kippled. I've got it! Do

33   you like horseshoes?

34   ROB: I prefer Reeboks. Betty Jo, it seems that our tastes are

35   so different that I'm beginning to doubt that we can find

1   sufficient commonality for any mutually enjoyable
2   activity without some sort of catalyst.
3   BETTY JO: I have an uncle who is a cattle-ist. He raises
4   Herefords and Black Angus on a big ranch in west Texas.
5   But he's too far away to do us any good.
6   ROB: What I'm trying to say is this: I think we must address
7   the obvious fact that this date is not working out. You
8   seem to be a very fine girl, and our failure to find a
9   common interest is certainly not your fault. Yet it seems
10   that our heterogeneous tastes may prevent our sustain-
11   ing an evening of pleasant companionship. *(BETTY JO*
12   *stares blankly at ROB for a moment, then picks up the dictionary*
13   *and begins searching the pages.)* What are you doing, Betty
14   Jo?
15   BETTY JO: I'm looking up that word.
16   ROB: What word?
17   BETTY JO: Heterogeneous. I know I can't spell it, but I
18   thought I might get lucky and find a picture of one. It's
19   a Greek with a high IQ, isn't it?
20   ROB: Heterogeneous? Uh, no. It is merely an alternate term
21   for different. You won't find a picture. But my point is —
22   BETTY JO: That's OK. I think I was following your point
23   pretty well. I was just afraid that word might have thrown
24   me off the scent — you know, like a jack rabbit does when
25   it jumps up in front of a coon dog. I guess I have to agree.
26   You and I don't seem to plow in the same fields. It almost
27   seems like we don't even live on the same planet. I never
28   saw anyone so heterogeneous. I'm sure sorry it's turning
29   out this way.
30   ROB: I regret it, too. I wonder what our friends Joe and Mary
31   had in mind when they recommended that we get
32   together?
33   BETTY JO: Yeah, me too. To hear them tell it, you and I are
34   just like two bluejays on a barb-wire fence. Do you
35   suppose they set us up together as a big practical joke?

1 ROB: That would certainly be uncharacteristic of them.
2 They are not the type to risk deliberately hurting
3 someone merely for the humorous effect. Well, I shall
4 depart and leave you to more profitable pursuits. Good
5 night, Betty Jo. *(He opens the door and begins to leave.)*
6 BETTY JO: Good night, Rob. Joe and Mary can't say we didn't
7 try, can they?
8 ROB: Absolutely not. Fine people they are; matchmakers
9 they're not. Incidentally, I'm curious; how did you make
10 their acquaintance?
11 BETTY JO: I met them at church.
12 ROB: Then you must attend the West Side Church. I go to
13 Wilmington Avenue, myself. I met them at an intercity
14 Faith Council meeting.
15 BETTY JO: Really! Soon after you came in, I had a hunch you
16 might be a Christian — in spite of your weird — uh — I
17 mean, heterogeneous tastes. I really got to know Joe and
18 Mary at their Tuesday evening home study meetings.
19 We've been studying the first chapter of John.
20 ROB: *(Excitedly)* Have you?! That explains why Joe has been
21 so interested in the nature and activity of the pre-existent
22 Christ lately.
23 BETTY JO: If you like that sort of thing, you would really
24 enjoy these studies, Rob. Last week we discussed what
25 it means when John calls Jesus "The Word." That term
26 kinda gave me a handle on how we can know what the
27 Father is like through what the Son says.
28 ROB: Good point! You've got quite a mind underneath that
29 country charm. It just occurred to me that your idea
30 could be expressed in another way: Jesus is God
31 incarnate, just as words are thoughts incarnate.
32 BETTY JO: What a great way to put it! You really plant those
33 fancy words of yours in a straight row, Rob. I'll have to
34 remember that for our next study group meeting.
35 ROB: Don't give me the credit. I was merely expanding on

1   your own very stimulating and exciting idea. We should
2   get together and discuss — *(ROB and BETTY JO both*
3   *suddenly stop in their tracks and look at each other wide-eyed*
4   *and open-mouthed.)*
5   **ROB and BETTY JO:** *(In unison)* I think we've found what we
6   have in common.
7   **BETTY JO:** Close that door, Rob. Don't even think of leaving.
8   Just plop down there on the couch while I get my Bible
9   and ask Mom to fix us some sandwiches. We're going to
10   have a better evening than either of us imagined.
11   **ROB:** *(Smiling broadly)* Wal, ah reckon yer raht. We're gonna
12   have more fun than a duck in a rain barrel. *(They both*
13   *laugh as the lights fade to blackout.)*
14
15
16
17
18
19
20
21
22
23
24
25
26
27
28
29
30
31
32
33
34
35

A COMEDY IN ONE ACT BY T. M. WILLIAMS

Midnight Choirboys

When you're locked in, *sing out!*

Midnight Choirboys

MIDNIGHT CHOIRBOYS

A comedy in one act about Paul and Silas in prison.

(Acts 16:16-34)

Cast

Roman Guard

Brastus (The Philippian jailer)

Egorius (Assistant to Brastus)

Paul (The Apostle)

Silas (His companion)

Garbini ⎤

Crispus |

Tony ⎬—(Prisoners)

Angelo |

Finias ⎦

Dorothea (Tony's wife)

Costumes:

ROMAN GUARD — Classic Roman soldier's uniform. BRASTUS — Severe but neat Roman-styled tunic with trim at collar, sleeves, and hem. Pajamas or nightshirt in his final entrance. EGORIUS — Clean but plain Roman-styled tunic. PAUL — Neat, clean biblical robe. SILAS — Neat, clean biblical robe similar to Paul's. The actor may want to add padding to his back as protection against the whip blow delivered by the jailer on page 103. (A ski vest, for example, or a doubled bath towel pinned inside his robe.) PRISONERS — Colorless, ragged, dirty shifts. DOROTHEA — Plain but clean and neat robe.

Props:

Seven sets of prisoner's chains to be worn on wrists. These chains must be capable of being opened or slipped off by the wearers. A whip, sword, and candle for Brastus. The whip should not be a real one, but should be made from a light, harmless material. Cotton rope, for example, can be dyed brown to resemble leather and attached to a wooden dowel handle painted the same color. Seven bowls, seven pieces of bread, a tray and a water pitcher. A "baby" for Dorothea (a large doll bundled up to look like a real baby). Stocks to secure the ankles of Paul and Silas (these can be made easily from wood — see sketch). Five musical pitch pipes. Loose straw on floor of prison cell. Lumber, containers, and miscellaneous junk that can be dropped backstage to create a clatter to simulate the noise of an earthquake.

Setting:

A prison cell in Philippi. The staging need not be elaborate unless the producers choose. The prison interior can be suggested by two or three barred windows painted on cardboard, cut out, and attached to the wall and the entrance/exit doors. (See sketch on page 97.) Or, if a more complete set is preferred, see the suggested design on page 97.

SUGGESTED CONSTRUCTION FOR SET
WITH FALLING BEAM

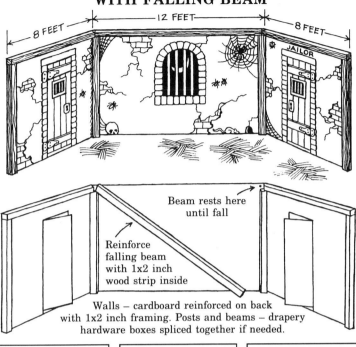

Beam rests here
until fall

Reinforce
falling beam
with 1x2 inch
wood strip inside

Walls – cardboard reinforced on back
with 1x2 inch framing. Posts and beams – drapery
hardware boxes spliced together if needed.

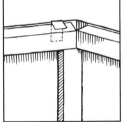

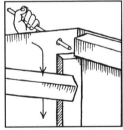

A strip of packing tape attached to top of beam and back of set will hold beam in place.

Stagehand behind set removes tape and, with dowel inserted through hole, pushes beam over edge of post, causing it to fall to floor.

The other end of beam wired to background wall through holes reinforced with duct tape.

STOCKS

Two strips of
2 x 4 inch wood

Metal
hinge

Padlock fixture
(without padlock)

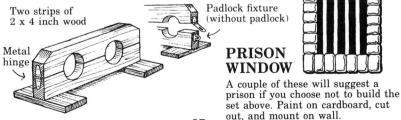

PRISON
WINDOW

A couple of these will suggest a prison if you choose not to build the set above. Paint on cardboard, cut out, and mount on wall.

97

1   *(The play opens in an austere prison cell. Prisoners GARBINI,*
2   *CRISPUS, and TONY are sitting idly or leaning against the*
3   *walls. FINIAS is lying down, gasping for breath. Once in a while*
4   *he feebly asks for water. ANGELO is reclining with his shoulders*
5   *against the wall. He is holding his right arm and wincing in pain.*
6   *With much clamor and roughness, a ROMAN GUARD*
7   *enters right and throws PAUL and SILAS to Center Stage where*
8   *they stumble and fall to the floor. As this is in progress,*
9   *BRASTUS enters left followed closely by EGORIUS.)*
10 **ROMAN GUARD:**   **Here are a couple more prison rats for you,**
11   **Brastus. Your instructions are to keep them in the**
12   **deepest part of the prison and guard them especially well.**
13   **They have already been flogged.**
14 **BRASTUS:**   **Already flogged? Aw, I've asked you guys not to**
15   **do that! Bring them straight here and let me flog them.**
16   **I've got all the equipment and I do it much better than**
17   **you can with those namby-pamby little whips of yours.**
18   **And besides, I enjoy it.** *(EGORIUS giggles and snorts.)*
19 **ROMAN GUARD:**   **They have been flogged, Brastus. Your job**
20   **now is just to keep them here. You know what happens**
21   **to jailers who let their prisoners escape — they get**
22   **shortened by a head.**
23 **BRASTUS:**   **You're wasting your time warning me, soldier.**
24   **I've never lost a prisoner. I've had a lot of them die, but**
25   **I've never lost one.**
26 **ROMAN GUARD:**   **I know that. Otherwise there would be**
27   **nothing but empty space above your shoulders. I'll be**
28   **back to check on these two in the morning. They'd better**
29   **be here or —** *(He draws his finger across his throat in a cutting*
30   *motion. BRASTUS responds by putting his hand to his own*
31   *throat as ROMAN GUARD exits right.)*
32 **BRASTUS:**   **All right, you two scumbags, listen up. Stand up**
33   **when I'm talking to you!** *(He kicks PAUL and SILAS as they*
34   *struggle to their feet.)* **I have little welcome gifts for the two**
35   **of you — bracelets. Hold out your wrists.** *(EGORIUS*

1 *clamps chains on their wrists.)* **Now, don't you feel pretty?**
2 **Haw! Haw! Now, listen up, pill bugs. I don't know what**
3 **you did to get thrown in here and I don't care. But this**
4 **prison is my own little kingdom and I'm the law here.**
5 **The only law. And my number one rule is that prisoners**
6 **don't cause trouble while in my prison. At all! Now, if**
7 **you're quiet and don't ask for anything and don't bother**
8 **me, we'll get along just fine. But if you cause a smidgin**
9 **of trouble or even look like you're thinking about it, I**
10 **have ways of making your life miserable** *(He twists SILAS'*
11 *arm painfully)* **or short.** *(He sticks his sword under PAUL's*
12 *chin.)* **Technically, it's against the law to kill a prisoner**
13 **but accidents do happen. Right, Egorius?** *(EGORIUS*
14 *giggles and snorts.)* **You see, no one really cares what**
15 **happens in here. Do you cockroaches get the picture? I**
16 **said, do you understand me?**
17 **PAUL:** **I believe we comprehend the general scope of your**
18 **expectations. We shall make every reasonable effort to**
19 **avoid causing you any inconvenience.**
20 **BRASTUS:** **Good.** *(He turns to exit.)*
21 **SILAS:** **Uh, sir, we haven't eaten all day. Would you be so kind**
22 **as to tell us when dinner is —**
23 **BRASTUS:** *(Turns quickly and knocks SILAS across the room.)*
24 **What did I just tell you? There you go causing trouble**
25 **already. Next time it's the stocks for you, slimeball!**
26 *(EGORIUS giggles and snorts. BRASTUS and EGORIUS exit*
27 *left.)*
28 **SILAS:** *(Groaning and wincing)* **Oh, my poor back!**
29 **PAUL:** **Here, let me help you.**
30 **GARBINI:** *(Steps forward and slaps PAUL on the back.)* **Howdy,**
31 **boys. Welcome to the Philippian Hilton. Ha! Ha! What are**
32 **your names?**
33 **PAUL:** *(Groaning and wincing from the back slap)* **My name is**
34 **Paul, and this is my associate Silas.**
35 **GARBINI:** **Mighty pleased to meetcha. I figure since we're all**

1 going to be living together for quite a spell, we ought to
2 get to know each other. We'll introduce ourselves to you,
3 then you can tell us all about yourselves. My name's
4 Garbini. I'm in for bilking poor widows out of their money.
5 CRISPUS: I'm Crispus. They got me for armed robbery.
6 TONY: My name's Tony. I stole a loaf of bread to keep my wife
7 and four kids from starving after I had been out of work
8 for over two months. I sure wish I knew what happened
9 to my poor little family. I'm worried about them.
10 ANGELO: My name is Angelo. My crime is drunken and
11 disorderly conduct. When I drink, I get rambunctious,
12 you see. Last time I started a fight and tore up the whole
13 tavern. Broke my arm in the process. Hurts like an ox is
14 standing on it. *(Lifts sleeve.)* See, the bone is almost poking
15 through.
16 PAUL: That's terrible. Won't the jailer get you a physician?
17 *(All prisoners laugh except FINIAS.)*
18 GARBINI: Are you serious? You might as well ask for a king-
19 sized bed with satin sheets.
20 CRISPUS: Or a warm bath with extra towels.
21 TONY: Or room service with pheasant under glass.
22 GARBINI: Or a manicure and a massage.
23 ANGELO: Or a chariot and chauffeur to take you to the theater.
24 CRISPUS: Or overnight laundry service.
25 TONY: Or after-dinner entertainment with jugglers, acrobats,
26 and dancing girls.
27 PAUL: But if a physician does not attend to Angelo promptly,
28 that arm could become infected, and — well — he could
29 die.
30 CRISPUS: Now, that would really hurt ol' Brastus' feelings.
31 Yes, sir; to have one of his own dear prisoners die would
32 really break our dear keeper's heart. *(All PRISONERS*
33 *laugh except FINIAS.)*
34 FINIAS: Water . . .
35 SILAS: What's wrong with him?

1 GARBINI: That's Finias. In for attempted murder. He's got
2 the plague.
3 PAUL: He is obviously consumed with a dangerously high
4 fever. Why don't they at least bring him some water?
5 CRISPUS: Hey, Tony. Call up room service and have them
6 send up a bucket of ice water for Finias. And while they're
7 at it, have them stick a bottle of champagne in it.
8 PAUL: All right, all right, I get the picture quite clearly. But
9 look at him. He's perspiring like a compressed sponge.
10 Here, I shall at least wipe off his forehead.
11 CRISPUS: *(Grabs PAUL's arm to hold him back.)* Stay away from
12 him, or you'll come down with what he's got. We don't
13 want the plague spreading through the whole prison.
14 GARBINI: Well, now you know all about us. We are just one
15 big, happy family here. In a moment we'll find you a nice
16 spot against a wall and rake up a little straw for you to
17 sleep on. But first, tell us about yourselves. What
18 dastardly deed got you dumped in here?
19 ANGELO: And the more dastardly the better; right, guys?
20 *(CRISPUS, GARBINI, and TONY respond affirmatively.)*
21 PAUL: Very well. As I told you, my name is Paul, and this is
22 my associate, Silas. We were walking down the street
23 minding our own business when a certain young female
24 began to follow us, taunting us incessantly. We soon
25 found that she was a commercial fortune teller managed
26 by two keepers who profited immensely from her occult
27 activity.
28 CRISPUS: Did she have kinda long, dark hair?
29 PAUL: Yes, she did.
30 CRISPUS: About medium height with big, brown eyes?
31 SILAS: Yes, as a matter of fact.
32 CRISPUS: About eighteen years old?
33 PAUL: Yes, I would say that is a close approximation.
34 CRISPUS: Wore loud, flashy clothes?
35 SILAS: That's right, she did.

1 CRISPUS: And did she kinda wiggle when she walked?

2 PAUL: Uh, well, yes. I suppose she did have certain ambula-

3 tory excesses that could be characterized in that way.

4 Apparently you know this young woman.

5 CRISPUS: Nope. Never seen anyone like that in my life.

6 TONY: I have. She's all around the market every day. I've

7 always thought she was weird and obnoxious, but those

8 guys make a fortune on her. I wonder how she can know

9 all the things she knows?

10 PAUL: She was possessed by an evil spirit.

11 GARBINI: No kidding! How do you know that?

12 SILAS: We cast it out of her. She is just a normal girl, now.

13 Her keepers got us thrown in here because we ruined

14 their business.

15 CRISPUS: No fooling! Can you guys really cast out evil

16 spirits?

17 PAUL: It is not actually we who do it; it is the power of Christ

18 working in us.

19 GARBINI: Don't tell me you guys are Christians?

20 SILAS: *(Smiling)* Yes, we certainly are.

21 CRISPUS: You mean you're a couple of them narrow-minded

22 bigots that pass judgment on other people's religion and

23 morals if they don't believe like you?

24 SILAS: Why, no, we —

25 GARBINI: I know what you Christians are like; you're all

26 fanatics. You think we all oughtta kowtow to some

27 invisible power in the sky who makes you follow a long

28 list of rules and sends you to hell if you don't.

29 SILAS: Yes, we believe in God, but he's not like —

30 TONY: What kind of riffraff will they let in here next?

31 CRISPUS: Really! It takes all the fun out of being in jail when

32 we have to associate with low-lifes like you. *(PRISONERS*

33 *all turn away from PAUL and SILAS and go back to their own*

34 *places.)*

35 GARBINI: You hairballs find your own places to sleep and

1   **get your own straw if you can find it. You'll get no help**
2   **from me.**
3   **CRISPUS:**   **Or me.**
4   **ANGELO:**   **Or me.**
5   **TONY:**   **Or me.**
6   **FINIAS:**   **Water . . .**
7   **PAUL:**   **Well, there seems to be a little space over here**
8   **adjacent to Angelo. Perhaps we could squeeze in there.**
9   **ANGELO:**   **No way! No Christian is gonna bed down by me.**
10   **SILAS:**   **How about over here by Tony? Maybe he could move**
11   **over just a bit.**
12   **TONY:**   **Forget it. I don't want to spend the night listening to**
13   **a sermon.** *(PAUL and SILAS look toward CRISPUS.)*
14   **CRISPUS:**   **Don't even think about it.** *(PAUL points to the space*
15   *next to GARBINI. SILAS nods affirmatively and they walk*
16   *toward it.)*
17   **GARBINI:**   *(Stands threateningly in their path.)* **Go ahead. Make**
18   **my day.**
19   **PAUL:**   *(Sighs.)* **Well, I suppose we shall just have to lay here**
20   **in the middle of the floor.** *(They begin to settle themselves on*
21   *the bare floor when BRASTUS and EGORIUS enter left.)*
22   **BRASTUS:**   **Chow time!** *(EGORIUS, giggling and snorting, gives*
23   *each PRISONER except FINIAS a piece of bread and pours water*
24   *into their bowls. The PRISONERS noisily wolf down their food*
25   *and water. BRASTUS to PAUL and SILAS)* **Here are your**
26   **water bowls. Take good care of them. Break them and**
27   **all the water you get is what you can hold in your hands.**
28   *(EGORIUS giggles and snorts. BRASTUS with mock courtesy)*
29   **Are you gentlemen quite comfortable here? Is there**
30   **anything I can do to make your stay more pleasant?**
31   **SILAS:**   **Well, yes, since you mention it. Do you have anything**
32   **for my sore back?**
33   **BRASTUS:**   **I sure do. Just turn around and I'll see what I can**
34   **do for you.** *(SILAS turns. BRASTUS takes his whip and lays a*
35   *severe blow across SILAS' back.)*

1   **SILAS: OOOooowww!** *(EGORIUS giggles and snorts. All*
2   *PRISONERS laugh at SILAS.)*
3   **BRASTUS: Will there be anything else?**
4   **SILAS: No, sir.**
5   **BRASTUS: No? Very well, then. Enjoy your meal. Haw! Haw!**
6   *(BRASTUS and EGORIUS exit left as EGORIUS giggles and*
7   *snorts.)*
8   **FINIAS: Water . . .**
9   **PAUL: It appears that he forgot to feed Finias.**
10   **GARBINI: He didn't forget. They don't go near that man. In**
11   **fact, they avoid him like the plague. Ha! Ha!**
12   **PAUL:** *(To SILAS)* **I'm not as hungry as I thought, Silas. I**
13   **suppose I could make it on a half piece of bread.**
14   **SILAS: . . . and a half bowl of water? So could I.** *(They both halve*
15   *their bread, drink half their water and pour the remainder into*
16   *SILAS' bowl. They take the bowl and two half-pieces of bread*
17   *to FINIAS and hand feed him.)*
18   **PAUL: Poor fellow; he's burning up.** *(He wipes FINIAS'*
19   *forehead with a corner of his own robe. He and SILAS place*
20   *their hands on FINIAS' head as PAUL prays.)* **Lord, we pray**
21   **that you will heal this man Finias of his disease and**
22   **restore him to full health. In the name of Jesus we pray,**
23   **amen.**
24   **FINIAS:** *(Slowly sits up, rubs his eyes and looks around.)* **Hey,**
25   **guys, I think my fever just broke. In fact, I feel pretty**
26   **good. To tell the truth, I feel great!** *(He stands and flexes*
27   *his muscles.)* **I've never felt better in my life. Man, you**
28   **guys have really got the magic touch.**
29   **SILAS: It wasn't us; it was the power of God.**
30   **FINIAS: Whatever it was, I really appreciate it. I was roasting**
31   **like a peanut. Wouldn't have lasted much longer.**
32   **ANGELO: I don't suppose you guys — or your God — could**
33   **do anything about my arm?**
34   **PAUL: Let's see that arm.** *(He and SILAS place their hands on*
35   *ANGELO's arm as PAUL prays.)* **Father, we ask you to heal**

1 Angelo's broken arm. Please knit the bones together and
2 make the arm as good as new. We pray in Jesus' name,
3 amen. Hold up your arm, Angelo.
4 ANGELO: Hmm, looks OK. And do you know what? The
5 pain is gone. I — I think you've done it, Paul. Here, let's
6 road test it. Anybody want to arm wrestle? Come on,
7 Crispus. *(ANGELO and CRISPUS arm wrestle and ANGELO*
8 *wins easily.)* Would you look at that? I can hardly believe
9 it. Man, this is really something! *(Knock at door, Stage*
10 *Right)*
11 GARBINI: Who could that be? No one ever comes here on
12 purpose. *(Knock sounds again, louder. Enter BRASTUS and*
13 *EGORIUS Stage Left.)*
14 BRASTUS: Who the devil could that be? *(He opens door a crack*
15 *and looks out.)* It's a woman. Did any of you grease slicks
16 ask your wife or sweetheart to come here? You all know
17 that personal visits are against the rules.
18 PRISONERS: No, no. Of course not. Not me, sir. *(Etc.)*
19 BRASTUS: *(Again looking through cracked door)* Who are you?
20 *(He closes door.)* It's Tony's wife. Get him out of here,
21 Egorius.
22 TONY: Please, sir, let me see her for just a moment. I won't
23 take long —
24 BRASTUS: What kind of discipline would I have in here if I
25 started breaking rules and making exceptions? Out with
26 him, Egorius! *(EGORIUS giggles and snorts as he roughly*
27 *hustles TONY out at exit left. BRASTUS opens door and speaks*
28 *with great courtesy.)* Please come in, my lady. *(Enter*
29 *DOROTHEA holding an infant wrapped in a blanket.)*
30 DOROTHEA: Oh, thank you, sir. My name is Dorothea. I need
31 very much to see my husband Tony for just a moment,
32 please. It is very important.
33 BRASTUS: I'm very sorry, my dear. It would give me the
34 greatest pleasure to see you and your husband share a
35 moment together, but unfortunately, there are very strict

1   **rules against family visitors in this prison.**

2   **DOROTHEA:**   **Oh, dear, the poor boy must be frantic with**

3   **worry. Things were in such bad shape when he got**

4   **arrested; you see, we were homeless and hungry, and he**

5   **has no idea what has happened to us since he was taken**

6   **away. It would ease his mind so much if I could just tell**

7   **him.** *(She is on the verge of tears.)*

8   **BRASTUS:**   **Now, now, my dear. I'm not as hard as some**

9   **people think I am.** *(He casts a dirty look at the PRISONERS.)*

10   **Why don't you just tell me what you want to tell Tony**

11   **and I will personally deliver the message to him?**

12   **DOROTHEA:**   **Oh, would you, sir? That would be so kind of**

13   **you. Just tell him not to worry about us at all because**

14   **we are well and doing fine. A good Christian family found**

15   **us in our cave and took us all into their home for as long**

16   **as Tony is in jail. So we are warm and have plenty to eat.**

17   **And most important, tell him that he has a new daughter.**

18   **She was born five days ago. I wanted so much for Tony**

19   **to see her. Just look at her, sir; isn't she beautiful? See,**

20   **she's got Tony's eyes and cute little dimples in her cheeks.**

21   **BRASTUS:**   **Awww, just wook at the wittow thing. What a**

22   **wovvy wittow doll. Kitchie-kitchie-koo. Say heowoh to**

23   **wittow ol' Bwastus. Kitchie-kitchie-kootchie-koo.**

24   **DOROTHEA:**   **And sir, please tell Tony to be as good as he can**

25   **so he can get out soon. There's a steady job waiting for**

26   **him the moment he walks free. Would you tell him all**

27   **that, sir? Oh, and one more thing; tell him that I love him**

28   **very, very much and can't wait to have him come home**

29   **to me.**

30   **BRASTUS:**   **Of course I'll tell him, my dear. You can depend**

31   **on it. Tony is a very lucky man to have a wife like you,**

32   **and I'll tell him that, too. Rest assured that I will take**

33   **good care of Tony and send him back to you safe and**

34   **sound. Now, you just don't worry your pretty little head**

35   **about a thing.**

1 DOROTHEA: Oh, thank you, sir. Thank you very much. I'm
2 so grateful to you, and Tony will be, too. Good-bye. *(Exit*
3 *DOROTHEA to right.)*
4 BRASTUS: Good-bye, Dorothea. Egorius! Bring Tony back in
5 here. *(Enter EGORIUS, left, roughly prodding and shoving*
6 *TONY in front of him.)* Come here, Tony. Your wife has
7 asked me to pass along some news.
8 TONY: Yes? Yes? What did she say? How did she look? How
9 are the kids? Do they have food? Where are they living?
10 How do they —
11 BRASTUS: If you'll shut your flapping mouth for a second,
12 I'll tell you. But you're not going to like it. Things are not
13 going well at all. Your wife really looked bad — thin as
14 a skeleton, pale, tired-looking, and her skin was all
15 blotchy and kind of green. It was hard for her to talk for
16 all the coughing fits, and when she did talk, it was so
17 mumbly I couldn't always make it out.
18 TONY: Oh, no! She's got the plague! Poor Dorothea. But how
19 are the kids? Did she say anything about the kids?
20 BRASTUS: She had to sell them all into bondage just to keep
21 them alive. She sold them separately to foreigners
22 passing through. You will probably never see them again.
23 TONY: Sold them? No! It can't be true! How about our baby?
24 Has it come yet? Is it a boy or girl?
25 BRASTUS: Stillborn. What did you expect in her condition?
26 She buried it three days ago.
27 TONY: *(Sinks to the floor in tears.)* Oh, no, no, no! Our baby . . .
28 our dear, poor baby . . . oh, Dorothea, Dorothea . . . how
29 terrible this must be for her . . . and I can't be with her
30 when she's hurting so much. This is just terrible!
31 BRASTUS: She told me to tell you one more thing.
32 TONY: What?
33 BRASTUS: She doesn't love you any more. She has found
34 another man — one who can provide for her better than
35 you ever did. She said you could rot in jail forever as far

1 **as she is concerned. She's leaving the country with him.**
2 **She came to tell you good-bye forever, Tony.** *(TONY buries*
3 *face in hands and sobs heavily.)* **I guess you know that all**
4 **this is your own fault. None of it would have happened**
5 **if you hadn't turned thief and left your poor wife to fend**
6 **for herself.**
7 PAUL: **Don't believe him, Tony. None of what he is telling**
8 **you is true. I saw your wife while she was here and heard**
9 **every word she said. She is healthy and beautiful. Your**
10 **entire family is well, warm, and well-fed. They are being**
11 **cared for by a Christian family that has —**
12 **BRASTUS:** *(Slaps PAUL across the mouth, sending him sprawling.)*
13 **Shut up, you lying fool!**
14 PAUL: **And you have a beautiful, healthy, new baby daughter.**
15 *(BRASTUS kicks PAUL.)*
16 SILAS: **. . . with dimples and your eyes.**
17 **BRASTUS:** *(Slaps SILAS, sending him sprawling.)* **You slime-**
18 **balls have had it!**
19 PAUL: **And she loves you very much.** *(BRASTUS kicks PAUL*
20 *again.)*
21 SILAS: **And there's a job waiting for you when you get out.**
22 *(BRASTUS kicks SILAS brutally.)*
23 **BRASTUS:** *(Livid with anger)* **Egorius, slap these two bags of**
24 **carrion in the stocks.** *(EGORIUS, giggling and snorting,*
25 *clamps the ankles of PAUL and SILAS in the stocks as*
26 *BRASTUS continues speaking.)* **You numbskulls are slow**
27 **learners. Maybe this little piece of modern educational**
28 **technology will help you grasp a few things that don't**
29 **seem to be getting through to your crippled brains.**
30 **Lesson one is that I'm in charge here. Lesson two: don't**
31 **contradict what I say or do in this prison. Lesson three:**
32 **prisoners that give me trouble are usually carried out of**
33 **here in a wooden box. Maybe by morning you'll be a little**
34 **smarter. I'm going to bed now and I don't want to hear**
35 **a peep out of you peanut brains. Do you hear me?** *(He*

1   *raps them on the head with his whip handle.)* **I said, do you**
2   **hear me?**
3   SILAS: We hear, we hear.
4   PAUL: And we will henceforth make a sincere effort to
5   comply with your penal code.
6   BRASTUS: You'd better. Now, good night, boys. Sleep well.
7   Haw! Haw! *(Exit BRASTUS left, followed by EGORIUS,*
8   *giggling and snorting.)*
9   TONY: Uh, Paul, Silas, I appreciate what you did for me.
10   And I — I'm sorry for the way I treated you.
11   ANGELO: That goes for me, too. I appreciate your fixing up
12   my arm.
13   FINIAS: And curing me of the plague.
14   CRISPUS: I guess we were wrong about you guys.
15   GARBINI: You're not what we thought Christians were like.
16   You really seem to have it all together. The power to heal
17   that your God has given you is really miraculous, but to
18   me the way you stood up to that monster Brastus is even
19   more impressive. That was a very brave thing to do. We
20   all owe you one.
21   PAUL: Thank you, gentlemen, but you don't owe us anything.
22   Everything we have done for you is by the power of God.
23   CRISPUS: Can we get that power, too?
24   SILAS: It's for everybody who wants it. He can give you the
25   power to rule yourself, to love each other, to be patient,
26   and to be joyful wherever you are.
27   GARBINI: How do we get it?
28   PAUL: Accept Jesus as your Lord, repent of your sins, and be
29   baptized.
30   FINIAS: That's it?
31   SILAS: That's it. Of course, baptism is a little problem right
32   now, but do the rest and God will take care of you.
33   TONY: That is good news.
34   ANGELO: Great news! Actually, it's even better than getting
35   my arm fixed.

1   **BRASTUS:**   *(Voice Off-stage)* **You mangy rats get quiet in there**
2   **or I'll come in and gag every one of you.**
3   **GARBINI:**   **Yes, sir. We'll tone it down, sir.** *(All are quiet for a*
4   *moment.)*
5   **SILAS:**   **Paul, isn't it wonderful how God works?**
6   **PAUL:**   **I was just thinking the same thing. Appalling circum-**
7   **stances often produce superb results. As a consequence**
8   **of our squalid incarceration, God now has five new**
9   **members in his kingdom.**
10   **SILAS:**   **Hallelujah!**
11   **PAUL:**   **Silas, I think I feel a song coming on.** *(He begins to sing*
12   *a hymn.)*
13   **SILAS:**   **Uh, Paul — Paul. Just a moment. You're a little flat.**
14   **Does anyone here have a pitch pipe?**
15   **GARBINI:**   **Yeah, I've got one here.**
16   **FINIAS:**   **Got mine right here in my pocket, I think.**
17   **CRISPUS:**   **Let's see, I had one. Oh, here it is.**
18   **ANGELO:**   **Here's mine. The F sharp doesn't work, but otherwise,**
19   **it's fine.**
20   **TONY:**   **Here, you can use mine.**
21   **SILAS:**   **Hit me a B flat, someone.** *(All sound a B flat on their*
22   *pitch pipes.)* **OK, Paul, got that? Now, let's try again.** *(PAUL*
23   *and SILAS begin the song in duet. Gradually, the other*
24   *PRISONERS join in and continue to the end of the song.)*
25   **BRASTUS:**   *(Voice Off-stage)* **You scumbags cut out that**
26   **caterwauling in there. This is the last time I'm warning**
27   **you!**
28   **SILAS:**   **Well, I guess it's time to call it a day, guys. Good night,**
29   **Garbini.**
30   **GARBINI:**   **Good night, Crispus.**
31   **CRISPUS:**   **Good night, Finias.**
32   **FINIAS:**   **Good night, Tony.**
33   **TONY:**   **Good night, Angelo.**
34   **ANGELO:**   **Good night, Paul.**
35   **PAUL:**   **Good night, Silas.** *(Soon all PRISONERS are snoring.*

1　*After a few moments, an earthquake hits. The sudden clatter of*
2　*falling lumber, boxes, and other debris is heard Off-stage. The*
3　*lights flicker. The PRISONERS pantomime the earthquake's*
4　*movement by lurching from side to side. During the following*
5　*dialog they unobtrusively slip the chains from their wrists.)*
6　**GARBINI:　What's happening?**
7　**CRISPUS:　Brastus must be snoring again.**
8　**FINIAS:　No! It's an earthquake!**
9　**ANGELO:　Look, the door is open!**
10　**PAUL:　And our stocks are loose.** *(PAUL and SILAS open their*
11　*stocks.)*
12　**TONY:　And so are our chains. We can escape! Come on, guys.**
13　*(Off-stage clatter continues.)*
14　**SILAS:　Don't do it! Look at the stones falling out there in the**
15　**hallways. We'd be crushed like stomped grapes. Let's all**
16　**get over here under this beam until it's over.** *(They huddle*
17　*together in corner until earthquake stops. Enter BRASTUS, left,*
18　*in pajamas, holding a candle in one hand and his sword in the*
19　*other. He is followed by EGORIUS who is not giggling and*
20　*snorting, but cowering in fear.)*
21　**BRASTUS:　Oh, no! They're all gone — escaped!** *(Sinks on knees*
22　*to floor.)* **It's all over for me. I'll be executed for losing my**
23　**prisoners. I can't let them do that to me; I'll save myself**
24　**the humiliation and take care of it right now.** *(Takes sword*
25　*in both hands and places the point to his stomach.)* **Good-bye,**
26　**cruel world . . .**
27　**PAUL:　*(Yells.)* Stop! Don't do it! We're all here.**
28　**GARBINI:　Aw, if he really wants to do it, let him go ahead.**
29　**BRASTUS:　You're all here?**
30　**PAUL:　Every one of us.**
31　**BRASTUS:　You could have let me kill myself, and then all of**
32　**you could have escaped. But instead, you actually saved**
33　**my life — and after the way I treated you. Why?**
34　**PRISONERS:　Yeah, why, Paul?** *(Etc.)*
35　**PAUL:　Because it was the right thing to do.**

1   **BRASTUS:** *(Tearfully)* **Things are all backwards. Here I am,**
2   **free, healthy, well-fed, comfortable, and in charge; yet**
3   **I'm always irritable, upset, and angry.** And I would have
4   **killed you with half an excuse. And there you are, beaten**
5   **to shreds, bloody, sore, starving, chained, abused, and**
6   **yet you're so happy you can't help but sing. What's wrong**
7   **with this picture?**
8   **PAUL:**   **We have Jesus in our lives. And you can, too.**
9   **BRASTUS:**   **Yes, yes, I want that. What do I have to do?**
10   **PAUL:**   **It's very simple, Brastus; just believe that Jesus is the**
11   **Son of God and make him the Lord of your life.**
12   **BRASTUS:**   **And how about my family and servants?**
13   **SILAS:**   **They can all become Christians. Bring them in and**
14   **we'll tell them all about it.**
15   **BRASTUS:**   **Egorius, go tell my wife and daughter to come in**
16   **here.** *(Exit EGORIUS left, humming the same hymn the*
17   *PRISONERS sang.)* **This is wonderful. I've known for a**
18   **long time that something was wrong with my life, but I**
19   **just couldn't quite put my finger on what it was.**
20   **GARBINI:**   **We could have suggested a few things, sir.**
21   **BRASTUS:**   **Well, I want you gentlemen to know that I am**
22   **turning over a new leaf. I'm going to clean all this rancid**
23   **straw out of the prison and put in new Beautysleep**
24   **mattresses.** *(Cheers from the PRISONERS)* **I'm going to add**
25   **central heat.** *(More cheers)* **And I'm hiring a gourmet chef**
26   **to cook you three square meals a day.** *(Cheers)* **I'm**
27   **bringing in the best doctors to treat your wounds.** *(Cheers)*
28   **And I'm burning up the stocks and throwing away my**
29   **whip.** *(The PRISONERS cheer wildly.)* **Men, I'm turning this**
30   **place into a four-star prison. Felons will be begging**
31   **judges to send them here. They may even beg for**
32   **convictions so they can come here. Now, let me ask you,**
33   **is there anything else any of you need?**
34   **SILAS:**   **Brastus, you will be happy to know that these men**
35   **have committed their lives to Jesus, too. Do you think you**

1   **could find a place where they and your family could all**
2   **be baptized together?**
3 **BRASTUS:** **Of course; there's a water tank out in the court-**
4   **yard. Come, gentlemen; follow me.** *(All exit right, singing the*
5   *same hymn.)*
6
7
8
9
10
11
12
13
14
15
16
17
18
19
20
21
22
23
24
25
26
27
28
29
30
31
32
33
34
35

PONTIUS PILATE'S PRESS CONFERENCE

Was he telling the truth?
Or was he hiding a
cover-up of major
proportions?

Pontius Pilate's Press Conference

PONTIUS PILATE'S PRESS CONFERENCE

Colorful media personalities (with striking
similarities to contemporary journalists!) question the
Governor about Jesus' last days.

Cast

Pontius Pilate (Governor of Judea)

Press Secretary

Roman Guard

Roman Guard (Non-speaking part)

Tom Brokejaw

Dan Lather

Barbara Falters

Jane Paltry

Frank Gizzard

Peter Skinnings

George Willful   —(Newspaper reporters)

Walter Crankcase

Ted Topple

Sam Donkeyson

Bryant Gumbo

Diane Sawhorse

Notes:

The names of the reporters in this play are obvious parodies
of prominent news personalities. It will enhance the humor if the
actors learn to imitate the voices and mannerisms of these personalities. If any of the celebrities on which these parodies are
based are no longer active in the media at the time of your performance, you can easily come up with your own parody of some other
reporter as a substitute. Well-known local media personalities
may be used as well as those on the national networks.

The size of the cast may be increased or decreased as needed
by adding to or trimming the list of reporters to fit the number
of actors in your group. Lines may be reassigned accordingly.

Costumes:

PONTIUS PILATE — an elegant, white, Roman-styled robe. PRESS SECRETARY — A Roman-styled robe. REPORTERS — New Testament period robes in varying colors, some in Roman style, others in Judean style. FRANK GIZZARD — a brightly colored blazer over his robe. ROMAN GUARDS — Classic Roman soldier uniforms.

Props:

A writing pad and pencil for each reporter. A magazine for Frank Gizzard. A walking cane for Walter Crankcase.

Setting:

The stage is set with one folding chair for each reporter, facing a podium. A seal on the podium reads, "GOVERNOR OF JUDEA" in letters encircling a Roman fasces (see illustration).

1   *(As the play opens, the REPORTERS are seated in their chairs,*
2   *some making notes on their writing pads, others chatting quietly*
3   *with each other. FRANK GIZZARD is reading a magazine.*
4   *WALTER CRANKCASE is sleeping and snoring softly. After a*
5   *moment, the two ROMAN GUARDS enter and take their places*
6   *about four feet apart, a few steps behind the podium. They are*
7   *followed immediately by the PRESS SECRETARY and*
8   *PONTIUS PILATE. The PRESS SECRETARY steps up to the*
9   *podium as PILATE waits at one side.)*
10   **PRESS SECRETARY: Ladies and gentlemen of the press,**
11   **welcome to the governor's press conference. Governor**
12   **Pilate will first make a brief statement, after which he**
13   **will take questions from you predators — I mean,**
14   **reporters. When you are called, please stand, state your**
15   **name, the name of your paper, and ask your question. I**
16   **now present to you his honor, Pontius Pilate, Governor**
17   **of Judea.** *(PILATE steps to the podium as the PRESS*
18   *SECRETARY steps to the side. The REPORTERS stand and*
19   *applaud, then take their seats again.)*
20   **PILATE: Friends, Romans, Countrymen. I am sure that each**
21   **of you has heard the rumors of strange and supernatural**
22   **events that have been circulating since the execution of**
23   **that Jewish troublemaker Jesus just over two weeks ago.**
24   **I have appointed a blue ribbon panel to conduct an**
25   **investigation of these rumors, and I am pleased to inform**
26   **you that their report proves conclusively that nothing**
27   **supernatural or extraordinary has occurred at all. The**
28   **events surrounding the Crucifixion, as strange as they**
29   **seemed at the time, were all the results of completely**
30   **natural causes and very easily explained.**
31   **Furthermore, I can assure you that the Roman**
32   **government is on top of things and fully in control of the**
33   **situation. And we can reasonably expect the uncertainty**
34   **of the past several days to subside until very soon the**
35   **whole matter will be completely forgotten forever. It will**

1   be as if this Jesus of Nazareth never existed.

2   Now I will be happy to take your questions. You're

3   first, Tom.

4 BROKEJAW: Tom Brokejaw with the *Jerusalem Journal.*

5   Governor, at midday after Jesus had been nailed to the

6   cross, a darkness like a moonless night covered the land

7   for about three hours. Were your investigators able to

8   explain this?

9 PILATE: Yes, they were, Tom. The chief astronomer at

10   Jerusalem University informed them that the sudden

11   darkness was caused by a solar eclipse. There was

12   nothing abnormal or supernatural about it.

13 BROKEJAW: But sir, I interviewed the same astronomer

14   myself and he told me that there has not been an eclipse

15   visible in Judea for over a year.

16 PILATE: Obviously you interviewed him before my investi-

17   gators did. You see, he is subject to memory lapses and

18   my investigators, along with a couple of sturdy Roman

19   soldiers, *(He gestures to ROMAN GUARDS, who grin broadly)*

20   had to jog his memory a bit to get him to recall that

21   indeed an eclipse had occurred on that day.

22 BROKEJAW: It seems incredible to me that an astronomer

23   could forget an eclipse, and equally incredible that the

24   almanac did not predict this one.

25 PILATE: Well, Tom, it seems that almanacs are a little like

26   reporters; they miss a few facts now and then, too. Heh,

27   heh. *(To PRESS SECRETARY)* Henry, make a note to have

28   those almanacs recalled and reprinted to include the

29   eclipse. You're next, Dan.

30 LATHER: Dan Lather with the *Caesarea Sun-Times.* It was

31   reported that at the very moment Jesus died, the great

32   curtain that encloses the secret holy chamber of the

33   Jewish Temple ripped right down the middle without

34   being touched. Three priests fainted on the spot and a

35   fourth ran out the door and hasn't been seen since. Did

1   your investigators discover the cause of this strange
2   phenomenon?
3   PILATE: Yes, they did, Dan. They found that the curtain was
4   woven back when Judah returned from captivity. That
5   makes it over five hundred years old. At that age, a sneeze
6   could have ripped it apart.
7   LATHER: But that curtain was huge — almost a half-cubit
8   thick. Age would not have caused it to rot all the way
9   through, and certainly not from top to bottom, and not
10   suddenly, and not at that particular moment.
11   PILATE: You are forgetting the earthquake we had that day,
12   and the turbulent weather conditions.
13   LATHER: But the earthquake did not damage the temple at
14   all, and the wind could not have reached the enclosed
15   holy place where the curtain is located. There must be
16   another answer.
17   PILATE: *(Nervously rubs his hands together as if trying to get*
18   *something off of them — a gesture which he repeats with*
19   *increasing frequency throughout the play.)* If you want me to
20   answer your questions, you had better not question my
21   answers. Next question, please. Yes, Barbara.
22   FALTERS: Barbara Falters with the *National Inquisitor.*
23   Isn't it true, Governor, that there is trouble between you
24   and your wife over this man Jesus?
25   PILATE: Don't be silly. She didn't even know the man.
26   FALTERS: But isn't it true that she had a dream predicting
27   trouble if you executed him?
28   PILATE: *(Irritably)* What if she did? I don't make my decisions
29   on the basis of my wife's nightmares; I make them on the
30   basis of what makes me look good to Caesar — I mean,
31   on the basis of, uh, truth and — and — what's that other
32   word? Uh, justice. Yeah, that's it — justice. On
33   particularly hard cases, I sometimes just flip a coin. Heh,
34   heh.
35   FALTERS: But according to the Jerusalem society grapevine,

1	there may be a little rift in the governor's household. We
2	hear that Mrs. Pilate has not spoken to you since the day
3	of the execution.
4	PILATE: If that were true, it would certainly prove false her
5	prediction that only bad would come of Jesus' death. Next
6	question, please. Yes, Jane.
7	PALTRY: Jane Paltry with the *Galilee Gazette*. A number of
8	independent sources reported that graves in the
9	Jerusalem cemeteries opened up on that day and many
10	people who had been buried were seen walking about.
11	How do you explain this?
12	PILATE: *(Rubbing his hands)* Why are you wasting our time on
13	such nonsense? No rational person can believe that dead
14	people can come back to life! These were obviously
15	groundless reports brought on by mass hysteria. The
16	people around here are very superstitious, you know.
17	And when you have an earthquake and a sudden
18	darkness happening at the same time, naturally their
19	imaginations ran wild. Every time two people bumped
20	in the darkness, each thought the other was a zombie or
21	a mummy. It is just that simple, Jane.
22	PALTRY: But there were no reports of hysteria or fear, sir.
23	That is what makes these sightings seem so strange.
24	Instead of reporting zombies or boogie men, these people
25	insist that they saw their dead friends, relatives, and
26	well-respected citizens alive again — absolutely the
27	opposite of what you would expect from people under
28	the influence of fear and hysteria.
29	PILATE: *(As he rubs his hands)* Why are you pushing this,
30	Jane? We don't need a panel of experts to tell us that
31	when you die you're dead forever. Do you think I'm a
32	perfect fool?
33	PALTRY: Nobody's perfect, sir.
34	PILATE: Next question — uh, you over there — yes, you in
35	the red blazer.

1   GIZZARD: Frank Gizzard with *Gladiators Illustrated.* Do

2   you think your team will win the Super Chariot Bowl

3   Sunday?

4   PILATE: What?

5   PRESS SECRETARY: *(Steps in front of PILATE.)* Mr. Gizzard,

6   what kind of question is that? The governor is not here

7   to talk sports; this is a political press conference. Please

8   stick to the subject.

9   GIZZARD: You mean he isn't Don Shulamite, coach of the

10   Philippi Wheelers? Is this not the coach's pre-game

11   interview?

12   PRESS SECRETARY: Of course not! It's the governor's press

13   conference. Don't you know the governor of Judea when

14   you see him? Where were you when we made the opening

15   announcement?

16   GIZZARD: Uh, heh, heh. I was looking at my magazine's new

17   swimsuit issue. And you know how it is; governors and

18   coaches change so often it's hard to keep up with who's

19   in charge of what. Excuse me, ladies and gentlemen; I'm

20   obviously at the wrong press conference. I must have

21   missed my turn in the hallway. *(He gets up to leave.)* Which

22   way to the sports arena?

23   ROMAN GUARD: Down the hall and to your left.

24   GIZZARD: Thanks. By the way, if any of you would like a copy

25   of the swimsuit issue, I have extras for sale. It shows girls

26   wearing itsy bitsy veils that just barely cover their noses.

27   *(All the male REPORTERS reach for their money and say, "I'll*

28   *take one," "Right over here," "One for me," etc.)*

29   PRESS SECRETARY: Stop this, all of you! Out, Gizzard! We'll

30   have a little decorum here, please. *(Exit GIZZARD.)* You

31   may continue with your questions, ladies and gentlemen.

32   *(PRESS SECRETARY steps back to his place as PILATE steps*

33   *up to the podium again.)*

34   PILATE: You're next, Peter.

35   SKINNINGS: Peter Skinnings with the *Megiddo Mirror.* A

1   similar rumor to the one Jane mentioned says that Jesus
2   of Nazareth, the very man you crucified that day, also
3   rose from the dead three days later. They say he has been
4   seen many times in many places by over five hundred
5   people. Do you have an explanation, sir?
6   PILATE: Of course, Peter; the explanation is obvious. You
7   must remember that Jesus was heading up a small
8   religious movement when we executed him. Naturally,
9   his disappointed followers would like to have seen that
10 movement continue, but the death of their leader pretty
11 much put a stop to recruiting. So, to maintain their
12 momentum and attract a following, they simply stole the
13 body from the tomb, then claimed he had come back to
14 life.
15 SKINNINGS: Why haven't your men been looking for that
16 body? Finding it would certainly stop the rumors.
17 PILATE: I know that! Do you think I'm a blithering idiot?
18 SKINNINGS: Of course not, sir. I have never once seen you
19 blither.
20 PILATE: I can assure you that we are putting great effort into
21 finding the body of Jesus. And I am confident that we
22 will dig it up very soon.
23 SKINNINGS: But Governor, it ought to be fairly easy to find
24 a dead body. Those things are not easy to hide for long.
25 Once my wife's cat hid a dead mouse under our bed, and
26 a couple of days later, we had no trouble locating it at all.
27 PILATE: *(Rubbing hands)* If you are implying incompetence
28 on the part of the Roman government, I represent it — I
29 mean — I resent it. But if you are suggesting that rumors
30 of the resurrection of Christ might be true, I would like
31 to sell you some ocean-front property in the Sahara.
32 SKINNINGS: I was not trying to imply or suggest anything,
33 Governor. I'm just surprised that all the power and
34 resources of the Roman government can't find a dead
35 body in a crowded city, especially when finding it would

1   .   end what must be an embarrassing situation for you.

2   PILATE: I would not be embarrassed if you nitpicking

3   reporters were not out to make me look bad. If you would

4   just report the news we give you instead of digging

5   around for the truth, we could keep a lid on — uh — I

6   mean, we could keep the people from being confused by

7   facts. So, get off it! Next question, George.

8   WILLFUL: George Willful with the *Roman Tribune*. Governor,

9   you seem to be making a distinction between facts and

10   truth. Could you explain to us just what you mean by the

11   term "facts"?

12   PILATE: Gladly, and you reporters should take this down

13   and remember it well. The facts are what the Roman

14   government says they are and nothing more.

15   WILLFUL: And what is truth?

16   PILATE: Funny you should ask that. During my interrogation

17   of Jesus, I asked him the same question.

18   WILLFUL: And what was his answer?

19   PILATE: Well, it was a rather silly answer when you think

20   about it. Jesus said he was the truth. But truth is a

21   concept, an idea, an abstraction. How can truth be a

22   person? It just doesn't make sense.

23   WILLFUL: It has something to do with his claim to be the Son

24   of God, wouldn't you think? Believers think that God is

25   the standard for truth, righteousness, and goodness.

26   Anything that does not measure up to him is false, wrong,

27   and evil.

28   PILATE: That's all nothing but hogwash. In my rise to

29   political power, I've learned that there are really no such

30   things as good or bad, right or wrong, true or false. There

31   is no unchangeable, rock-solid standard that we can rely

32   on to make our judgments. Right is simply whatever

33   works, or is politically expedient, or accomplishes your

34   purpose, or makes you feel good, or advances your career.

35   Wrong is whatever you get caught at. Yes, Walter.

1   CRANKCASE: Walter Crankcase with the *Dead Sea Evening*
2   *News.* Governor, do you plan to raise Social Security
3   benefits this year? *(He cups his hand to his ear to hear the*
4   *answer.)*
5   PILATE: Yes, Walter, we plan to raise them about, like, say
6   three percent.
7   CRANKCASE: What? You plan to phase them out and hike
8   the May rent?
9   PILATE: *(Much louder)* No, Walter, I said you'll get an increase.
10 CRANKCASE: What? We'll get it in Greece? But I don't live in
11   Greece; I live in Judea. Do you mean you have set up a
12   Social Security office in Greece and I have to go all the
13   way across the Mediterranean to —
14 PRESS SECRETARY: *(Steps to the podium as PILATE steps back.)*
15   Mr. Crankcase, we're getting off the topic —
16 CRANKCASE: What's this about the tropics? Are you setting
17   up an office there, too?
18 PRESS SECRETARY: *(Very loudly)* Mr. Crankcase, the purpose
19   of this press conference is to give you the straight hype
20   on Jesus.
21 CRANKCASE: What? To give us the rate hike for geezers?
22   Good! That's all I wanted to hear. I don't know why you
23   young whippersnappers always have to beat around the
24   bush before you give us a simple, straight answer.
25   *(CRANKCASE sits down. The PRESS SECRETARY steps*
26   *aside. PILATE returns to the podium.)*
27 PILATE: Next question — Ted.
28 TOPPLE: Ted Topple with the *Lebanon Cedar Post.* Governor,
29   how was it possible that the body of Jesus could be stolen?
30   The official report says that a unit of Roman soldiers was
31   posted to watch the tomb from the moment Jesus was
32   placed there to prevent just this sort of thing from
33   happening.
34 PILATE: The guards fell asleep. *(A general stir with exclama-*
35   *tions of surprise arises from among the REPORTERS.)*

1   TOPPLE: They fell asleep? Roman guards all fell asleep at
2   the same time while on official duty? Surely you are not
3   serious, sir.
4   PILATE: That is their testimony; it is on record, so it is the
5   truth.
6   TOPPLE: But Governor, don't you find it incredible that an
7   entire unit of guards would fall asleep at the same time?
8   PILATE: Well, nobody's perfect, you know. They had had a
9   busy day, and guard duty can be terribly boring. Besides,
10   it was a warm, calm night and there may have been a
11   little alcoholic beverage involved. You know how it is;
12   boys will be boys.
13   TOPPLE: But isn't sleeping on guard duty a capital offense?
14   PILATE: Well, uh, yes, it is.
15   TOPPLE: And have these guards been executed?
16   PILATE: *(Rubbing hands)* Well, uh, no, not exactly.
17   TOPPLE: Not exactly? What does that mean? Have they been
18   partly executed or sort of executed?
19   PILATE: Well, uh —
20   TOPPLE: Maybe you mean they are in prison awaiting
21   execution.
22   PILATE: Uh, no.
23   TOPPLE: Certain inside sources have told me that the
24   Jewish religious leaders paid the guards to say they had
25   been sleeping on guard duty in order to cover up the real
26   truth about what happened that night. Furthermore,
27   these sources say that the same Jews then paid you to
28   get the guards off the hook. Is there any truth to these
29   reports, sir?
30   PILATE: Of course not! I am not a crook. Ask the guards
31   themselves.
32   TOPPLE: I have tried to do that, Governor, but these
33   particular guards seem to have disappeared. Would you
34   like to tell us where they —
35   PILATE: Enough from you, Topple. Next question. OK, Sam.

1   DONKEYSON: Sam Donkeyson with the *Wailing Wall Street*
2   *Journal.* According to the official government reports,
3   those guards were not punished at all. They were
4   reassigned to new posts outside the country. Is that true,
5   Governor?
6   PILATE: What a stupid question, Donkeyson. If it's in the
7   official report, it's got to be true. That's what truth is,
8   remember — whatever is in the official report.
9   DONKEYSON: My question is, why weren't those guards
10   punished, and why were they shipped out of the country?
11   PILATE: Oh, come now, Donkeyson. Rome dominates most
12   of the known world and soldiers are shipped from one
13   country to the other all the time. It's silly to look for some
14   deep, dark, sinister reason for why any given soldier is
15   sent to any given place. You're getting a little paranoid,
16   aren't you?
17   DONKEYSON: But to find that these particular guards were
18   all sent away at this particular time has all the earmarks
19   of a cover-up, as if they were being shuttled away to keep
20   them from being questioned. Now, isn't it true that you
21   did this because you knew their answers could be
22   embarrassing to your administration? Aren't you trying
23   to cover up the truth to prevent an Eastergate scandal
24   of major proportions?
25   PILATE: Donkeyson, you are the rat in my pantry at every
26   press conference. I get sick and tired of your smart-aleck
27   mouth always trying to make me look like a nincompoop.
28   DONKEYSON: Oh, I can't take credit for that, Governor. You
29   seem to handle it pretty well on your own.
30   PILATE: Are you showing contempt for my office, Donkeyson?
31   DONKEYSON: Oh, I hope not, sir. I've been trying my best
32   not to let it show.
33   PILATE: *(To GUARDS)* Throw that man out of here and
34   confiscate his notes. *(GUARDS escort DONKEYSON from*
35   *press conference.)* That's something I've wanted to do for a

1   long time. You're next, Bryant.

2   GUMBO: Bryant Gumbo with the *Bethlehem Star*. Governor,

3   if you can't tell us why the guards at the tomb were not

4   executed for sleeping on duty, perhaps you will tell us

5   how they could know that Jesus' followers stole the body

6   if they were all sleeping when the theft supposedly

7   occurred.

8   PILATE: *(Exasperated)* What in thunder else could have

9   happened?

10   GUMBO: My point is, they could not have known what

11   happened if they were asleep while it was happening.

12   PILATE: Your point is clear, Gumbo. I'm not blind or stupid.

13   GUMBO: We know you are not blind, sir.

14   PILATE: It's obvious that you word hackers are too bone-

15   headed to realize the implications involved in rejecting

16   the testimony of the guards. Can't you idiots see that

17   either those disciples stole the body just like the guards

18   said, or this Jesus really did rise from the dead? And if

19   he rose from the dead, we really did have a God on our

20   hands and we did not show him the best hospitality. Do

21   you gentlemen want to deal with the consequences of a

22   truth like that? I think not. So we have come up with our

23   own truth which is quite a bit easier to deal with, even

24   if there are a few holes in it here and there. Can't you

25   see that I simply cannot allow my subjects to believe that

26   Jesus is alive? I must forbid it in the name of Caesar.

27   Let's see, who's next? OK, Diane.

28   SAWHORSE: Diane Sawhorse with the *Hebron Herald*. The

29   Jewish religious leaders who arrested Jesus charged him

30   with starting riots, plotting against the government, and

31   religious heresy. Did you prove these allegations to be

32   true?

33   PILATE: Not a single one of them. Those holy shams were out

34   to get Jesus and they thought they could railroad me

35   into believing their trumped-up charges. But I didn't get

1   to be governor by being stupid; I got here by bribing
2   Caesar. Actually, Judea wasn't my first choice — too dry
3   and hot, and too far from where all the action is. I wanted
4   to be governor of the Riviera, but it cost twice as much
5   as Judea and I couldn't afford it.
6 SAWHORSE: I understand, sir. But back to the charges
7   against Jesus; you said they were trumped up.
8 PILATE: Yes, the moment those conniving Jews set foot in
9   my hall, I could see that they were green with envy over
10   the influence Jesus had with the people. With mass
11   conversions from their religion to his, he was a threat to
12   their pocketbooks. They didn't have enough evidence
13   against him to convict a jaywalker.
14 SAWHORSE: Well, then, since you sentenced Jesus to death,
15   you obviously had other evidence against him. Could you
16   tell us what that evidence was?
17 PILATE: I had him executed because it was the politically
18   correct thing to do.
19 SAWHORSE: Why? Were you afraid the Jews would start
20   riots if they didn't get what they wanted? Were you afraid
21   that if word of trouble in Judea got out to Caesar your
22   career would be on the line?
23 PILATE: *(Rubs hands increasingly.)* My own reputation had
24   nothing to do with it. I was merely looking out for the
25   best interests of my people. Justice is not always as cut
26   and dried as you would think. Sometimes you have to
27   make very hard choices between equally bad options. In
28   the case of Jesus, I had to weigh the rights of a single,
29   unimportant individual against the greater good of peace
30   and harmony for the whole society.
31 SAWHORSE: Do you mean to say that you actually executed
32   an innocent man, and you knew it all the time?
33 PILATE: Why do you insist on putting it that way? I tried to
34   give Jesus a fair trial, but he wouldn't do anything to
35   defend himself. Just stood there like a dumb sheep when

1   a single word could have made him a free man. Then I
2   had him beaten, hoping those bloodthirsty Jews would
3   have a little pity and let him go. Might as well expect a
4   spider to pity the fly in its web.
5   SAWHORSE: You're all heart, sir.
6   PILATE: And that's not all I did for him. We traditionally
7   release one prisoner to the Jews during their Passover
8   celebration. I let them choose between Jesus and
9   Barabbas, the worst criminal we've had in years. But
10   would you believe it? They chose Barabbas! They'd rather
11   have him terrorizing the countryside again than to have
12   Jesus healing and working miracles. The fools! But at
13   least I did what I could for him. His death was not my
14   fault.
15   SAWHORSE: Then whose fault was it? You are the only one
16   in Judea with the authority to pronounce the death
17   sentence. If he was innocent, you could have set him free.
18   PILATE: *(Distraught, rubs his hands continually.)* No! Please,
19   don't say that. Can't you see? I had to do it; the people
20   wanted it. All right, so he was innocent. And yes, I knew
21   it. I could tell it in everything about him — his bearing,
22   his calmness, his patience, his unblinking gaze, looking
23   at me as if he could see every thought, every sin, every
24   lie I was telling myself to rationalize taking his life just
25   so I wouldn't have to deal with that howling mob of
26   animals.
27   SAWHORSE: But you washed your hands in front of that
28   crowd to show that you accepted no responsibility for
29   his death. Aren't you sticking to that claim?
30   PILATE: *(With composure collapsing, looks at hands and rubs*
31   *them in anguish.)* Yes, I washed them, but I couldn't get
32   them clean. Look! They are dripping with blood — his
33   blood. I can feel it on my hands all the time. I have washed
34   them and washed them, over and over and over, but it
35   doesn't help. I still feel the blood. My hands, oh, my poor

1 hands! Is there any god who will hear me? Caesar!
2 Jupiter! My hands ... the blood ... please help me ...
3 *(PILATE buries his face in his hands and sobs uncontrollably.*
4 *The PRESS SECRETARY steps to the podium and gently moves*
5 *him toward the exit.)*
6 **PRESS SECRETARY:** Ladies and gentlemen, as you can see,
7 the governor has not been feeling too well lately. It's the
8 stress of his office, you understand. I hope you will
9 consider that as you report on this conference.
10 **SKINNINGS:** Wait! One more question, please. Jesus claimed
11 to be the Son of God. In the light of all that has happened
12 since his death, have you seriously considered that this
13 claim might be true?
14 **PRESS SECRETARY:** Mr. Skinnings, this conference is over.
15 Each of you will just have to answer that question for
16 yourself. *(REPORTERS stand as PRESS SECRETARY leads*
17 *PILATE to exit and lights fade to blackout.)*
18
19
20
21
22
23
24
25
26
27
28
29
30
31
32
33
34
35

THE GREAT ESCAPE

He was coming out on a wing and a prayer

A COMEDY IN ONE ACT BY T. M. WILLIAMS

The Great Escape

THE GREAT ESCAPE

A thoroughly fun one-act about Peter's prison
experience and angel-assisted rescue.

(Acts 12:1-17)

Cast

Mary (Hostess to a prayer vigil)

John Mark (Mary's son)

Rhoda (A servant)

Sidius ⎤

Perfidia

Amos

Judith

Howie ⎬—(Guests in Mary's home)

Letha

Mordecai

Germaine

Sophie ⎦

Spurious ⎤
⎬—(Roman soldiers)
Fibius ⎦

Peter (The Apostle)

Angel

Costumes:

MARY, JOHN MARK, RHODA, GUESTS, and PETER —
Bible-times robes. ROMAN SOLDIERS — Classic Roman soldier
uniforms. ANGEL — A long, white robe with a gold band around
head.

Props:

Twelve chairs, a bench to accommodate three people, two
sets of handcuffs, a pocket-sized paperback book, a crossword puzzle book, a pencil, a wand.

Settings:

Scenes 1 and 3 — a room in the home of Mary and her son John Mark in Jerusalem. The play is suitable for bare stage performance using folding chairs. If your staging area has an entrance/exit door, stick a round, black dot on it at eye level to represent a peephole. If there is no door, you may either pretend one is there or construct a free-standing door with framing and cardboard as shown in the sketch on page 137. Windows cut out of cardboard and attached to stage walls would also add to the atmosphere (see sketch, page 137). For a more ambitious production, a suggested set with construction hints is provided on page 137.

Scene 2 — a Roman prison cell in Jerusalem with a bench large enough to seat three at Center Stage. The addition of barred windows painted on cardboard will help give the stage the look of a prison (see sketch, page 137). Suggestions for a more elaborate set are given on page 137.

SCENES 1 AND 3

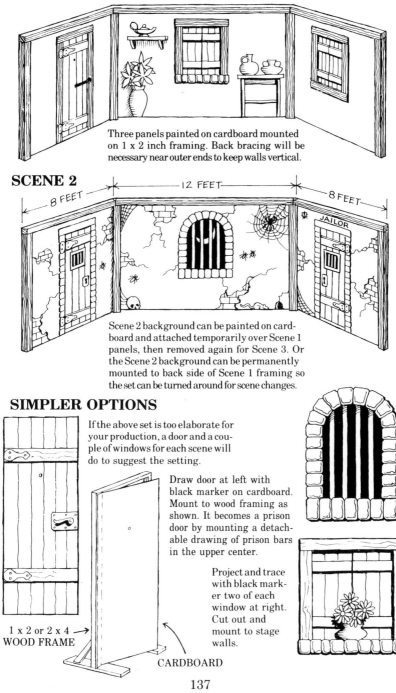

Three panels painted on cardboard mounted on 1 x 2 inch framing. Back bracing will be necessary near outer ends to keep walls vertical.

SCENE 2

8 FEET — 12 FEET — 8 FEET

Scene 2 background can be painted on cardboard and attached temporarily over Scene 1 panels, then removed again for Scene 3. Or the Scene 2 background can be permanently mounted to back side of Scene 1 framing so the set can be turned around for scene changes.

SIMPLER OPTIONS

If the above set is too elaborate for your production, a door and a couple of windows for each scene will do to suggest the setting.

Draw door at left with black marker on cardboard. Mount to wood framing as shown. It becomes a prison door by mounting a detachable drawing of prison bars in the upper center.

Project and trace with black marker two of each window at right. Cut out and mount to stage walls.

1 x 2 or 2 x 4 →
WOOD FRAME

CARDBOARD

137

1   *(The play opens with MARY, JOHN MARK, and RHODA setting*
2   *up chairs in a semicircle facing the audience.)*
3   MARY: *(Distraught)* **I just can't believe what is happening**
4   **these days. It's an awful time for Christians. First King**
5   **Herod has James beheaded, and now he has arrested**
6   **Peter. It's likely the same thing will happen to him.**
7   JOHN MARK: **Maybe not, Mother. I know Peter is a little**
8   **impulsive sometimes, but I've never known him to lose**
9   **his head.**
10   MARY: **John Mark, this is no time for jokes! It is very serious.**
11   **Peter's trial is tomorrow, and with that pompous,**
12   **egotistical, cold-hearted, self-serving tyrant Herod**
13   **sitting in judgment, Peter has about as much chance as**
14   **a chocolate chip cookie at a Weight Watchers' convention.**
15   JOHN MARK: **Not so loud, Mother, it's not safe to talk about**
16   **our ruler that way. The walls have ears, you know.**
17   RHODA: *(Suddenly alarmed, goes to wall and examines it.)* **Really?**
18   **I knew that tables had legs, chairs had arms, and roofs**
19   **had hips, but I didn't know that walls had ears. Where**
20   **do you think they are?**
21   JOHN MARK: **It's just a figure of speech, Rhoda.**
22   RHODA: **And speech has a figure? I didn't know that, either.**
23   JOHN MARK: **No, no, that means — oh, I don't have time to**
24   **explain it now. Mother, do you think we have enough**
25   **chairs?** *(Exit RHODA.)*
26   MARY: **A couple more ought to do it. Where did Rhoda go? It**
27   **sure is hard to find good help these days.** *(Yells.)* **Rhoda.**
28   **Rhoda!** *(Enter RHODA with two more chairs.)* **Rhoda, go get**
29   **two more — oh, you have them already. Good. Put them**
30   **over there at the end.**
31   RHODA: **Mistress Mary, I think it's wonderful that Peter is**
32   **getting out of jail tonight. And it's wonderful that you —**
33   MARY: *(Interrupting excitedly)* **Peter's getting out of jail? What**
34   **do you mean, girl?**
35   JOHN MARK: **Have you heard something we haven't?**

1   RHODA: No, not yet, anyway. But that's why you're having
2   this prayer party tonight, isn't it? I'm sure that when
3   we've finished with our praying, Peter will be as free as
4   a dandelion seed.

5   JOHN MARK: *(Aside to MARY)* How naive. Isn't that just like
6   a child?

7   MARY: Rhoda, just because we are praying for Peter to be
8   released doesn't necessarily mean that it will happen. We
9   want him released, of course, but God may have other
10   plans. And he knows what is best for all of us, including
11   Peter. You'll understand more about such things when
12   you're older and have been praying as long as I have.
13   *(Knock at door)* Oh, they're here. John Mark, get the door,
14   please.

15   JOHN MARK: Yes, Mother. *(Opens door.)* Come in, come in —
16   all of you. *(Enter SIDIUS, PERFIDIA, AMOS, JUDITH,*
17   *HOWIE, LETHA, MORDECAI, GERMAINE, and SOPHIE. All*
18   *greet JOHN MARK and MARY as they enter.)*

19   MARY: I'm so glad all of you could come. Please find a chair
20   and make yourselves comfortable. *(All sit.)*

21   PERFIDIA: Oh, we wouldn't have missed this for anything,
22   Mary. It's just too awful what is happening to our church
23   leaders — first James, and now Peter. Without men like
24   them, the church will be like a chicken with its head cut
25   off.

26   LETHA: Please, Perfidia, I wish you wouldn't put it quite
27   that way.

28   PERFIDIA: *(Flustered)* Oh, dear! I didn't mean — that is, what
29   I meant to say was that without Peter we don't have a
30   prayer. I mean, of course, we do have a prayer, don't we?
31   But right now it seems that prayer is about all we have —
32   not that prayer isn't enough, you understand, but — oh,
33   dear — what I'm trying to say is, we'll all miss Peter's
34   leadership. He had such a good head on his shoulders —
35   oh, my — I mean —

1   AMOS: We all know what you mean, Perfidia. The church will
2   certainly miss Peter. But in some ways I think it will be
3   good for the church that he is gone — not that any of us
4   would wish it, of course. But I think we depended on him
5   too much. The church just left everything in his hands
6   as if he was divinely annointed. He was just a man like
7   the rest of us, but we all acted as if he could walk on water.
8   RHODA: He once did, you know.
9   SIDIUS: But Amos, with Peter and James both gone, who
10   can we turn to? Where can we find leaders of their caliber?
11   AMOS: From among ourselves. As a matter of fact, I have a
12   little untapped leadership ability myself. I used to head
13   up a contingent of twenty-three hardy, well-disciplined
14   members of one of our most respected developmental
15   units.
16   JUDITH: He means the North Jerusalem Cub Scout Den.
17   AMOS: Well, Judith, keeping those urchins in line took more
18   leadership ability than you would think.
19   JUDITH: Like I've always said, if you're looking for someone
20   with a little leadership ability, Amos is your man. He's
21   got about as little as anyone I know.
22   AMOS: Thank you, my dear.
23   LETHA: It's James and Peter now, but any one of us could be
24   next. I'm sure they watch us all the time. Oh, Mary, I do
25   hope you have all the windows covered. And we've got
26   to keep our voices down. In fact, what would you think
27   of our just having a silent prayer? The walls have ears,
28   you know.
29   MARY: These are bad times for Christians, bad times.
30   MORDECAI: Well, now, I wouldn't say that. My business has
31   never been better.
32   SIDIUS: That's because you happen to be the only under-
33   taker in the church, Mordecai.
34   MORDECAI: Yes, and I'm performing a valuable service for us.
35   SIDIUS: But it's a service no one really wants.

1   MORDECAI: That's not so. People are just dying to do business
2   with me.
3   SIDIUS: You're taking advantage of our misfortunes.
4   MORDECAI: Hey, give me a break. Can I help it if I happen
5   to be in a business that makes a little profit when
6   everyone else is, uh, going under? It's a dirty job, but
7   someone's got to do it, you know.
8   SIDIUS: Someone's got to do it, but someone shouldn't enjoy
9   it so much.
10   MORDECAI: But we've all been taught to enjoy our vocation
11   and be happy in our calling.
12   SIDIUS: I know, but there are limits. You're the only under-
13   taker I know who whistles while he works.
14   MARY: Enough bickering, you two. We've got to get our
15   thoughts back on Peter.
16   SIDIUS: Sorry, Mary. I was just getting in a little dig. Get it —
17   a little *dig*?
18   GERMAINE: You are so right, Mary; we've got to think of our
19   poor brother Peter, sitting there in Herod's prison,
20   waiting for the axe to fall. And his poor wife; I wonder
21   if she is prepared to be a widow?
22   SOPHIE: I sure hope Peter took out life insurance.
23   MORDECAI: I just hope he took out burial insurance.
24   SIDIUS: You would.
25   RHODA: After we're finished praying, he won't need any
26   kind of insurance. Our prayers will keep him alive.
27   MORDECAI: Isn't the simple, naive faith of a child refreshing?
28   Rhoda, our prayers will keep him alive if it is God's will.
29   HOWIE: If God's will is going to happen anyway, why bother
30   to pray?
31   SOPHIE: Prayer allows us to participate in God's will. It
32   gives our actions meaning. We must ask in faith, then
33   simply trust God for the answer.
34   MORDECAI: If it is God's will.
35   GERMAINE: But it must be God's will for Peter to live. He is

1   such a tower of strength. We need him badly.

2   MORDECAI: But everyone's got to die sometime. Death is

3   nature's way of escape from the IRS.

4   SIDIUS: And nature's way of keeping you in business.

5   MORDECAI: *(Hurt)* You've got me all wrong, Sidius. Funeral

6   direction is not just a business with me, it's a serious

7   undertaking. It's my way of serving my fellow Christians.

8   Why, I've already offered Peter's widow — I mean, wife —

9   a three-percent discount on the funeral if she signs up

10   to let me do hers, too. That is, if she will die within the

11   year after Peter's funeral. I have to protect myself against

12   inflation, you know.

13   LETHA: Oh, how touching. I think I'm going to cry.

14   SIDIUS: Yeah, Mordecai is all heart.

15   MORDECAI: Well, I am all heart, Sidius. Last week I buried

16   a man who had a good friend who was so grieved that

17   he wanted to put a thousand pieces of silver in the coffin

18   to be buried with his friend. I was so touched that I told

19   the man I'd match his generous gesture by adding a

20   thousand of my own.

21   SIDIUS: You mean you put a thousand of your own silver

22   coins in that coffin?

23   MORDECAI: Well, yes, same as. I deposited the thousand his

24   friend left me in the bank, then wrote a check for two

25   thousand which I placed in the coffin.

26   SIDIUS: I should have guessed. Mordecai, I wouldn't trust

27   you as far as I could throw a gravestone.

28   MORDECAI: Sidius, you really hurt my feelings when you

29   say things like that. Why, I'll be the last person on earth

30   to let you down.

31   JOHN MARK: OK, OK, you two; it's time to lay aside your

32   differences and get down to some serious praying. We'll

33   let each of you take turns, beginning with Howie and

34   going around the room. Now remember, the sincere

35   prayers of a righteous person gets things done —

1   **MORDECAI:** If it is God's will.

2   **JOHN MARK:** Yes, Mordecai, if it is God's will. Howie, would

3   you lead us off, please?

4   **HOWIE:** Of course. *(He stands and noisily clears his throat.)* **Let**

5   **us pray. Our holy, righteous, and ever-to-be-adored**

6   **Father who art in heaven. We, a contrite and humble**

7   **band of believers come before your august and glorious**

8   **throne in heartfelt supplication, begging you to hear our**

9   **collective petition. We now lift up before your hallowed**

10   **presence our dear and beloved brother Peter. We beseech**

11   **you to look down upon him in your tender mercy and**

12   **grant him the comfort that only you can afford in this,**

13   **his hour of trial and tribulation** . . . . *(Lights dim on Scene*

14   *1 as HOWIE is praying.)*

15

16   **Scene 2**

17

18   *(Lights come up on the stark interior of a Roman prison, bare*

19   *except for a bench. Enter PETER, SPURIOUS, and FIBIUS.*

20   *PETER is handcuffed at each wrist between the two soldiers.)*

21   **SPURIOUS:** All right, jailbird, this is your home until the

22   headsman calls. Let's all just sit here on this bench and

23   wait.

24   **FIBIUS:** No funny stuff, now. Just behave yourself and there

25   will be no trouble, you hear? *(They sit on bench.)*

26   **SPURIOUS:** Now, tell us your name.

27   **PETER:** My name is Simon Barjonah.

28   **SPURIOUS:** Any nicknames?

29   **PETER:** Well, I have a very dear friend who called me Peter.

30   **FIBIUS:** Do you know what they will call you after tomorrow?

31   **PETER:** No, what?

32   **FIBIUS:** Shorty! *(He and SPURIOUS laugh uproariously.)*

33   **SPURIOUS:** Actually, beheading is not as bad as some people

34   think. In fact, it has several advantages.

35   **PETER:** Really? Like what?

1   SPURIOUS: Well, just think what you will save on haircuts.

2   FIBIUS: And razor blades.

3   SPURIOUS: And it's the only sure cure for a headache.

4   PETER: That all sounds well and good, but there's one thing

5   I'm a little worried about.

6   FIBIUS: What's that?

7   PETER: Where will I put my hat? *(He laughs uproariously.)*

8   SPURIOUS: Why will you need a hat?

9   PETER: To protect me from the hot sun. I'm a fisherman by

10   trade.

11   SPURIOUS and FIBIUS: *(Wrinkling their noses)* We knew that.

12   FIBIUS: What are you in the slammer for?

13   PETER: For preaching.

14   SPURIOUS: For preaching? Now, I've heard of some bad

15   sermons, but never one bad enough to be jailed for.

16   FIBIUS: What happened, did your sermon go over twenty

17   minutes?

18   SPURIOUS: Or did you preach on gluttony the Sunday after

19   Thanksgiving?

20   PETER: No, no, nothing like that. I was simply preaching

21   about Jesus.

22   FIBIUS: Jesus? You mean that Jewish carpenter Governor

23   Pilate had crucified? What's there to preach about him?

24   He's dead and gone.

25   PETER: Oh, no; he rose from the dead three days after he was

26   buried.

27   SPURIOUS: No wonder they put you in jail. If you believe

28   stuff like that, you're just too stupid to be running loose.

29   PETER: But it's true. I was with him myself after he came

30   back to life. *(SPURIOUS and FIBIUS laugh and slap their*

31   *knees a few times, jerking PETER's hands with the movement.)*

32   FIBIUS: Peter, you're not only stupid, you're crazy. You've

33   been having hallucinations.

34   PETER: Then there were over five hundred other people

35   hallucinating with me. That's how many saw him alive.

1   SPURIOUS: You mean there are five hundred more crazies
2   like you out there? We're going to have to build more
3   prisons.
4   PETER: They are not crazy. They are witnesses to the greatest
5   event that ever occurred in human history.
6   FIBIUS: *(Irritated)* Now look here, Peter, this sort of thing just
7   doesn't happen and every sane person knows it. Besides,
8   I heard that Governor Pilate posted a guard of Roman
9   soldiers at that man's tomb. If Jesus had come back to
10   life, they would have seen it and reported it.
11   PETER: Those guards claimed they fell asleep that night.
12   *(SPURIOUS and FIBIUS laugh and slap knees with same effect*
13   *on PETER's hands as before.)*
14   SPURIOUS: Peter, do you know what happens to Roman
15   soldiers who sleep on duty? The same thing that's going
16   to happen to you in the morning. They get the head bone
17   disconnected from the neck bone. And I happen to know
18   one of those soldiers, and he still has to shave and get
19   haircuts. For that reason alone, we know your story can't
20   be true. Roman soldiers simply do not sleep on duty.
21   FIBIUS: Right, Spurious. So there's no more need to talk
22   about it. I'm going to read for a while. *(He pulls out a*
23   *paperback book.)*
24   PETER: What are you reading?
25   FIBIUS: *The Decline and Fall of the Greek Empire.* *(SPURIOUS*
26   *pulls out a book and pencil.)*
27   PETER: And what are you reading?
28   SPURIOUS: I'm not reading. I'm working on crossword
29   puzzles. Now, get quiet.
30   *(After several seconds of silence, SPURIOUS drops his pencil*
31   *and reaches to the floor and retrieves it with the hand manacled*
32   *to PETER. This action pulls PETER off balance and, by chain*
33   *reaction, jerks the book from FIBIUS' hand. FIBIUS reaches to*
34   *the floor for his book, pulling PETER off balance in his direction*
35   *and, by chain reaction, again jerking the pencil from SPURIOUS'*

1   *hand. SPURIOUS and FIBIUS look at each other.)*

2   **FIBIUS: OK, on the count of three: one, two three.**

3   *(SPURIOUS and FIBIUS bend forward simultaneously to*

4   *retrieve pencil and book, causing PETER to lean forward, tip*

5   *off balance, and tumble to the floor, pulling SPURIOUS and*

6   *FIBIUS with him. After two or three awkward and*

7   *uncoordinated attempts, all three stand up. SPURIOUS and*

8   *FIBIUS turn around, rotating away from PETER in order to*

9   *step back to the bench. This move causes PETER to be backward*

10   *to them with his arms stretched across their backs. Realizing*

11   *that this is not working, SPURIOUS and FIBIUS rotate to face*

12   *forward again, and all three step backward toward the bench.*

13   *They bump against the bench, it overturns, and they fall*

14   *backward over it, sprawling on the floor. With much awkward*

15   *fumbling, they manage to set the bench upright and sit on it in*

16   *the same position as when they first entered.)*

17   **FIBIUS: Spurious, this time please hold your pencil in your**

18   **fist.**

19   **SPURIOUS: Sure, Fibius; and if you drop that book again,**

20   **I'll stuff it where the only way you can read it is with**

21   **your eye teeth.** *(SPURIOUS and FIBIUS lean forward in front*

22   *of PETER and glare at each other.)*

23   **PETER: Please, boys, don't fight over me.** *(SPURIOUS and*

24   *FIBIUS resume puzzle and book, each throwing an occasional*

25   *dirty look at the other until they become absorbed in puzzle-*

26   *solving and reading.)*

27   **SPURIOUS: What's a four letter word for "unit of electricity"?**

28   **PETER: What?**

29   **SPURIOUS: Watt. Yeah, that's it.** *(He writes in puzzle book then*

30   *thinks for several seconds.)* **What's a four letter word for**

31   **"cistern"?**

32   **PETER: Well, uh . . .**

33   **SPURIOUS: Yeah, that's it — well. Thanks, Peter.** *(He writes*

34   *the word in his book, then starts thinking again.)*

35   **PETER: Fibius, would you brush that fly off my nose?**

1   **FIBIUS:**   **No way! Leave me alone.** *(PETER tries to blow the fly*
2   *from his nose.)*
3   **SPURIOUS:**   **What's a four letter word for "footwear"?**
4   **PETER:**   *(About to sneeze)* **Ah ... ah ... AH ... SHOOO!**
5   **SPURIOUS:**   **Shoe. Yeah, that's it again, Peter. You're good at**
6   **this.** *(He writes it down. After several seconds of silence, PETER*
7   *nods a few times and falls asleep.)* **What's a noise made by a**
8   **buzz saw?** *(PETER snores loudly.)* **How do you spell that?**
9   *(PETER snores again.)* **Just like it sounds, huh?** *(Enter*
10   *ANGEL, tiptoeing quietly to bench behind the three. ANGEL*
11   *touches FIBIUS with wand, causing him to drop his book and*
12   *slump into sleep, snoring loudly with PETER. ANGEL turns*
13   *toward SPURIOUS and is about to touch him with wand.)* **Give**
14   **me a word that means pickle.**
15   **ANGEL:**   **Uh, how about "cucumber"?**
16   **SPURIOUS:**   **No, that doesn't fit.**
17   **ANGEL:**   **How many letters?**
18   **SPURIOUS:**   **Eleven.**
19   **ANGEL:**   **Hmmm. Pickle ... pickle ... oh, I've got it —**
20   **"predicament."**
21   **SPURIOUS:**   **Predicament? Oh, of course, of course; that's it.**
22   **If you're in a pickle, you're in a predicament.**
23   **ANGEL:**   **You got that right, Buster.** *(Touches SPURIOUS with*
24   *wand, causing him to drop book and pencil and fall asleep,*
25   *snoring loudly with PETER and FIBIUS. ANGEL makes a face*
26   *and puts hands over ears, then begins shaking PETER by the*
27   *shoulder.)* **Peter, wake up.**
28   **PETER:**   *(Snorts and jerks.)* **Hm? Oh, uh, let's see ... wake up**
29   **... uh, try "arouse," A-R-O-U-S-E.**
30   **ANGEL:**   **No, Peter, *wake up!***
31   **PETER:**   *(Still mostly asleep)* **Um, uh, try "stir," S-T-I-R.**
32   **ANGEL:**   **Peter, this is not a puzzle word; *wake up!***
33   **PETER:**   *(Awakens, looks at ANGEL.)* **Who are you?**
34   **ANGEL:**   **Never mind that right now. We've got to get you out**
35   **of here.**

1   **PETER:**   You're an angel, aren't you?

2   **ANGEL:**   No, I'm Frosty the Snowman. Now hurry. We need to

3   **go.** *(He easily unlocks handcuffs from PETER's wrists.)*

4   **PETER:**   **What are you doing here?**

5   **ANGEL:**   **There's been a prayer alert. A group of Christians**

6   **is meeting at Mary's house to pray for your release. I was**

7   **on duty when the prayer came in, so I got dispatched**

8   **here. Come on, let's go.** *(They start toward exit when ANGEL*

9   *stops and touches his temple with his finger to signify that he*

10   *has an idea, and grins broadly.)* **Wait just a minute, Peter.**

11   *(ANGEL tiptoes back to SPURIOUS and FIBIUS and locks their*

12   *hands together, grinning all the while. ANGEL and PETER*

13   *exit.)*

14   **FIBIUS:**   *(Dreaming, finds SPURIOUS' hand and begins to hold*

15   *it.)* **Oh, Gwendolyn, Gwendolyn, what soft, sweet hands**

16   **you have.**

17   **SPURIOUS:**   *(Talking in sleep)* **Stop it, Peter; go back to sleep.**

18   **FIBIUS:**   *(Holds SPURIOUS' hand and strokes it with his free*

19   *hand.)* **And what a lovely bracelet. It complements the**

20   **beauty of your exquisite skin so nicely . . .**

21   **SPURIOUS:**   **Peter, you're dreaming. Turn over.**

22   **FIBIUS:**   **Oh, Gwendolyn, Gwendolyn, being with you is like**

23   **heaven. I can't live without you!** *(He kisses SPURIOUS'*

24   *hand passionately and loudly.)*

25   **SPURIOUS:**   *(Awakens and sees what is happening.)* **Fibius! What**

26   **do you think you're doing?** *(SPURIOUS jerks his hand away,*

27   *sending FIBIUS sprawling and himself as well. They land in a*

28   *heap on the floor.)* **Where's Peter?**

29   **FIBIUS:**   **Where's Gwendolyn?** *(They hold up their wrists,*

30   *shackled together, and look at them in dismay.)* **I think we are**

31   **in a predicament.**

32   **SPURIOUS:**   **Yep, a real pickle, I'd say.** *(Lights dim on Scene 2.)*

33

34

35

1   **Scene 3**

2

3   *(The setting is the same as in Scene 1. All participants in the*

4   *prayer party are sitting in their chairs, bowed in prayer as the*

5   *curtain opens. SOPHIE is just closing the prayer.)*

6   **SOPHIE:**   ... **and in conclusion, Lord, we pray that you will**

7   **grant our beloved Peter his much wanted freedom from**

8   **the grasping clutches of the cold hand of death ...**

9   **MORDECAI:**   **If it is God's will.**

10   **SOPHIE:**   ... **yes, of course; if it be thy holy, divine, and**

11   **righteous will. Through the name of our Lord and Savior**

12   **Jesus Christ, we offer this humble but heartfelt prayer.**

13   **Amen.**

14   **ENTIRE GROUP:**   **Amen.** *(Knock sounds at the door.)*

15   **JUDITH:**   **Who could that be at this hour?**

16   **PERFIDIA:**   **Maybe it's someone from church just coming late.**

17   **HOWIE:**   **Surely not this late.**

18   **LETHA:**   **Maybe it's Herod's men.**

19   **AMOS:**   **Yeah! Maybe he had spies following us and they're**

20   **out there now, just waiting for us to finish.**

21   **GERMAINE:**   **Or maybe they have been out there listening to**

22   **us all the time.**

23   **SOPHIE:**   **What are we going to do?**

24   **LETHA:**   **John Mark, what are you going to do?**

25   **JOHN MARK:**   **Mother, what are you going to do?**

26   **MARY:**   **Uh, well, uh ... Rhoda, go see who is at the door.**

27   **JOHN MARK:**   **Meanwhile, maybe we'd better continue our**

28   **prayers.**

29   **HOWIE:**   **On the other hand, maybe we'd better not. What if**

30   **they come in and catch us red-handed?** *(RHODA looks out*

31   *of the peephole in the door. Her eyes widen and she comes back*

32   *to the others.)*

33   **RHODA:**   *(Greatly excited)* **He's here! He's here! Our prayers**

34   **have been answered. He's here!**

35   **LETHA:**   **Who's here?**

1   **RHODA:**   **Peter! Peter is out of prison and he's here.**

2   **MARY:**   **Rhoda, you mustn't joke about such things.**

3   **RHODA:**   **I'm not joking. Peter is really here.**

4   **JUDITH:**   **You're hallucinating, girl. Peter is chained and**

5   **locked up deep in prison behind eight layers of guards.**

6   **No one gets out of Herod's prison; no one.**

7   **RHODA:**   **But he did get out. He's here, I tell you.**

8   **MORDECAI:**   **Impossible!** *(Aside)* **I hope.**

9   **SOPHIE:**   **Maybe she saw Peter's ghost.**

10   **LETHA:**   **Yeah! I've heard awful stories about ghosts that**

11   **stalk the night, returning to haunt old familiar places**

12   **and knocking at midnight on doors of houses where they**

13   **knew someone.** *(Knock at door comes again, louder. All hush*

14   *and look toward door.)*

15   **HOWIE:**   *(Terrified)* **What are we going to do?**

16   **SOPHIE:**   **Yes, Mary, what are you going to do?**

17   **MARY:**   **Uh, John Mark, what are you going to do?**

18   **JOHN MARK:**   **Uh, I'll answer —** *(His voice breaks. He clears*

19   *throat.)* **I'll answer it.** *(He goes to the door and looks out the*

20   *peephole. His eyes widen and he turns back to the others.)* **It's**

21   **Peter! He's here!**

22   **LETHA:**   **Oh, dear, it's just as I thought — Peter's ghost!**

23   **AMOS:**   **Or his angel.**

24   **JOHN MARK:**   **No, there's no mistake about it; Peter — the**

25   **real, live Peter is out of prison and he's here, head and**

26   **all. Hallelujah! Our prayers have been answered!** *(Finally,*

27   *all believe him and begin to respond with exclamations of joy*

28   *and wonder.)*

29   **MORDECAI:**   *(Aside)* **Bummer! This is going to cost me a**

30   **bundle. I already printed the obituary and hired an**

31   **organist.**

32   **SIDIUS:**   **Ladies, gentlemen, this is wonderful. God has given**

33   **Peter back to us. I think we all had a lesson to learn**

34   **about prayer. When we started tonight, none of us really**

35   **believed it would do any good. In our minds Peter was**

1 **as good as gone. We were just praying because we knew**
2 **we were supposed to pray. Only one of us really believed**
3 **that our prayers would work, and that was our dear little**
4 **Rhoda.** *(ENTIRE GROUP responds affirmatively: "He's right,"*
5 *"That's true," "Hallelujah!" "God bless little Rhoda," etc. as*
6 *RHODA looks down shyly and rubs the toe of her shoe on the*
7 *floor. A very loud knock at door.)*
8 **MARY: Oh, my goodness, we completely forgot about Peter!**
9 **John Mark, go let him in at once.**
10 **JOHN MARK: Gladly, Mother.** *(He opens door. Enter PETER. All*
11 *crowd   around   him   with   handshakes,   hugs,   cheers,   and*
12 *exclamations of praise as the lights fade to blackout.)*
13
14
15
16
17
18
19
20
21
22
23
24
25
26
27
28
29
30
31
32
33
34
35

JOE BOB

Not even
rich Texans
can live
by money,
cattle, and
oil alone.

A COMEDY IN TWO ACTS BY T. M. WILLIAMS

Joe Bob

JOE BOB

The story of Job in a two-act comedy set in 20th century Texas.

(Job 1-42)

Cast

Cameraman

Rev. Jimmy Trivit (A slick televangelist)

Joe Bob Worth (A Texas cattleman)

Mary Bell Worth (His wife)

Commercial actress

Zeke ⎤
Hank ⎬ (Hired hands)
Slim ⎦

Telegram delivery person

Fed-Tex delivery person

Jake Aikman (An IRS agent)

Aikman's assistant 1

Aikman's assistant 2 ⎤
Aikman's assistant 3 ⎬ (non-speaking parts)
Aikman's assistant 4 ⎦

Postman

Dr. Pilzer (Joe Bob's family physician)

Bubba ⎤
Tommy Earl ⎬ (Joe Bob's friends)
Billy Ed ⎦

This play has a large cast of twenty actors, but it can be easily performed with half that number or even as few as seven by having some of the actors play more than one part. Most of the supporting characters appear on stage sequentially, and there are never more than seven players on stage at once. (See the scene beginning with Aikman's entrance on page 169.) Several of the parts are brief walk-ons with no more than a line or two to be spoken, making the doubling or tripling of some parts fairly painless. For example, Aikman's four assistants could also be delivery

155

persons, hired hands, Dr. Pilzer, Joe Bob's three friends, or all the above.

Costumes:

CAMERAMAN — normal casual wear. REV. TRIVIT — sharp suit, flashy tie with matching handkerchief, "big" hair. MARY BELL — elegant suit, clip-on earrings, an easily removable bracelet, a wedding ring, a coat (which she dons later in the play). JOE BOB — (Act I) western cut suit, bolo tie, and boots, (Act II) a scruffy bathrobe over a dirty T-shirt and pajama bottoms. COMMERCIAL ACTRESS — a flashy, form-fitting dress. ZEKE — overalls and work shirt. HANK and SLIM — worn jeans, western shirts and hats. DELIVERY PERSONS — appropriate uniforms. JAKE AIKMAN and DR. PILZER — business suits. AIKMAN's ASSISTANTS — worn jeans, T-shirts, "gimme" caps. JOE BOB's FRIENDS — neat casual wear.

A Word About Dialect:

For easy readability this script is not written in "Texan," but in normal English. However, performance will be greatly enhanced if the following characters, at least, speak with a Texas drawl: Joe Bob, Mary Bell, Zeke, Hank, Slim, Bubba, Tommy Earl, and Billy Ed. Joe Bob is a college graduate, but even educated Texans, while using good grammar, often retain their drawls (witness U.S. Senator Phil Gramm, who holds a Ph.D.)

To give you an idea of how to "Texanize" the dialog, here are a couple of excerpts from the script rewritten in drawl.

JOE BOB: Yore fergittin', Mary Bell, we've still got tuns of muny in th' Cattleman's Nash'nul Bank. Mah friend Bill Wiggins runs thet bank an' he's been tendin' orr muny lack a sheep-dawg, herdin' it around frum CDs to trusts to savin's jist t' keep up with th' best int'rest rates. (From page 168)

ZEKE: Yo' got t' rumember, Mr. Joe Bob, this here laff ain't th' reel thang. This here world is jist th' brandin' yard whar God rounds up 'is herd and puts his brand on them that's his'n. We shuddn't expect th' brandin' yard t' be lack hevvin. But we kinda fergit thet . . . (From page 186)

Some sample words and their Texas equivalents:

think: thank	isn't: iddn't
thing: thang	iron: arn

get: git   chair: cheer
just: jist   my: mah
barbwire: borb war   I: ah
poor: pore   our: orr
your: yore   like: lack
fire: far   life: laff (*a* as in *half*)
doesn't: duddn't   ranch: rainch
hired: hard   for: fer

Drop the *g* on words ending with *ing.*

Props:

Television camera (see sketch on page 158 for suggested construction); "Havitol" product (a cereal-sized box with the word *Havitol* lettered logo style on the front); a small, cheap Bible; a checkbook and pen; a severely pruned potted plant; a healthy, blooming plant of the same variety; a doorbell; two telegrams; two letters in overnight envelopes (large cardboard envelopes saying "Fed Tex"); IRS badge; IRS documents; a framed diploma; two letters in #10 envelopes; a telephone; a bottle of pills; a suitcase; a scratching stick; two sacks of groceries.

Sound Effects:

Telephone and doorbell rings.

Setting:

Act I — a living room with elegant appointments: large paintings, potted plants, fine furniture, and a very large fireplace. (See sketch on page 158 for suggested construction.)

Act II — the same room stripped bare except for the fireplace.

FIREPLACE

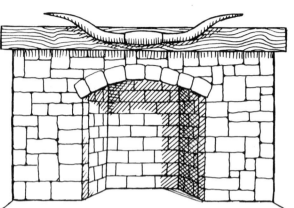

Make enlarged film copy of sketch at right. Project onto cardboard and trace in broad-tipped black marker or black poster paint. Paint as suggested below. Cut out and mount to back wall of stage.

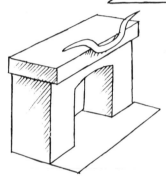

DIMENSIONAL OPTION

Fireplace can be flat, as shown above, or constructed in three dimensions, as shown at left.

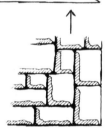

To achieve the illusion of dimension on the fireplace stones, add a strip of light, warm gray to the bottom and left side of each stone, as shown in corner enlargement above. If you choose the flat, non-dimensional fireplace, paint a shadow just under the edge of the mantle and inside the firepit. Colors:

Stones — off white
Shadows on stones — warm gray
Mantle — brown
Longhorns — tan

TV CAMERA

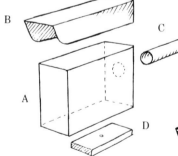

A. Crisp-edged cardboard box approximately 8" x 12" x 16".

B. Cut and fold cardboard hood and glue to top of box.

C. Cut hole in front of box. Insert cardboard tube (aluminum foil core) and glue into place.

D. Drill hole in 1" x 4" block of wood. Glue and staple to box.

Paint camera hood black and apply large mailbox letters to sides. Paint box, lens tube, and mounting block metallic silver. Paint viewfinder area on back of camera black. Add decorative stripes around base of box and to end of tube with black plastic tape. Mount on heavy camera tripod.

1   **Act I**

2

3   *(As the play opens, JOE BOB and MARY BELL are sitting stiffly*

4   *on their divan. REV. JIMMY TRIVIT sits in the chair beside*

5   *them. They are all smiling broadly at the television camera which*

6   *is manned by the CAMERAMAN.)*

7   **CAMERAMAN:**   ... five, four, three, two, one — you're on the

8   **air.** *(Points to TRIVIT.)*

9   **REV. JIMMY TRIVIT:**   Hello to all you folks out there in TV

10   land. This is Rev. Jimmy Trivit again, welcoming you to

11   Lifestyles of the Rich and Faithful. Tonight I'm bringing

12   you another inspirational interview with highly

13   successful Christians. We are in the beautiful home of

14   Joe Bob and Mary Bell Worth, who will tell us all about

15   how turning to Jesus made them wealthy, healthy,

16   successful, and happy. And you will find out how the

17   same thing can happen to you. So, don't touch that remote

18   control; we'll be back with the Worths' story right after

19   this important message. *(Enter COMMERCIAL ACTRESS.*

20   *She stands away from TRIVIT and THE WORTHS. CAMERA-*

21   *MAN turns camera to her.)*

22   **COMMERCIAL ACTRESS:**   Are you tired of having to choose

23   between wealth and religion? Are you tired of conflicts

24   between your good times and the Good Book? Are you

25   seeking a way to blend faith with fortune? Then I have

26   just what you are looking for. *(She holds up Havitol product*

27   *box for camera.)* It's Havitol, a soothing new product

28   especially formulated to relieve your irritated conscience;

29   to help you sleep better at night after a long day of

30   indigestible ethics.

31   Havitol contains more of the active ingredient

32   Simulated Grace to make you feel better faster. And

33   Simulated Grace has no unpleasant side effects — no

34   demands, no commitment, and no pangs of conscience.

35   And best of all, it costs much less than the real thing —

1　　　no tithing required.
2　　　　　Just send your check or money order for $19.95 plus
3　　　$10 for postage and handling to Jimmy Trivit Ministries,
4　　　Box 666, New Haven, Tennessee. *(ACTRESS freezes —*
5　　　*smiles to camera as it swings away from her and back to TRIVIT,*
6　　　*then she exits. CAMERAMAN points to TRIVIT.)*
7　TRIVIT:　Today's program comes to you from the spacious,
8　　　elegant living room of Joe Bob and Mary Bell Worth's
9　　　eight thousand square foot, eight bedroom mansion,
10　　　complete with olympic-size pool and tennis courts, all
11　　　located on their huge ranch out here in west Texas. Yes,
12　　　God has been good to the Worths, but things have not
13　　　always been so good, have they, Mary Bell?
14　MARY BELL:　No, they haven't, Rev. Jimmy. When Joe Bob
15　　　and I first married, we were as poor as buzzards on a
16　　　shut-down highway.
17　TRIVIT:　And why were things so tough then?
18　JOE BOB:　Well, we got married when I was a junior at Texas
19　　　A & M. It's always a little hard trying to go to school and —
20　TRIVIT:　I didn't know you were an Aggie, Joe Bob. I just
21　　　heard a new Aggie joke I think you'll love. Did you hear
22　　　the one about the Aggie who walked into a room with a
23　　　pig under his arm? Someone said, "Hey, where did you
24　　　get that?" And the pig said, "I won him at a raffle." Haw,
25　　　haw, haw, haw! Won him at a raffle — the pig says. Haw,
26　　　haw, haw! Well, back to your early life. How did you two
27　　　get by during those hard times?
28　MARY BELL:　We just barely did. I worked nights at the
29　　　corner drugstore, and Joe Bob worked evenings and
30　　　weekends fixing fences on a local ranch.
31　JOE BOB:　We had nothing but an old, beat-up pickup with no
32　　　reverse gear, and the fenders were tied on with bailing
33　　　wire. Rattled like an armadillo needing a grease job.
34　MARY BELL:　And the roof of our one-room apartment leaked
35　　　so badly that when it rained, it took all our pans to catch

1   the water. Sounded like the spittoons at a spitters'
2   convention.
3   JOE BOB: And we just barely had enough to keep from
4   starving. I remember when we used to fill up on nothing
5   but crackers and water for lunch so we'd swell up and
6   feel too full to want supper.
7   TRIVIT: My goodness; you really did have it rough. But then
8   what happened in your life to change all that?
9   MARY BELL: Well, we started going to a little church at the
10   edge of town, then one night we turned our lives over to
11   Jesus. And suddenly everything started getting better
12   for us.
13   JOE BOB: After I graduated, we scraped up the down
14   payment for a little piece of land and a few head of
15   Hereford, and everything just started falling into place
16   like alfalfa seeds in a straight furrow. Our cattle started
17   multiplying and bringing good prices, so we hauled in
18   more. Then we started buying up some of the acreage
19   next to ours, which allowed us to gradually graze more
20   and more cattle. Well, things just sort of kept on going
21   like that until —
22   MARY BELL: Until now we have over one hundred thousand
23   acres of the best grazing land in Texas and over seven
24   thousand head of cattle. Then several years ago we
25   started drilling for oil, and pretty soon our wells started
26   coming in like God just turned the faucets on.
27   TRIVIT: Praise the Lord and hallelujah! Ain't God wonderful!
28   And you still have not told us the whole story. Tell us
29   about your family.
30   JOE BOB: Well, we have two fine kids, a boy and a girl. Our
31   son Jim Bob is —
32   MARY BELL: A senior at the University of Texas. He was
33   voted most handsome, most likely to succeed, student
34   body president, had a 4.0 grade point average, and is the
35   starting quarterback on the baseball team.

1   JOE BOB: The football team, dear.

2   MARY BELL: Yes, that too.

3   TRIVIT: Hallelujah! God is really grand! And what about

4   your daughter?

5   JOE BOB: Well, Suzanne has been in college for almost a year

6   and —

7   MARY BELL: She has already been elected most beautiful on

8   campus, made the dean's list, and is captain of the drill

9   team. She is also a candidate for homecoming queen.

10   TRIVIT: Praise the Lord! Oh, praise the Lord! *(To camera)*

11   Folks, you see what happens when you accept Jesus into

12   your life? You can be just like Joe Bob and Mary Bell.

13   You, too, can be rich, successful, happy, beautiful, and

14   saved. And it's so easy. All you have to do is lay your

15   hands on your TV right now and repeat after me: Lord,

16   I want you to come into my heart right now. Give me

17   wealth beyond compare. Make me successful in business.

18   Give me health, good looks, happiness, and good times.

19   I pray in the holy name of our precious Lord Jesus, amen.

20   Now, folks, I've told you many times on these programs

21   that God wants you to be healthy, rich, and happy. But

22   he only answers prayers that come from a faithful heart.

23   To show God your faith and ensure an answer to the

24   prayer you just prayed, you need to send a generous love

25   offering to Jimmy Trivit Ministries, Box 666, New Haven,

26   Tennessee. For an offering of five dollars or more, I will

27   send you a copy of my new book, *How to Get What You*

28   *Want From God.* So, until next time, this is Rev. Jimmy

29   Trivit saying, hold out your hands, 'cause God is ready

30   to pour! Good night, everyone. *(He freezes with a big smile*

31   *on his face as COMMERCIAL ACTRESS enters and takes her*

32   *former position. CAMERAMAN swings camera from TRIVIT*

33   *to ACTRESS and points to her as the cue to begin speaking.)*

34   COMMERCIAL ACTRESS: We're glad you could be with us

35   today for another inspiring interview on Lifestyles of the

Rich and Faithful. Don't forget to order your supply of Havitol, *(She holds up product for camera)* and, as a special bonus if you order now, we will send you Rev. Trivit's own translation of the New Testament — The New Comfort Version, especially edited to ease the pressure on your spiritual life. *(She holds up Bible for camera.)* **Rev. Trivit has removed troublesome passages such as the rich man's problem with the eye of the needle, the parable of the rich fool, the story of Ananias and Sapphira getting zapped for lying about real estate prices, and the entire book of James. And the New Comfort Version is the only translation fully endorsed by the National Association of Millionaires.**

So, don't delay. Send your check or money order today for only $19.95 plus $10 for postage and handling to receive a month's supply of Havitol and your very own copy of the New Comfort Version of the New Testament. That address again is Jimmy Trivit Ministries, Box 666, New Haven, Tennessee. *(ACTRESS freezes and smiles into camera.)*

CAMERAMAN: Cut. That's a wrap, folks. It's in the can.

TRIVIT: Good. Go ahead and load up the camera. I'll be out in just a minute. *(Exit CAMERMAN and ACTRESS.)* Joe Bob, Mary Bell, thanks so much for being on my program. I really appreciate it. Now, I feel sure that after all the good exposure I'm giving you on national television, you'll want to bless my ministry with a little love offering of your own. Just a token amount — something like, say twenty-five thousand dollars?

JOE BOB: Well, I don't know, Rev. Trivit. We give pretty generously to our church and to quite a passel of charities and missionaries. I don't much think —

MARY BELL: Oh, come on, Joe Bob; don't be such a miser. *(She gets out her checkbook and quickly writes a check.)* Here, Rev. Jimmy — a check for fifty thousand dollars.

1   TRIVIT: *(Greedily takes check.)* **Oh, that's wonderful, Mary Bell.**
2   **I really appreciate this.**
3   MARY BELL: **Now, do you think you could get yourself on the**
4   **prayer line to have our daughter elected homecoming**
5   **queen? The election is next week.**
6   TRIVIT: **I'll be glad to, Mary Bell. After a generous offering**
7   **like this, how could God refuse? He's obligated.** *(He rises*
8   *to leave.)* **Well, good-bye for now.** *(JOE BOB and MARY*
9   *BELL rise and they all shake hands.)* **Have a good day and**
10   **praise the Lord.** *(Exit REV. TRIVIT.)*
11   JOE BOB: **Well, I'm sure glad that's over. This tie is choking**
12   **me like a chicken snake on a prairie dog.**
13   MARY BELL: *(Angrily)* **Ooooh! I've never in my life been so**
14   **humiliated.**
15   JOE BOB: **What are you talking about?**
16   MARY BELL: **You, that's what! You weren't going to give Rev.**
17   **Trivit a love offering. Didn't you hear anything he said?**
18   **God has made us rich because we have given a lot of**
19   **money to his businesses.**
20   JOE BOB: **God's businesses?**
21   MARY BELL: **You know, his churches, charities, missionaries,**
22   **TV ministries and all that. If we stop giving now, God**
23   **might decide to repossess all our things. What on earth**
24   **were you thinking?**
25   JOE BOB: **Really, now, Mary Bell, I don't think God works**
26   **quite like that. You make it sound like God has some sort**
27   **of protection racket or rent-to-own scheme going. We do**
28   **our giving because we love God, not to get something**
29   **back.**
30   MARY BELL: **Well, I don't intend to take any chances. And**
31   **besides, when you don't give to people like Rev. Trivit,**
32   **they think you don't have the money. It's not good for**
33   **our image.**
34   JOE BOB: **Maybe we need to think a little less about our**
35   **image and a little more about putting our money where it**

1   can do the most good.
2 MARY BELL: I can't think of any place better to put it than
3   in the hands of preachers who have God's ear and can
4   put in a good word for us.
5 JOE BOB: But don't you ever wonder if Trivit is really on the
6   up and up? Sometimes he seems about as artificial as a
7   K-Mart Christmas tree.
8 MARY BELL: Nonsense. He's got to be for real. He's got rich
9   preaching, hasn't he? *(Doorbell rings.)*
10 JOE BOB: I'll get it. *(Opens door.)* Howdy, Zeke. Come on in.
11   *(Enter ZEKE carrying a severely pruned potted plant.)*
12 ZEKE: Howdy, Mr. Joe Bob, Miz Mary Bell. 'Scuse me for
13   interrupting. I'll just set this here plant back where I got
14   it.
15 MARY BELL: Oh, my goodness! What have you done to it?
16 ZEKE: I done pruned it a bit, Ma'am.
17 MARY BELL: Pruned it? You've ruined it. There's nothing
18   left but a bare stalk. You've killed my favorite plant.
19 JOE BOB: *(Aside to MARY BELL)* Why, Mary Bell, you always
20   said that plant looked like a porcupine with its tail in a
21   light socket.
22 MARY BELL: Hush! He doesn't have to know that. *(To ZEKE)*
23   I loved that plant, and look what you've done to it.
24 ZEKE: The plant was dying, Ma'am. You saw the poor critter;
25   it was all stalk and no blooms. And the leaves was starting
26   to droop and turn sort of putrid yellow-like.
27 MARY BELL: Sure, I knew that, and I was taking care of it. I
28   doubled its dose of vitamin-rich plant food, fertilizer, and
29   soil minerals. In a few days I'd have had it blooming like
30   honeysuckles on a barbwire fence.
31 ZEKE: In a couple of days that plant would have been deader
32   than a bear rug. You're overfeeding it; that's been the
33   whole problem. The little sucker's been pigging out like
34   a hog in a corn bin. It's all going to stalk and not making
35   any blooms.

1   MARY BELL: It sure can't bloom now. Where would it put a
2   bloom?
3   ZEKE: Patience, Ma'am, patience. Give 'er a little time and
4   she'll have enough blooms to make a lifetime career for
5   some lucky honeybee. I guarantee it. Well, I'll be
6   moseying along now. Y'all have a good day. *(Exit ZEKE.)*
7   MARY BELL: Stupid hired hand. That's the silliest thing I
8   ever heard. When you want something to grow, you feed
9   it the best you've got. When you want it to die, you whack
10   it down to a bare stick.
11   JOE BOB: Let's just give it a little time and see what happens.
12   *(Doorbell rings.)* I'll get it. *(He opens door.)* Come on in here,
13   Hank. What's wrong with you? You look like you just ran
14   over your best coon dog.
15   HANK: Boss, I really got terrible news.
16   JOE BOB: What's wrong, Hank?
17   HANK: It's your cattle, boss. They're gone. All dead; every
18   last one of them.
19   JOE BOB: Gone? Dead? What do you mean, Hank?
20   HANK: We had them all in the south pasture, and —
21   JOE BOB: All seven thousand of them at once?
22   HANK: Yep. We been clearing out the mesquite in the east,
23   they done grazed out the west, and the north has been
24   dry as lizard's spit since July. Anyhow, up come one of
25   them there sudden storms with boiling clouds blacker'n
26   a panther stalking at midnight, and thunder rumbling
27   around in them like they hadn't et in three days. Then
28   sudden-like there was three or four popping cracks of
29   lightning, and them cattle took off like they was shot out
30   of a deer rifle — straight up the slope and over the ledge
31   into Coyote Canyon. They're all gone, boss.
32   JOE BOB: *(Stunned)* All seven thousand of them?
33   HANK: Not even a calf left, boss. I sure am sorry. Well, I
34   reckon there's nothing more I can say. I'll be gittin' now.
35   *(Exit HANK.)*

1 JOE BOB: This is terrible! We've lost all our cattle, Mary Bell.
2 MARY BELL: Oh, that's no big deal for us. You've got so many
3   other irons in the fire now I've wondered if we shouldn't
4   get out of the cattle business anyway.
5 JOE BOB: But I've always thought of myself as a cattleman.
6 MARY BELL: Now you'll just have to start thinking of
7   yourself as an oil man. We make more off of oil than cattle
8   anyway, you know. *(Doorbell rings. JOE BOB opens door.*
9   *Enter SLIM.)*
10 SLIM: Howdy, boss. You better sit down. I've got some pretty
11   awful news for you.
12 JOE BOB: What is it, Slim?
13 SLIM: Your oil wells are gone.
14 JOE BOB: What do you mean, oil wells gone? Oil wells don't
15   just root themselves out of the ground and run away.
16 SLIM: No, boss, but they do burn pretty good. And that's
17   what's happening right now. Every last one of them is
18   on fire, burning like brimstone.
19 JOE BOB: Come on, Slim, how can thirty-seven oil wells all
20   catch fire at the same time?
21 SLIM: We don't rightly know, boss. I reckon there's been some
22   kind of foul play. We seen tire marks around and evidence
23   of dynamite. We figure your ornery neighbor whose wells
24   all come up dry might have hired it done.
25 JOE BOB: Well, thanks for telling me, Slim. You'd better call
26   the sheriff, I reckon.
27 SLIM: I'll do that, boss. I'm sure sorry this happened. *(Exit*
28   *SLIM.)*
29 JOE BOB: At least those wells were insured. I'll just call up
30   my insurance agent and have him file a claim.
31 MARY BELL: Insurance?! Oh, no!
32 JOE BOB: Mary Bell, what do you mean, "Oh, no"?
33 MARY BELL: I just remembered something I forgot to do.
34   *(Starts crying.)* Oh, Joe Bob, I'm so sorry.
35 JOE BOB: Sorry for what, Mary Bell? Come on — out with it.

1   **MARY BELL:** *(Bawling)* **I forgot to mail the insurance payment.**

2   **JOE BOB:** *(Comforts her.)* **There, there, don't worry about**

3   **that. Insurance companies always give a thirty-day grace**

4   **period.**

5   **MARY BELL:** *(Really bawling)* **But it was due six weeks ago.**

6   **JOE BOB:** **I see. That means our cattle were not insured**

7   **either, doesn't it? Nor our house, cars, land, anything.**

8   **MARY BELL:** **Wah!**

9   **JOE BOB:** **Oh, that's all right, Mary Bell. Don't worry your**

10   **pretty little head about this. We've still got our**

11   **investments, which are considerable, as you know.**

12   **MARY BELL:** *(Snuffling)* **Yeah, you're right. We're not down**

13   **yet. You've got enough stocks that we'll never have to**

14   **worry about money. We can live very well for the rest of**

15   **our lives off your investments, can't we?** *(Doorbell rings.*

16   *JOE BOB opens door.)*

17   **TELEGRAM DELIVERY PERSON:** **Telegram for Joe Bob**

18   **Worth.**

19   **JOE BOB:** **Thank you.** *(Takes telegram, closes door, opens envelope.)*

20   **Well, speak of the devil; this is from our stockbroker.**

21   **Uh-oh. It says, "All your stocks have fallen below**

22   **purchase prices. Margin due. Remit one hundred**

23   **thousand dollars immediately."**

24   **MARY BELL:** **Well, so much for retiring on investments.**

25   **Where are you going to get the money to pay the margin?**

26   **JOE BOB:** **You're forgetting that we've still got tons of money**

27   **in the Cattleman's National Bank. My friend Bill Wiggins**

28   **runs that bank and he's been tending our money like a**

29   **sheepdog, herding it around from CDs to trusts to savings**

30   **to keep up with the best interest rates. I'll just cash in a**

31   **CD or two, pay the margin, and we'll still have several**

32   **million left.** *(Doorbell rings. JOE BOB opens door.)*

33   **FED-TEX DELIVERY PERSON:** **Overnight letter for Joe Bob**

34   **Worth. Sign here, please.**

35   **JOE BOB:** *(Signs and takes letter.)* **Thank you.** *(Closes door.)*

1   **According to the law of averages, this should be good**
2   **news.** *(Opens envelope and reads silently.)* **Well, so much for**
3   **the law of averages. Here, you read it.** *(Hands letter to*
4   *MARY BELL and sits down.)*
5   **MARY BELL:** *(Reading)* **"We regret to inform you that the**
6   **Cattleman's National Bank has failed. You had CDs,**
7   **trusts, and other deposits in this bank totaling**
8   **$17,867,423.46. Of this amount, one hundred thousand**
9   **dollars is covered by FDIC insurance. We regret to tell**
10   **you that all above this amount must be written off as a**
11   **total loss. Sincerely, Robert C. Johnson, Agent, Federal**
12   **Deposit Insurance Corporation."** *(Crumples paper and*
13   *throws it to the floor.)* **Do you know what this means, Joe**
14   **Bob? We're broke — flat broke. We've got a total of one**
15   **hundred thousand dollars left to our name, and we've**
16   **got to shell out that to pay off your bad investments. And**
17   **it's all your fault. Anyone who doesn't know any better**
18   **than to put all his money into one bank needs to have**
19   **his garden weeded.**
20   **JOE BOB:**   **But Bill Wiggins is an old friend.**
21   **MARY BELL:**   **And just look where that good ol' boy, scratch-**
22   **each-other's-back, friends-do-business-with-friends, stupid**
23   **male bonding, hairy-chested macho code has got you:**
24   **penniless — flat broke. Why didn't you parcel out our**
25   **money in hundred thousand lots to banks all over Texas?**
26   **Then it all would have been insured.**
27   **JOE BOB:**   **OK, OK, so I made a little mistake. But we're not**
28   **broke, Mary Bell — far from it. You're forgetting that we**
29   **have one hundred thousand acres of top Texas grazing**
30   **land. I'll just sell off a little acreage and make ourselves**
31   **liquid again. No problem.** *(Doorbell rings. JOE BOB opens*
32   *door. Enter JAKE AIKMAN without invitation, followed by four*
33   *ASSISTANTS. ASSISTANTS immediately start picking up*
34   *furniture and carrying it out.)* **What is going on here?**
35   **JAKE AIKMAN:**   **Are you Joe Bob Worth?**

1   JOE BOB: Why, yes, but —
2   AIKMAN: *(Flashes badge.)* **Jake Aikman, Internal Revenue**
3   **Service. I'm here to collect the taxes you underpaid in**
4   **1979, '80, and '81.**
5   JOE BOB: What are you talking about? I've always paid my
6   taxes.
7   AIKMAN: Heh, heh, heh. You may have thought you were
8   paying your taxes, but your accountant was ripping you
9   off. He hid half your assests in phony bookkeeping and
10   only paid us a fraction of what you owed. Heh, heh.
11   JOE BOB: My accountant did that? Harvey was my best
12   friend.
13   MARY BELL: Good ol' boy male bonding again.
14   AIKMAN: Harvey Belman has been under investigation for
15   months, but we just discovered what he did to you last
16   week. He thought he could get by with it, but trying to
17   put one over on the IRS is like trying to sneak a sunrise
18   past a rooster.
19   JOE BOB: How much do I owe?
20   AIKMAN: Heh, heh, heh. You know, if we had discovered this
21   problem back when it happened, you'd have only owed
22   a few hundred thousand. But now, with penalty and in-
23   terest adding up all these years, you owe us quite a pile,
24   heh, heh. Yes, quite a pile.
25   JOE BOB: Come on, Aikman, how bad is it?
26   AIKMAN: Heh, heh, heh, heh. I have the figure right here, but
27   I always hate to show it right off the bat. I like to sort of
28   linger a bit and savor the moment.
29   JOE BOB: Give me that, you sadist! *(Grabs paper from*
30   *AIKMAN's hand and looks at it.)* **Holy hereford! This is more**
31   **than my whole ranch is worth.**
32   AIKMAN: I know that, Mr. Worth, but I suppose it will just
33   have to do. Heh, heh. I have authorization to seize your
34   entire acreage except for the half acre this house sits on.
35   *(Chuckles as he shows JOE BOB a paper.)* **And here is my**

1   **authorization to take your household goods,** *(More*
2   *chuckles as he shows another paper)* **your automobiles,** *(More*
3   *chuckles as he shows another paper)* **your boat and plane,**
4   *(Another paper)* **your paintings and sculptures** *(Another*
5   *paper)* **and all your clothing. Heh, heh, heh, heh, heh.**
6   **MARY BELL:** *(Alarmed)* **Even what we're wearing?**
7   **AIKMAN: Unfortunately, I have to let you keep the clothes**
8   **you have on, but I can take the jewelry. Here, I'll have**
9   **those earrings,** *(He plucks them from MARY BELL's ears with*
10   *some difficulty as she resists)* **and that bracelet.** *(He takes*
11   *bracelet as she resists.)* **Now, give me that ring.**
12   **MARY BELL: But that's my wedding ring.**
13   **AIKMAN: Right. Give it to me.**
14   **MARY BELL: No, you can't have it.**
15   **AIKMAN: Yes, I can.** *(He forcibly removes ring from MARY BELL's*
16   *finger.)*
17   **MARY BELL: Oowww!** *(Angrily)* **Why don't you just go ahead**
18   **and take the house, too?!**
19   **AIKMAN: I would love to, Mrs. Worth, but the law forbids it.**
20   **Unfortunately, we must allow a man to keep his**
21   **homestead. It's a stupid law and we're working on**
22   **changing it.**
23   **MARY BELL: Ohhh! You are perverse!**
24   **AIKMAN: Well, thank you, Mrs. Worth. Heh, heh.**
25   **ASSISTANT NO. 1: Look what I found, Mr. Aikman.** *(Hands*
26   *AIKMAN a framed certificate.)* **Mr. Worth's Texas A & M**
27   **diploma. He's an Aggie.**
28   **AIKMAN: Well, what do you know about that. Say, Mr. Worth,**
29   **do you know how to tell if an Aggie's been using your**
30   **computer? By the white-out on your screen. Ha, ha, ha,**
31   **ha, ha, ha. Pretty good one, eh? Well, we're just about**
32   **done here, so we'll be on our way now. Have a nice day.**
33   **Heh, heh, heh.** *(Exit AIKMAN followed by FOUR*
34   *ASSISTANTS carrying the last items of furniture. JOE BOB*
35   *begins to sit in large, easy chair just as TWO ASSISTANTS pick*

171

1   *it up to remove it, and he lands on the floor, where he sits, chin*
2   *on hands.)*
3   **JOE BOB: Harvey, my best friend; I just can't believe it.**
4   **MARY BELL:** *(Sits on floor.)* **What has happened to us? We're**
5   **about as low as a wart on a bullfrog's toe.**
6   **JOE BOB: Not really, Mary Bell. Look on the bright side;**
7   **we've still got our family.** *(Doorbell rings.)*
8   **MARY BELL: Uh, oh.**
9   **JOE BOB:** *(Opens door.)* **Yes?**
10 **POSTMAN: Special delivery for Joe Bob Worth.** *(Hands letter*
11 *to JOE BOB.)*
12 **JOE BOB:** *(Closes door, opens letter, and reads.)* **It's from the**
13 **University of Texas. "Dear Mr. Worth: We regret to inform**
14 **you that your son Jim Bob has been permanently**
15 **dismissed from the university due to his arrest yesterday**
16 **for drug possession and use. He is presently in the Travis**
17 **County jail pending trial. The state is convinced that**
18 **they have an airtight case against him, and that**
19 **conviction is inevitable. Sincerely, James R. Finston,**
20 **Dean of Men."**
21 **MARY BELL: Well, so much for family. Now we're not only**
22 **broke, we're disgraced.**
23 **JOE BOB: I'd better call Jim Bob and see what we can do for**
24 **him. Meanwhile, remember that we've still got Suzanne.**
25 **We can certainly be proud of her.** *(Telephone rings.)*
26 **MARY BELL: I'll get it.** *(Into phone)* **Hello. What? You can't**
27 **mean it! No! No! No! I can't believe it. Oh, no, it just can't**
28 **be true!** *(She starts crying and hangs up phone.)*
29 **JOE BOB: Mary Bell, what's wrong?**
30 **MARY BELL:** *(Bawling)* **It's Suzanne.**
31 **JOE BOB: Suzanne? What's happened to her?**
32 **MARY BELL:** *(Sobbing)* **Our daughter . . . Suzanne . . . she . . .**
33 **she has . . . eloped. Booo hoooooo . . . .**
34 **JOE BOB: There, there, now; maybe that's not so bad. I mean,**
35 **after all that's happened to us today, this we can deal with.**

1   And we might even like the boy.

2   MARY BELL: *(Still crying)* No, no, no! You don't understand.

3   She married a — a — an Episcopalian! *(Or substitute any*

4   *denomination. She bawls.)*

5   JOE BOB: *(Immediately bawls with her.)* Our only daughter . . .

6   how could she?

7   MARY BELL: *(Snuffling as she recovers.)* Now we have hit

8   bottom, Joe Bob. We're down to nothing, absolutely

9   nothing.

10 JOE BOB: Not really; we've still got our health. *(Doorbell*

11 *rings. JOE BOB opens door.)* Howdy, Dr. Pilzer. Come on

12 in here. *(Enter DR. PILZER. JOE BOB offers a handshake,*

13 *which DR. PILZER obviously avoids.)*

14 DR. PILZER: Howdy, Joe Bob. I can't shake hands with you;

15 you're contagious.

16 JOE BOB: Contagious? What do you mean?

17 DR. PILZER: I got the results of your tests. That itching you've

18 been having in your side is cactus fever. And it's going

19 to get worse, lots worse.

20 JOE BOB: How's that, Doc?

21 DR. PILZER: Pretty soon that rash is going to spread all over

22 your body, and you'll itch like you're sitting in a barrel

23 of goose feathers. Then sores will break out all over and

24 you'll scratch like a chicken after a grubworm. And when

25 you scratch, those sores will hurt like cactus spines are

26 stuck in them.

27 JOE BOB: That sounds awful. What can I do for it?

28 DR. PILZER: I can't cure it, but I've got something here that

29 will ease the symptoms. *(Pulls bottle from pocket.)* Extract

30 of Mesquite root ointment. It's only eighty-seven dollars

31 and fifty cents.

32 JOE BOB: I don't have eighty-seven dollars and fifty cents.

33 DR. PILZER: Oh, sure; Joe Bob Worth doesn't have eighty-

34 seven dollars and fifty cents like Amarillo doesn't have

35 jack rabbits. Come on, Joe Bob, enough jokes. I'm in a

173

1   hurry.

2   JOE BOB: I'm afraid I'm serious, Dr. Pilzer. We've just been
3   hit with a run of rotten luck. I have no income and no
4   assets. It's kind of like I've been trampled by a herd of
5   wild buffaloes.

6   DR. PILZER: OK, I'll sell it to you for four dollars and ninety-
7   five cents. *(Aside to audience)* I'll still make a couple of
8   dollars profit.

9   JOE BOB: I don't have any money at all. I'm flat broke. But I
10   need the medicine. Could you give it to me on credit?

11   DR. PILZER: With no income and no assets? No way!

12   JOE BOB: But what can I do about the rash?

13   DR. PILZER: *(As he exits)* Scratch.

14   MARY BELL: *(Angrily)* How could God let this happen to us
15   after all we've done for him?

16   JOE BOB: I don't know. I really don't know.

17   MARY BELL: Well, I know this: God has failed us. After all
18   we've done for him, look what he does for us in return:
19   he sets us up for a big crash. He makes us think he is
20   blessing us, then he yanks the rug right out from under
21   our feet and we land flat on our — uh — faces. Joe Bob,
22   I've had it with God.

23   JOE BOB: Mary Bell, you can't mean that.

24   MARY BELL: Oh, yes I can. If this is what God does to loyal
25   supporters after years of service — just throws them
26   away like a sneezed-in tissue — then I don't want any
27   part of him. I would not have spent my life resisting
28   temptation, pouring hard-earned money into collection
29   plates and watching Billy Graham crusades if I'd known
30   he wouldn't bless me in return. I want to go on record
31   right now; I renounce Jesus. Yes, I utterly renounce him,
32   and God, too. And you will do the same if you have any
33   sense left — but of course, he may have taken that from
34   you too — not that it would be any great loss. *(MARY BELL*
35   *turns and stalks out of the room.)*

1 JOE BOB: *(Calls after her.)* **Listen, I know you are hurting, and**
2 **I can certainly understand why. But we can't renounce**
3 **Jesus. Who else is there to turn to? I don't understand**
4 **all this either. The pat answers surely aren't working**
5 **right now, but God is still God, and there's bound to be**
6 **a purpose in all this that we'll understand down the line.**
7 **We've got to keep on serving him.**
8 **MARY BELL:** *(Voice Off-stage)* **We've been serving him all our**
9 **married lives, and now look what we've got to show for**
10 **it — nothing, absolutely nothing.**
11 **JOE BOB:** That's not true, Mary Bell. We've still got each
12 other. *(Enter MARY BELL, coat on, suitcase in hand.)*
13 **MARY BELL:** Good-bye, Joe Bob.
14 **JOE BOB:** What are you doing?
15 **MARY BELL:** What does it look like I'm doing? I'm leaving
16 you. If you're hanging on to that God of yours after what
17 he's done to us, I'm out of here. *(Exit MARY BELL.)*
18 **JOE BOB:** *(Calls after her.)* **Mary Bell!** *(Quieter)* **Mary Bell . . .**
19 *(Bows head and covers face with hands as lights dim on Act*
20 *I.)*
21
22 **Act II**
23
24 *(Act II opens with JOE BOB sitting in the fireplace. He is spotlit,*
25 *but the rest of the room is gloomy and dark. His clothes are*
26 *covered with ashes. His hair is uncombed, and there are splotchy*
27 *sores on his hands, face, and neck. He holds a stick in his hand*
28 *which he uses to scratch himself, moaning and gritting his teeth*
29 *as he does it. Knock at door.)*
30 **JOE BOB:** Come in. *(Enter BUBBA carrying a sack of groceries.)*
31 Howdy, Bubba.
32 **BUBBA:** Howdy, Joe Bob. Your doorbell doesn't seem to work,
33 so I just knocked.
34 **JOE BOB:** I know. The electricity is off. I couldn't pay the bill.
35 **BUBBA:** I came because I heard you was stove up. I thought

1   I'd drop in and cheer you up a spell. Say, I heard this
2   new Aggie joke. There was this guy with a brain disease
3   and he was going to get a brain transplant, you see. So
4   they told him he could get a Yale brain for ten thousand
5   dollars, a Harvard brain for twenty thousand, an Oxford
6   brain for fifty thousand, or an Aggie brain for five million
7   dollars. So this guy says, "Five million dollars for an Aggie
8   brain? Why so high?" And they tell him, "Do you know
9   how many Aggies it takes to make up one brain?" Ha, ha,
10   ha, ha. Pretty good, huh? Hey, what are you doing sitting
11   in the fireplace like that?
12 JOE BOB: I got cactus fever. Rubbing ashes on it seems to
13   ease the pain a bit.
14 BUBBA: I brought you a few things for the pantry.
15 JOE BOB: Thanks, just put them anywhere. I'd offer you a
16   seat, but good ol' Uncle Sam took all the chairs.
17 BUBBA: That's OK, I'll just sit on the floor. *(He places sack on*
18   *floor and sits.)* So, how have you been?
19 JOE BOB: You've got to be kidding.
20 BUBBA: Oh, uh, heh, heh. I guess that wasn't such a good
21   question. Uh, how's the family? No — how's business? Er,
22   I mean, how's the weather?
23 JOE BOB: It's OK, Bubba. Don't worry about hurting my
24   feelings. There's nothing about me that doesn't hurt
25   already. I feel like I've been pitched from a bucking
26   nightmare. I just wish I understood why all this is
27   happening.
28 BUBBA: Well, I wouldn't have brought it up, Joe Bob, but
29   since you asked the question, I'm going to let you have
30   it with both barrels. There's got to be sin in your life.
31 JOE BOB: Well, of course. You've hit the nail with your head,
32   there. I'm a sinner for sure, but a forgiven one, thank
33   God. I try to do right, but when I slip I always make
34   amends and confess to God. So I don't see how —
35 BUBBA: Come on, Joe Bob, who are you kidding? Things like

1 this don't happen to good people. You're hiding some
2 deep, dark secret, horrible sin, and that's why God has
3 got you in his frying pan. And he's going to turn up the
4 heat until you confess and come clean. Now, I want to
5 help you out of this, so, come on, what is your sin?

6 JOE BOB: Really, if I knew of some awful, hidden sin, I would
7 lay it face up on the table and hope God would help me
8 deal with it and turn things around. But my conscience
9 is clean.

10 BUBBA: OK, OK. I understand; it's something you just can't
11 bring yourself to talk about. So I guess I'll just have to
12 pull it out of you. You drink too much.

13 JOE BOB: I don't drink at all.

14 BUBBA: You're doing drugs.

15 JOE BOB: Not unless you count Pepto-Bismol.

16 BUBBA: You've killed someone and hidden the body.

17 JOE BOB: Don't be ridiculous.

18 BUBBA: You hate someone then. That's just as bad, you know.

19 JOE BOB: I don't hate anyone. I don't have warm feelings
20 toward Sam Donaldson, but I don't hate anyone.

21 BUBBA: It's a woman then. You've had an affair.

22 JOE BOB: Yes.

23 BUBBA: Aha! I knew it! You goodie-goodie types are the
24 sneakiest kind of skirt chasers. Who is she? When did it
25 happen?

26 JOE BOB: It was my wife Mary Bell. It lasted twenty-five years.

27 BUBBA: Aw, come on, Joe Bob, that doesn't count and you
28 know it. Hasn't there been someone else?

29 JOE BOB: Absolutely not.

30 BUBBA: You've stolen money. You cheat on your taxes. You
31 duplicate rented videos. You bet on football games.

32 JOE BOB: No, no, no and no.

33 BUBBA: I've got it; you tear the "Do not remove under
34 penalty of law" tags off of mattresses.

35 JOE BOB: Never.

1   BUBBA: I see it all now, Joe Bob. Your sin is as plain as the
2   wart on your dentist's nose, and it gets plainer with every
3   word you say.
4   JOE BOB: Really? What is it?
5   BUBBA: You're a liar. You haven't told me a word of truth.
6   JOE BOB: I've been telling you the absolute truth. Your
7   problem is that you're assuming there's always a
8   connection between immorality and misfortune. But
9   things just don't work that way all the time. Lots of fine,
10   upstanding Christians have been poor, sick, beat down
11   and wrung out all their lives. Then there are others who
12   have never seen a stained glass window from the inside
13   and who do all the things you've been accusing me of,
14   yet they live their whole lives in luxury and comfort. The
15   sun shines and the rain falls just the same on the good,
16   the bad, and the ugly. You ought to know that, Bubba.
17   *(Knock at door)*
18   BUBBA: I'll get it. *(Opens door.)* Why, howdy, Tommy Earl.
19   Come on in here. *(Enter TOMMY EARL with sack of*
20   *groceries.)*
21   TOMMY EARL: Howdy, Bubba. Howdy, Joe Bob. How've you
22   been?
23   JOE BOB: If I were a dog my tail wouldn't be wagging.
24   TOMMY EARL: I heard you had a little run of hard luck, so
25   I thought I'd drop in and cheer you up a little. I heard
26   this new Aggie joke I just got to tell you. It seems there
27   were these two Aggies walking past a Catholic church
28   just as a priest with his leg in a cast came hobbling out
29   the front door on crutches. One of the Aggies says, "What
30   happened to you, Father?" And the priest answers, "Oh,
31   I slipped in the bathtub and broke my leg." So after they
32   walk on by, one Aggie says to the other, "What's a
33   bathtub?" And the other Aggie answers, "I don't know;
34   I'm not a Catholic." *(TOMMY EARL and BUBBA laugh*
35   *uproariously.)* I brought you a few things, Joe Bob.

1   JOE BOB: Thanks, I appreciate it. Just set them there by the
2   others. Pick yourself a good spot on the floor and sit a
3   spell. *(TOMMY EARL sets groceries down and sits on floor.)*
4   BUBBA: I'm mighty glad you came by, Tommy Earl. I've been
5   trying to cheer up ol' Joe Bob myself but wasn't making
6   any headway. I was just telling him he needs to root out
7   whatever secret sin he's got that's making God bulldog
8   him like this.
9   TOMMY EARL: Bubba, you're about as subtle as a west
10   Texas cyclone. I hardly think that's the way to go about
11   cheering someone up. Besides, I'm downright sure there's
12   nothing wrong with Joe Bob's moral life. I've known him
13   for years, and he's as upright as a piano.
14   JOE BOB: Thanks, I appreciate that.
15   TOMMY EARL: No, sir, the Joe Bob I know would not touch a
16   sin with a ten-foot cattle prod. But that really doesn't
17   matter, does it? Because we don't earn our way to heaven
18   with deeds or pave our way to hell with sins. God saves
19   us because we believe, not because we're good. So, the
20   problem is not sin in your life, Joe Bob; obviously you've
21   lost your fervor for God somewhere along the line and
22   God is telling you that you need to restore your faith.
23   JOE BOB: Why are you two accusing me of such things? I
24   love God. I believe in him. I have faith.
25   TOMMY EARL: Come on, Joe Bob; you're about as innocent
26   as a diamondback rattler, and I have evidence. I saw you
27   nodding off to sleep during the sermon the Sunday before
28   all this happened. Obviously you've lost your interest in
29   spiritual things.
30   JOE BOB: Or maybe I lost interest in listening to a poorly
31   prepared preacher who droned on for an hour and twenty
32   minutes.
33   TOMMY EARL: If you were truly spiritual, you could have
34   listened till the cows came home.
35   JOE BOB: In fact, I believe I saw you nodding that Sunday, too.

1 TOMMY EARL: Oh, uh, well, that's different. I had been up
2   till after three the night before with a sick calf. But you
3   have shown other signs of drifting besides that. Didn't
4   you miss Wednesday night prayer meeting the week
5   before you got sick?
6 JOE BOB: Mary Bell and I drove over to Cowlick to visit a
7   sick friend.
8 TOMMY EARL: Was that more important than visiting the
9   house of the Lord? And about the same time, you dropped
10   out of the church volleyball team. Where is your
11   dedication, Joe Bob? *(Enter BILLY ED, unnoticed by the*
12   *others.)*
13 JOE BOB: I dropped out of volleyball because the men's
14   evangelism team started up and I joined that instead.
15 TOMMY EARL: Couldn't muster up enough dedication to do
16   both, eh?
17 JOE BOB: I couldn't muster up enough time to do both. They
18   both met at 7:30 on Tuesday nights.
19 TOMMY EARL: It looks to me like you've put your hand to the
20   plow and looked back.
21 BUBBA: Let's face it, Joe Bob; either you've got a serious
22   hidden sin or you've drifted away from the Lord. You
23   need to 'fess up to whichever it is and let God heal you.
24 JOE BOB: I almost wish you guys were right so I could confess
25   and see if it would put me out of my misery. But I honestly
26   don't know what I'm doing wrong. I've prayed to God to
27   show me, but he doesn't. I really can't understand why
28   all this is happening.
29 BILLY ED: I know what's wrong. *(All turn at his unexpected*
30   *voice.)*
31 BUBBA: Well, howdy, Billy Ed. We didn't know you had
32   snuck in.
33 BILLY ED: Y'all were busy talking and the door was unlocked,
34   so I just moseyed on in. I've been listening for quite a
35   spell, and you are all wetter than Waco after a liquor

1   election. You're playing fantasy games. It's silly to expect

2   a reason for Joe Bob's problems; there aren't any reasons.

3   Life is all just a big poker game. Sometimes you get good

4   cards, sometimes you get deuces and jokers. It's all up to

5   how the deck is shuffled. For a while Joe Bob had a long

6   run of good luck and drew all aces and kings. But it played

7   out, and now he's pulling bad cards with every hand.

8   What happens just happens, and that's all there is to it.

9   There's no controlling power, no providential destiny, no

10   all-seeing eye watching you, and certainly no God.

11   Everything is just chance and happenstance.

12   JOE BOB: What brings you out this way, Billy Ed?

13   BILLY ED: I came to cheer you up.

14   JOE BOB: I'm not sure I can take much more of that.

15   BILLY ED: Here's something that will help — a new Aggie

16   joke. Texas A & M and the University of Texas are playing

17   in this big football game. It's late in the fourth quarter,

18   and the timekeeper accidentally fires the final gun. Well,

19   the Longhorns leave the field, but the Aggies stay and

20   keep on playing. And five plays later they score. *(BILLY*

21   *ED, BUBBA, and TOMMY EARL laugh uproariously.)* **Don't**

22   you get it, Joe Bob? You see, it takes the Aggies five plays

23   to score even when there's no opposition. Get it?

24   JOE BOB: I get it, I get it.

25   BILLY ED: All seriousness aside, you could accept your

26   troubles a lot better if you'd quit looking for reasons and

27   just face the facts: there is no big Texas Ranger up there

28   in the sky looking down to give you extra oats when you

29   do good or pen you up when you do bad. Modern science

30   has shown us clearly that there is no God.

31   JOE BOB: Really? I didn't know that. But then my TV is gone

32   and I haven't read a paper lately.

33   BILLY ED: It wasn't lately. Charles Darwin figured out over

34   a century ago that man evolved from something kind of like

35   an amoeba. There was no God around and no God needed.

1   JOE BOB: Did Darwin have any ideas about where that
2   amoeba came from?

3   BILLY ED: Scientists since Darwin have figured that just the
4   right chemicals happened to mix under just the right
5   conditions to form a few simple cells. Then a bolt of
6   lightning shocked the little critters to life and they
7   immediately started reproducing and, well, here we are.

8   JOE BOB: You mean those first few cells came to life out of
9   dead matter? My old high school biology teacher told us
10   that sort of thing couldn't happen. He said it was a firm,
11   scientific law that life could only come from life.

12   BILLY ED: Sure, that's the way life always comes about now,
13   but the very first life obviously had to come from non-
14   living stuff.

15   JOE BOB: In other words, life started as an exception to the
16   scientific laws that have governed it ever since?

17   BILLY ED: Uh, well, I wouldn't put it quite that way —

18   JOE BOB: Has this claim been proved? Has anyone been able
19   to mix up those same first chemicals, jostle them into
20   cells, then shock them into life like they say it happened
21   in the beginning?

22   BILLY ED: Well, no, not yet. But top scientists have been
23   working on it and they're convinced that they will make
24   it happen sooner or later.

25   JOE BOB: If spontaneous life has never been proved, never
26   occurred in nature, and violates a known scientific
27   principle, why are they pushing it as a fact?

28   BILLY ED: Because it's the only choice they have since God
29   is out of the picture.

30   JOE BOB: If taking God out of the picture leaves them with
31   no choice but a nonscientific one, what's wrong with just
32   allowing the possibility that there may indeed be a God
33   who created life?

34   BILLY ED: There is no such possibility. Like I said, science
35   has proved that there is no God. They have explored the

1   universe from horn to hoof and haven't turned up hide
2   nor hair of any kind of deity. Nature created itself and
3   nature runs itself. What we can see with our eyes or
4   register on scientific instruments is simply all there is.
5   JOE BOB: That's sort of like a fish claiming that nothing
6   exists but its own pond. It takes a closed and narrow
7   mind to claim that what it can't see can't exist.
8   BILLY ED: But science has reached the point where it can
9   back that claim with all barrels loaded. The reach of
10   science is enormous and all-encompassing. We have
11   harnessed the atom. We've got footprints on the moon.
12   We have stomped out thousands of killer diseases. We
13   have explored the far reaches of the universe and the
14   subatomic world of particle physics. We've got our boot
15   prints in every corner of nature, yet we have found
16   absolutely no evidence of God.
17   JOE BOB: Of course not! It's silly to expect to find the God
18   who made nature inside the nature he made. You don't
19   expect to find the cook by poking around in his pudding.
20   God is not in nature; he is supernatural — outside and
21   above nature. Science is limited to the study of nature
22   only and has no means of probing into the supernatural,
23   no way to understand it, and no business making
24   proclamations about it.
25   BILLY ED: The only proclamation science has to make about
26   the supernatural is that it is superstitious nonsense on
27   a level with divining rods and rabbit's foot lucky charms.
28   There is no such thing as supernatural. Nature is all there
29   is.
30   JOE BOB: There's the old fish in his pond again. Proclama-
31   tions like that come from minds too arrogant to
32   understand their own ignorance. Billy Ed, can't you see
33   that you're believing in a contradiction? Your claim that
34   life began accidentally calls for basic, time-tested laws
35   of science to be plowed under. But my claim that God

1   created life accepts those same laws at face value. Yet,
2   in the name of science, we're being urged to brand all
3   religion as superstitious nonsense, when really it is the
4   believers who are upholding the validity of nature's laws.
5   Somewhere along the trail, good old common sense has
6   been waylaid, hogtied, and dragged off to the hanging
7   tree.
8   BILLY ED: How can you be so cocksure that the laws of
9   nature are so wagon-rut consistent? They may have
10   evolved over time. In the prehistoric world, it may have
11   been as natural as water running downhill for life to
12   come out of dead matter.
13   JOE BOB: That idea is about as scientific and rational as
14   rubbing on a magic lamp. It's like expecting a ball to
15   bounce higher than the point from which you drop it; or
16   like feeding a chicken one pound of grain and expecting
17   her to lay two pounds of eggs; or like expecting your
18   cattle to multiply without a bull in the herd. It is neither
19   scientific nor rational to believe that nature could give
20   us something for nothing like rabbits pulled out of a hat.
21   This universe has shown itself to be consistent, rational,
22   orderly, and running like a courthouse clock on steady,
23   predictable laws. Such a universe is not going to serve
24   up such irrational results as life coming from death, order
25   coming from chaos, or existence coming from oblivion.
26   Reason demands that it's all got to come from something
27   alive, orderly, and already in existence. There's got to be
28   a God, or nothing makes any sense at all.
29   BILLY ED: You've got a charley horse in your brain, Joe Bob.
30   I thought I could cheer you up with a little common sense,
31   but arguing with you is like trying to blow out a light
32   bulb. At first I felt sorry for you, but after listening to
33   your harebrained ravings, I've about decided you're
34   getting what you deserve.
35   JOE BOB: What does deserving have to do with anything? I

1 thought you said it was all chance and happenstance and
2 the luck of the draw.
3 BILLY ED: I've wasted enough time on you. I'm out of here.
4 *(He stalks out and slams the door behind him.)*
5 TOMMY EARL: I reckon I'm wasting my time, too. If you
6 want to keep on being a hypocrite, I reckon there's
7 nothing I can do about it. *(Exit TOMMY EARL.)*
8 BUBBA: The same goes for me, Joe Bob. I may as well head
9 out and leave you to the consequences of that sin you
10 won't confess. See you around. *(Exit BUBBA.)*
11 JOE BOB: Well, I certainly feel cheered up. Why, God? Why is
12 this happening to me? I don't understand . . . I just don't
13 understand. *(Knock at door)* Come in, it's open. *(Enter ZEKE,*
14 *carrying a blooming potted plant.)* Good ol' Zeke. You're the
15 only one who has stuck by me through all this. I don't
16 know what I would do without you. You paid the water
17 bill out of your own savings; you kept me from going
18 hungry; you — say, look at that plant! It really bounced
19 back, didn't it?
20 ZEKE: Yep, sure did. That's what pruning done for it. Like I
21 said, too much rich plant food puts all the growth in stalk
22 and branches instead of blooms. So I had to take it off
23 the fertilizer and cut away the stalky stuff and let it grow
24 back normal-like.
25 JOE BOB: Maybe that's what happened to me.
26 ZEKE: Could be, I reckon.
27 JOE BOB: But why? If God is good, and if he is great enough
28 to be in control, why does he let awful things like this
29 happen?
30 ZEKE: Well, I reckon God figured he couldn't have it both
31 ways. He couldn't give us humans real freedom and at the
32 same time keep bad things from happening. If we're really
33 free, it means we can choose to do good or bad, and if we
34 choose to do bad, he's got to stand back, grit his teeth, and
35 let it happen. Otherwise, it ain't really freedom.

1   JOE BOB: But I haven't chosen bad or evil.

2   ZEKE: No, I reckon you ain't. You're just the victim of other
3   people's evil.

4   JOE BOB: Why doesn't God do a little something to protect
5   good people from other people's evil so innocent people
6   don't suffer so much?

7   ZEKE: If he did that, our freedom would be like a mirage on a
8   west Texas road. It would be a sham. We'd all be puppets
9   with strings God could pull back on every time we started
10   to tell a lie, steal a pickup, or punch somebody out. We
11   wouldn't really be genuine, bona-fide, hundred-percent,
12   free human beings.

13   JOE BOB: Yeah, I guess I can see that. But still, it's hard to
14   understand why God can let so much bad happen to good
15   people.

16   ZEKE: Well, I wouldn't worry my head too much about that.
17   A God you could understand wouldn't really be much of
18   a God, would he?

19   JOE BOB: No, of course not. But somehow, I just expected
20   life to be more fair. I suppose I thought because I was a
21   Christian, things would go a little smoother for me.

22   ZEKE: You got to remember, Mr. Joe Bob, this here life ain't
23   the real thing. This here world is just the branding yard
24   where God rounds up his herd and puts his brand on
25   them that's his'n. We shouldn't expect the branding yard
26   to be like heaven. But we kinda forget that — keep trying
27   to pile up our own stash of hay in our own little corner,
28   always trying to keep from being crowded or trampled.
29   But the bottom line is, it's still just a branding yard and
30   the branding iron is bound to smart a bit. And we got to
31   keep on remembering that God has got the biggest,
32   greenest grazing pastures you can imagine waiting for
33   you on that big ranch he calls heaven. No drouth, no
34   hailstorms, no crop failures. No barbwire, neither. And
35   up there, you'll forget all about how you was stomped

1   on, jostled around, and crowded out down here in the
2   branding yard.
3   JOE BOB: You're right, of course; I've got to remember that.
4   Do you think my life will stay like this for the rest of my
5   days, Zeke?
6   ZEKE: Can't say. I reckon you've just got to do your part and
7   leave the rest to God.
8   JOB BOB: And what is my part?
9   ZEKE: Trust him. Obey him. Serve him. Love him.
10   JOE BOB: I want to do all that, but you've got to admit, it's
11   pretty hard after all he's let happen to me.
12   ZEKE: I know. But that's the whole idea. It's easy to love God
13   like a hound dog. You feed a hound dog regular and he'll
14   stick to you like a wood tick. He'll wag his tail, hunt with
15   you, and learn to fetch and roll over. But cut off the grub
16   and see how long he hangs around. We've got to love God
17   better than that. We've got to love him not just for what
18   he gives us, but for who he is.
19   JOE BOB: You're right. After all, he's pretty well got a
20   monopoly on the God business, doesn't he? It's his field
21   and his ball. I reckon it's kind of silly for us to expect to
22   have a hand in making up the rules.
23   ZEKE: Or to expect him to run this here universe of his just
24   the way we want it run.
25   JOE BOB: It would be like jumping from a plane without a
26   parachute to reject God now. Things are bad enough with
27   him; they would be miserable and hopeless without him.
28   Now is when I need him most. *(Knock at door)* Come in.
29   *(Enter MARY BELL. JOE BOB rises.)* Mary Bell! Come on in.
30   MARY BELL: I — I came back.
31   JOE BOB: Did you forget something?
32   MARY BELL: No, I came back to stay. At first, when we lost
33   everything so sudden-like, I was mad as a hornet in a
34   fruit jar. I guess I was so hurt I had to be angry with
35   someone, and since you gave me everything I had, you

1   were my target when I lost it all. But after the shock wore
2   off, I realized I loved you not just for what you gave me;
3   I loved you anyway. And bad as things were, they were
4   even worse without you. So, I came back — that is, if
5   you'll have me.
6 **JOE BOB:** *(Opens his arms; she goes to him and they embrace.)* **Of**
7   course I'll have you. Believe me, I know exactly how you
8   felt. Welcome home, Mary Bell. *(They continue embracing.)*
9 **ZEKE:** *(Clears throat.)* **Well, I reckon I'll be moseying.** *(Pause)*
10   **Adios, you two.** *(Pause)* **I said . . . oh, never mind.** *(Exit*
11   *ZEKE.)*
12 **JOE BOB:** *(Disengages from embrace.)* **Mary Bell, I just noticed**
13   something. I'm not itching any more. And look — the rash
14   is drying up! It seems I'm cured somehow!
15 **MARY BELL:** Oh, Joe Bob, that's wonderful! *(They embrace*
16   *again. Knock at door.)*
17 **JOE BOB:** I'll get it. *(Opens door. Enter JAKE AIKMAN in a*
18   *disgruntled mood, followed by FOUR ASSISTANTS.)*
19 **AIKMAN:** Here are your deeds. *(Slaps them into JOE BOB's*
20   *hand.)* **Where do you want your cotton-pickin' furniture?**
21 **JOE BOB:** What furniture?
22 **AIKMAN:** Your furniture, drat it! It seems we — that is, the
23   IRS computer — made a m — a mmmmis — made a
24   mmmm —
25 **ASSISTANT NO. 1:** A mistake.
26 **AIKMAN:** There were no errors in your tax forms after all,
27   I'm sorry to say. So they're forcing me to give you back
28   your ranch, your cars, your boat, plane, tractors, plows,
29   clothes, and even your jewelry, Ma'am. Bring it on in,
30   boys. *(ASSISTANTS begin bringing in furniture, which they*
31   *place in same positions as at beginning of play.)* **I sure do hate**
32   that this happened.
33 **JOE BOB:** Oh, that's all right. Everyone makes mistakes.
34   Don't worry about it.
35 **AIKMAN:** No, I mean I hate it that we're having to bring it

1   back. It hurts me right here. When they found the m — the
2   mmmm — the mmmmmii —
3   MARY BELL: The mistake.
4   AIKMAN: I told them we should keep all your stuff anyway.
5   You wouldn't have known the difference. And I think
6   they would have listened to me except that your
7   accountant had been making waves trying to get to the
8   bottom of your case. At least we should have got to keep
9   part of it to compensate for all our trouble. But the law
10   doesn't allow us to do that. Stupid law. We're working on
11   getting it changed. *(ASSISTANTS keep bringing in furniture*
12   *as play continues. AIKMAN moves to background and watches*
13   *silently, shaking his head sadly. When all furniture is in place,*
14   *AIKMAN and ASSISTANTS exit without a word.)*
15   JOE BOB: This is wonderful, Mary Bell. *(They embrace again.*
16   *Knock at door)* I'll get it. *(Opens door, enter SLIM.)*
17   SLIM: *(Excited)* Boss, I just heard you was getting your land
18   back. That means I got great news for you. We been
19   drilling over in the west pasture and it just blew in big.
20   And the geologist from the Land Commission says them
21   wells is sitting on top of an oil pool that oughta pump
22   till Judgment Day and maybe even longer. Says we can
23   drill fifty or sixty more wells out there. I was kind of sad
24   because I thought it would all belong to the government
25   after they took your land. But now that it's yours again,
26   you're going to be rich like you ain't never been before.
27   JOE BOB: Wow! Did you hear that? We're not broke anymore.
28   MARY BELL: Oh, Joe Bob, that's wonderful! *(They embrace*
29   *again. Knock at door)*
30   JOE BOB: I'll get it. *(Opens door. Enter HANK.)*
31   HANK: *(Hands JOE BOB a check.)* Here's the money for the
32   cattle you lost.
33   JOE BOB: What are you talking about?
34   HANK: Well, I did a little checking and found that your herd
35   was insured against natural disaster. So the insurance

1   company came out and investigated, and today they paid

2   off. Full value. No depreciation, no deductible, no

3   canceled policy.

4   **MARY BELL:** But I forgot to pay the premium.

5   **HANK:** Different policy, Ma'am. I been paying the cattle

6   policy myself.

7   **JOE BOB:** I really owe you one, Hank. This is really great! I

8   can start our herd again.

9   **MARY BELL:** It's wonderful, Joe Bob. *(They embrace again.)*

10   **HANK:** Well, I reckon I'll be gittin'. *(Pause)* I said, I suppose

11   I'll run along. *(Pause)* I'll see y'all later. *(Pause)* Oh, never

12   mind. *(Exit HANK. Knock at door)*

13   **JOE BOB:** I'll get it. *(Opens door. Enter POSTMAN and FED-*

14   *TEX DELIVERY PERSON.)*

15   **POSTMAN:** Special delivery for Joe Bob Worth.

16   **JOE BOB:** *(Takes envelope.)* Thank you. *(Exit POSTMAN. JOE*

17   *BOB opens envelope.)* It's from our stockbroker. *(Reads.)*

18   "Dear Mr. Worth: Your stock portfolio has made a

19   miraculous turnaround. Whereas a mere few weeks ago

20   your stocks had plunged to well below their purchase

21   prices, in the interim they have gained an average of two

22   hundred seventeen points, and are now higher than they

23   have ever been. Congratulations." *(Stops reading.)* What

24   do you know about that!

25   **MARY BELL:** Oh, Joe Bob, that's wonderful! *(They embrace.)*

26   **JOE BOB:** I'm beginning to sense a little dejá vu here.

27   **FED-TEX DELIVERY PERSON:** *(Clears throat.)* Uh, Mr. Worth.

28   *(Pause)* **Mr. Worth, sir.** *(Pause, then louder)* **Mr. Joe Bob Worth.**

29   *(Pause, then taps JOE BOB on shoulder.)* Um, Mr. Worth.

30   **JOE BOB:** Huh? Oh, yes — excuse me. I forgot you were here.

31   *(Takes envelope.)* Thank you. *(Exit FED-TEX DELIVERY*

32   *PERSON. JOE BOB opens envelope.)* It's about our son Jim

33   Bob. It says, "Dear Mr. Worth: We are pleased to inform

34   you that all charges against your son have been dropped.

35   He proved that the drugs in his possession were legiti-

1 mately prescribed by a qualified physician for treatment
2 of his allergies. He has been reinstated into the university
3 and will graduate with high honors this spring. We
4 apologize for the little error. Now, if you can see your
5 way clear to continue your pattern of generous
6 contributions to our school, we would certainly
7 appreciate —"
8 MARY BELL: Oh, Joe Bob, that's wonderful! *(They embrace.)*
9 JOE BOB: It's dejá vu all over again. You know, I think we've
10 got back even more than we had before.
11 MARY BELL: I know, and I'm grateful. But you know what?
12 It really doesn't matter so much to me anymore. I've
13 learned that the most important thing for God to do is
14 not to grant my wishes like a genie in a bottle, but just
15 to be God. From now on I'll serve him simply because he
16 is God, not for what he can do for me.
17 JOE BOB: Amen. *(Knock at door)* I'll get it. *(Opens door. Enter*
18 *TELEGRAM DELIVERY PERSON.)*
19 TELEGRAM DELIVERY PERSON: Telegram for Joe Bob
20 Worth.
21 JOE BOB: Thanks. *(Takes telegram, opens it. Exit TELEGRAM*
22 *DELIVERY PERSON.)* It says that Cindy is bringing her
23 new husband home to meet us.
24 MARY BELL: The Episcopalian? *(Or other demomination.)*
25 JOE BOB: I think that's the one she means.
26 MARY BELL: Oh, no. What can we do? An Episcopalian in
27 our family!
28 JOE BOB: Let's welcome him, Mary Bell. We can't expect to
29 have everything just like we want it. After all, my cousin
30 in El Paso married a Democrat.
31 MARY BELL: *(Shocked)* Really? I didn't know that! Why didn't
32 you ever tell me?
33 JOE BOB: I was afraid you would break off our engagement.
34 MARY BELL: Well, I'm not sure ...
35 JOE BOB: *(Distressed)* **Mary Bell!**

191

1   **MARY BELL:** *(Smiles broadly.)* **That was a joke, Joe Bob — a**
2   **joke. You're stuck with me till death do us part.** *(They*
3   *embrace as the lights fade to blackout.)*
4
5
6
7
8
9
10
11
12
13
14
15
16
17
18
19
20
21
22
23
24
25
26
27
28
29
30
31
32
33
34
35

A COMEDY IN ONE ACT BY T. M. WILLIAMS

FEERCE, PENNER, & SMITH

Have these bankers gone bonkers?

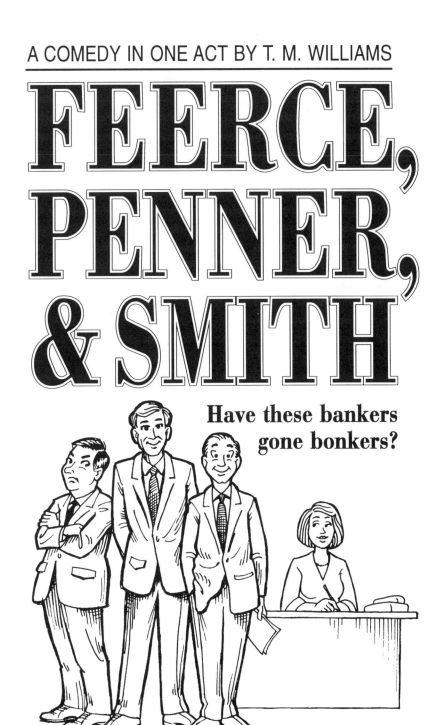

Feerce, Penner, and Smith

FEERCE, PENNER, AND SMITH

A modern-day retelling of the Parable of the Talents.
(Matthew 25:14-30)

Cast

John B. Stonefelter (President and CEO of Fidelity Bank & Trust)

Marsha Handley (Stonefelter's executive secretary)

Bill Feerce (Head of Bank Operations)

Ron (or Rose) Penner (Head of Trust Department)

Wilbur (or Wilma) Smith (Head of Checking & Savings)

Henry J. (or Henrietta) Farrington (Investor)

Ken Martin ⎤
⎬ — (Middle-aged couple)
Nancy Martin ⎦

Mildred Simpson (Elderly depositor)

Donna Murdock (Real estate broker)

Marty Bentley (Merchant marine captain)

Costumes:

All characters except Mildred Simpson and Marty Bentley should wear conservative, contemporary business clothing appropriate to their positions. MILDRED SIMPSON — should be dressed as a street person with frazzled, unkempt hair; dirty, ragged, ill-fitting skirt, shirt, and sweater or coat; worn-out shoes; hose loosely falling around ankles; a large wad of bubble gum in her mouth to represent a plug of tobacco. MARTY BENTLEY — should dress as a salty sea captain with light-colored pants; rubber-soled shoes; horizontally striped sweater; navy blue coat; a captain's hat.

Props:

Papers on desk, airline tickets, umbrella, briefcase, dress hat and topcoat for John B. Stonefelter. A telephone, pencil or pen, several papers on desk to be used as notes and receipts, and a wastebasket for Marsha Handley. A check and a wallet containing a driver's license for Henry J. Farrington. A ballpoint pen for Bill Feerce. A briefcase, a plot plan, and a proposal folder containing papers, including a letter for Donna Murdock. A large, worn, dirty carpetbag with shoulder straps; a worn blanket; ragged gloves; a ball of string; a bitten apple; money — many bills and a few coins; a square of carpet grass; a container of antifreeze; a rubber ducky; a Frisbee; an old newspaper; false teeth; peanuts; various other odds and ends as available, such as nuts and bolts, foil candy wrappers, wire, spoon, paper bag, plastic bottles, a coffee can, etc. for Mildred Simpson. If any of the items needed for her bag are too hard to find, substitute according to imagination and availability. A box of checks packed with a small piece of cardboard for Wilbur Smith. Four legal documents for Marty Bentley. A file folder for Ron Penner.

Sound Effects:

The ringing of a telephone several times throughout the script.

Setting:

Open office area of the Fidelity Bank and Trust Company, partitioned for one office, a secretarial cubicle, and a conference room. (See sketch below.) The office is richly furnished with a desk, chairs, and credenza. The secretarial cubicle is furnished with a small desk and chair, file cabinets, computer, typewriter, wastebasket, etc. as appropriate. On the desk are several papers, pencils, pens, etc. In the conference room is a large table with chairs. Several magazines are placed on top of the table. Appropriate pictures decorate the walls, a potted plant or two punctuate the interior. There are two exits: Stage Right and Stage Left. A coat rack is near the exit at Stage Left.

SUGGESTED SET DESIGN

STONEFELTER'S
OFFICE

CONFERENCE
ROOM

MARSHA'S
OFFICE

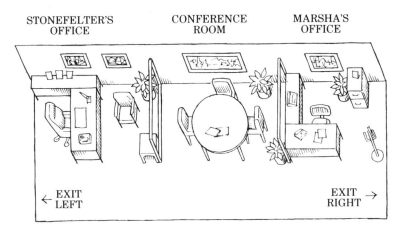

← EXIT
LEFT

EXIT →
RIGHT

The office dividers shown here must be transparent to allow a clear view of the action from all angles. Consider simple, 1" x 2" empty frames, painted in a decorator color to represent glass panels. These frames will be very unstable constructions that will need to be attached to the stage walls and furniture or hung with wire from the ceiling.

197

Scene 1

(The play opens with MARSHA HANDLEY and JOHN B. STONEFELTER On-stage. She is working at her desk. He is in the final stages of cleaning papers from the top of his. After putting the last paper in a drawer, he rises, looks over his office with satisfaction, picks up his briefcase and walks to MARSHA's desk.)

STONEFELTER: Well, Marsha, I believe I've just about got everything in order. My desk is clean for the first time I can remember. Have you got my airline tickets?

MARSHA: Right here, Mr. Stonefelter. Now, you just enjoy your trip and don't worry about a thing here.

STONEFELTER: *(Takes the tickets and puts them in his coat pocket.)* Thank you, Marsha. I'll try not to worry, but I've worked at this bank for thirty-seven years, and this will be the longest I've ever been away. Now that it's time to go, I'm beginning to wonder if our little scheme will work.

MARSHA: Of course it will work. We've got it planned like a NASA rocket launch. I will personally see to it that everything works.

STONEFELTER: You are one in a million, Marsha. I've been looking forward to retirement for several years, and I thought during that time it would become obvious who I should pick to take over my job. But I still have some questions about my three top managers. This little test we've devised ought to show me which of them is most capable. I just hope it works. Our retirement home is almost finished, and there are schools of bass out there in Lake Bluewater just waiting for my hook. I don't want to hang around this office any longer than I have to.

MARSHA: It will work, Mr. Stonefelter, it will work.

STONEFELTER: You did send my three friends their checks, didn't you?

MARSHA: Yes, Mr. Stonefelter.

STONEFELTER: And you have set up their appointments

1   with my managers?
2   MARSHA: Yes, Mr. Stonefelter.
3   STONEFELTER: And you are sure that my managers don't
4   suspect anything?
5   MARSHA: Yes, Mr. Stonefelter.
6   STONEFELTER: *(Alarmed)* They do?!
7   MARSHA: No, Mr. Stonefelter; they don't suspect a thing. You
8   are worrying too much, sir. It will work like laundry soap
9   in a TV commercial — everything will come out fine.
10   STONEFELTER: I surely do hope so.
11   MARSHA: I know so. *(She gets up, takes his hat, topcoat, and*
12   *umbrella from the hat rack, helps him on with his coat, places*
13   *hat on his head, and hangs umbrella over his arm.)* Now, get
14   out of here and leave it all to me. When you come back
15   in sixty days, we will know who should be the next CEO
16   of Fidelity Bank and Trust.
17   STONEFELTER: Very well, I'm convinced. I'm leaving and I
18   won't worry about a thing. Good-bye, Marsha. I'll see you
19   in two months. *(He walks toward door, hesitates, and turns*
20   *back toward MARSHA.)* Maybe I should make it thirty days
21   instead of sixty.
22   MARSHA: *(Exasperated)* Go, Mr. Stonefelter, go! If you don't
23   get out of here, our plan won't work at all. Now, shoo!
24   Scram! Git! Begone! Vamoose! Scat! Skedaddle!
25   STONEFELTER: OK, OK, I'm leaving. *(He exits left.)*
26   MARSHA: *(Returns to her desk and sits.)* Whew! If he'd stayed a
27   minute longer, I think I'd have left and let him carry off
28   his own scheme. *(She begins working with papers on desk.*
29   *Phone rings.)* Hello, Marsha Handley here. Henry J.
30   Farrington? Yes, I'm expecting him. Send him right on
31   in. *(Hangs up phone. After a short pause, enter HENRY J.*
32   *FARRINGTON from left.)*
33   FARRINGTON: Marsha Handley? I'm Henry J. Farrington. You've
34   probably heard of me — Farrington Manufacturing, Farring-
35   ton Investments, Farrington Enterprises, Farrington Oil —

1   MARSHA: No, I don't believe I have. But please come on in,
2   Mr. Farrington.
3   FARRINGTON: Surely you've heard of Farrington Tape and
4   Staple? Farrington Doorstops? Farrington Garbage Bag
5   Ties?
6   MARSHA: Well, uh, no, I'm afraid not, sir.
7   FARRINGTON: I've got to have a talk with our marketing
8   people. Miss Handley, I suppose you know why I'm here.
9   Your boss, John B. Stonefelter, sent me a check for one
10   million dollars — a million, mind you — and wants me to
11   invest it in his own bank. I've known that man for over
12   thirty years, and this is the craziest thing I've even seen
13   him do. It just doesn't make sense. Have you noticed him
14   exhibiting any other signs of irrational behavior? I can
15   recommend a good psychiatrist.
16   MARSHA: I know this seems a little unusual, Mr. Farrington,
17   but I can assure you that Mr. Stonefelter is sane and
18   rational and has very good reasons for what he's doing.
19   I'll call in Bill Feerce now. Remember, as far as Mr. Feerce
20   knows, you are investing your own money.
21   FARRINGTON: Yes, yes, I understand. No, I don't under-
22   stand at all, but I promised I would do this and I will do
23   it to humor the old fellow. He's done me a few favors over
24   the years.
25   MARSHA: Thank you, Mr. Farrington. *(On phone)* Mr. Feerce,
26   Mr. Farrington is here to see you. *(Hangs up phone.)* He
27   will be right with you. Just have a seat over there at the
28   conference table.
29   FARRINGTON: Thank you. *(He sits. Enter BILL FEERCE from*
30   *right.)*
31   FEERCE: Good morning, Mr. Farrington. I'm Bill Feerce,
32   Director of Bank Operations.
33   FARRINGTON: Good to meet you, Feerce. I'm Henry
34   Farrington. You've probably heard of me — Farrington
35   Manufacturing, Farrington Investments, Farrington

1   Enterprises, Farrington Oil —
2   FEERCE: Can't say that I have. But what can we do for you
3   today?
4   FARRINGTON: For starters, you might recommend a good
5   advertising agency. Actually, my real reason for coming
6   is this: I'm a little like an old bloodhound, you might
7   say — always on the prowl, sniffing out sound businesses
8   to put my money in. I've been watching your bank and
9   have noticed a steady rise in your assets and dividends.
10   To make a long story short, I want to purchase stock in
11   the Fidelity Bank and Trust Company.
12   FEERCE: We would be delighted to have you as a share-
13   holder. Just how much do you want to invest?
14   FARRINGTON: One million dollars.
15   FEERCE: One million dollars?
16   FARRINGTON: One million dollars.
17   FEERCE: One *million* dollars?
18   FARRINGTON: One million dollars.
19   FEERCE: One million *dollars?*
20   FARRINGTON: There seems to be an echo in here. Yes, one
21   million dollars. Here's my check. *(Hands check to FEERCE.)*
22   FEERCE: *(Takes check.)* One million dollars! That's a nice
23   investment. *(Looks at check, takes out his pen.)* Is everything
24   on here correct? Address? Phone number?
25   FARRINGTON: Yes, it is.
26   FEERCE: And could I see your driver's license, please?
27   *(FARRINGTON shows license as FEERCE jots down the*
28   *number on check.)* Thank you. I will have your stock
29   certificate drawn up and mailed to you. Meanwhile, Miss
30   Handley will give you a receipt. *(MARSHA begins typing a*
31   *receipt. The two men stand and shake hands.)* We are very
32   pleased to have you as part of our bank, Mr. Farrington.
33   We will do our best to make this a profitable investment
34   for you.
35   FARRINGTON: Thank you, Mr. Feerce. *(He walks toward exit*

1   *left.)*
2   **MARSHA:** Here is your receipt.
3   **FARRINGTON:** Thank you, Miss Handley. Maybe you've
4   heard of Farrington Farm Supply or Farrington Foods?
5   **MARSHA:** No, I guess I haven't.
6   **FARRINGTON:** *(Sighs.)* Well, good day to both of you. *(Exit*
7   *HENRY FARRINGTON.)*
8   **FEERCE:** What a nice surprise. *(Enter WILBUR SMITH.)*
9   **SMITH:** What was a nice surprise?
10   **FEERCE:** Hello, Smith. We just got a new investor. Mr. Henry
11   J. Farrington purchased a million dollars worth of our
12   stock.
13   **SMITH:** That is great! With that kind of increase in our
14   reserves, the FDIC will love us.
15   **MARSHA:** Is that what you want me to do with the money,
16   Bill — put it in bank reserves?
17   **SMITH:** Of course he does. What else can he do with it?
18   **FEERCE:** I was thinking of putting it in the investment pool.
19   **SMITH:** What? You've got a death wish, Feerce. Only Stone-
20   felter himself makes investments that size.
21   **FEERCE:** I know, but he's not here.
22   **SMITH:** What's that got to do with anything? He's coming
23   back, and if he finds you've overstepped your authority
24   and risked a million dollars that could solidify our
25   standing with the FDIC, you'll be in more trouble than
26   a stray cat at a dog show.
27   **FEERCE:** Who did he authorize to make investments, Marsha?
28   **MARSHA:** *(Innocently)* No one. No one at all.
29   **FEERCE:** No one? How strange. Sixty days is too long to go
30   without keeping our money working. A million dollars
31   is too much to let sit in reserves doing nothing. And the
32   FDIC is very happy with us already, Smith.
33   **SMITH:** But it never hurts to make them happier. And anyone
34   who would risk a million of the old man's money like it
35   was change for a vending machine needs to have his attic

1   cleaned. Don't say I didn't warn you, Feerce. *(Exit SMITH.)*

2 FEERCE: *(Pacing back and forth)* **It's true, Stonefelter didn't**

3   **give me explicit authority to invest, but apparently he**

4   **failed to give anyone that authority. I'm sure he has all**

5   **his investing programmed for his absence, but he could**

6   **not foresee a windfall like this dropping into our laps.**

7   **Authority or no authority, I've got to put that money to**

8   **work. Marsha, put Mr. Farrington's million in the**

9   **investment pool.**

10 MARSHA: **I'll do it, Bill.** *(Exit FEERCE. After a short pause,*

11   *MARSHA's phone rings.)* **Marsha Handley. Very well, send**

12   **them in.** *(Enter KEN and NANCY MARTIN.)*

13 KEN MARTIN: **Hello. I'm Ken Martin and this is my wife**

14   **Nancy.**

15 MARSHA: **Hi. I'm Marsha Handley. Glad to meet both of you.**

16   **I presume you have received the check Mr. Stonefelter**

17   **sent you and you know what to do?**

18 NANCY MARTIN: **Yes, we have very clear instructions. We**

19   **are to meet with a Mr. Penner and set up a trust fund**

20   **for our daughter Sally with the money Mr. Stonefelter**

21   **sent us.**

22 MARSHA: **And you are to take great care not to let Mr. Penner**

23   **know that this is a set-up. He is to think this is your own**

24   **money.**

25 KEN: **Right. We wouldn't do this for just anyone, but John**

26   **Stonefelter is an old family friend. And besides, it looks**

27   **like great fun.**

28 MARSHA: **Good. Just have a seat there at the conference**

29   **table and I'll call in Mr. Penner.** *(KEN and NANCY sit.*

30   *MARSHA dials phone.)* **Hello, Ron; Mr. and Mrs. Ken Martin**

31   **are here to see you.** *(She hangs up phone.)* **Mr. Penner will**

32   **be out in just a moment.** *(Enter RON PENNER.)*

33 PENNER: **Hello, Mr. Martin, Mrs. Martin. I'm Ron Penner,**

34   **Senior Trust Officer of the bank. What can I do for you?**

35 KEN: **Good morning, Mr. Penner. We want to set up a trust**

1   **fund for our daughter. Sally is sixteen now, and we want**
2   **to secure her future financially by putting a sum of money**
3   **in trust for her to receive, with interest, when she turns**
4   **twenty-one.**
5   **PENNER: We will be happy to set up a trust for your daughter.**
6   **How much do you want to place for her?**
7   **KEN and NANCY: Five hundred thousand dollars.**
8   **PENNER: Five thousand dollars? Very well, I'll —**
9   **NANCY: No, we said five hundred thousand dollars.**
10   **PENNER: *(Drops pencil and stutters.)* F-five hundred th-thousand**
11   **d-d-dollars?** .
12   **KEN: Five-zero-zero, zero-zero-zero.**
13   **PENNER: A half-million dollars. Do you mean it?**
14   **NANCY: Isn't that enough to start a trust fund?**
15   **PENNER: Well, if that's the best you can do. The poor girl**
16   **will just have to make the best of it.**
17   **KEN: We don't want our baby out on the street.**
18   **PENNER: With the interest she will earn from this trust, she**
19   **can buy the street and pave it with gold. We will be happy**
20   **to administer this trust for you. Let's go into my office.**
21   **I'll get the forms and take the information we need to**
22   **complete the transaction. *(PENNER, MR. and MRS.***
23   *MARTIN exit right. MARSHA's phone rings.)*
24 **MARSHA: Marsha Handley. Good, send her in.** *(Hangs up*
25   *phone. After a pause, enter MILDRED SIMPSON from left.*
26   *MARSHA looks at her, then bursts out laughing.)*
27 **MRS. SIMPSON: All right, all right, get it out of your system.**
28   **This was not my idea, you know.**
29 **MARSHA: Oh, I know, Mrs. Simpson. But you should see**
30   **yourself. I hardly recognized you. Your disguise is**
31   **perfect. No one would ever guess that you are on the**
32   **board of directors of a dozen major corporations. I truly**
33   **don't think I would have known you on the street.**
34 **SIMPSON: I don't know why I let John Stonefelter talk me**
35   **into this. I'm much too old for this sort of thing. John has**

1   got to be absolutely daft to have cooked up such a scheme.
2   Do you know what he did? He sent me a cashier's check
3   for $103,276.42. Asked me to cash it in small bills at another
4   bank, then bring it here and open a checking account
5   with it under an assumed name. If I didn't know that
6   John B. Stonefelter was as honest as a mirror, I would
7   think this was some kind of money laundering set-up.
8 MARSHA: Believe me, Mrs. Simpson, he has a good purpose
9   behind what he is doing.
10 SIMPSON: Oh, I know he does. And I'm not really complaining.
11   He did my late husband some big favors over the years —
12   even saved him from bankruptcy once — so I owe him a
13   favor or two. I just never expected him to ask me to do
14   something so off the wall. What if Mr. Smith recognizes
15   me? He has probably seen me in here from time to time.
16 MARSHA: I know. That's why Mr. Stonefelter wanted you to
17   disguise yourself. Don't worry, you'll do just fine. Have
18   a seat over there at the conference table and I'll call in
19   Mr. Smith. *(MARSHA dials phone as MRS. SIMPSON sits*
20   *and begins thumbing through a magazine.)* Hello, Wilbur.
21   There's a new depositor here who needs to see you. *(Pause)*
22   Well, I'm not sure New Accounts would know how to
23   handle this one. When you see her I think you will know
24   what I mean. *(Pause)* Good. Thank you. *(Hangs up phone.)*
25   Mr. Smith will be right in, Mrs. Simpson.
26 SIMPSON: Thank you. *(WILBUR SMITH enters right. He looks at*
27   *MRS. SIMPSON with obvious disgust and crosses stage to*
28   *MARSHA's desk.)*
29 SMITH: Marsha, what is that filthy bag lady doing in our bank?
30 MARSHA: Looks to me like she's reading a three-month-old
31   issue of *Banking Times*.
32 SMITH: Well, she can't use this bank for a library. Why didn't
33   you have Security throw her out?
34 MARSHA: What for? She hasn't done anything wrong. She
35   said she wanted to open a checking account.

1   SMITH: That's crazy. If she had any money she wouldn't be
2   dressed like that. Yuck! Well, I guess I'll have to talk to
3   her. *(He shudders.)* **After this is over we'll have to fumigate.**
4   *(He approaches MRS. SIMPSON.)* **Uh, Ma'am, uh, what did**
5   **you need here?**
6   SIMPSON: **Well, hello, sonny. Name's Betty.** *(She extends her*
7   *hand which SMITH gingerly shakes, holding it with only two*
8   *fingers, then wipes his hand on the back of his coat.)* **And the**
9   **first thing I need is a can to spit in.**
10   SMITH: **A can to spit in? Oh, really, now, Mrs. — uh — Betty;**
11   **I hardly think this is the appropriate place to —**
12   SIMPSON: **If you don't want this 'backy juice on your nice**
13   **carpet, you better get me a can.**
14   SMITH: **Uh, yes, yes, of course. Marsha, let me borrow your**
15   **wastebasket, please. You can discard it afterward.** *(He*
16   *places wastebasket beside MRS. SIMPSON. She uses it*
17   *occasionally.)* **There, and please don't miss. Now, quickly**
18   **tell me what you want here, then be on your way.**
19   SIMPSON: **I want to make a deposit.**
20   SMITH: **I'm sorry, but we have certain minimum amounts for**
21   **new accounts. I hardly think you could qualify. You'll be**
22   **better off stuffing your money in your stocking, or — or —**
23   **somewhere. Now, if you will just be on your way —**
24   SIMPSON: *(Makes no move to leave.)* **Just how much is this here**
25   **minimum of yours?**
26   SMITH: **One hun — uh — five hundred dollars. Yeah, five**
27   **hundred dollars.**
28   SIMPSON: **Well, I don't know . . . let me see just what I have**
29   **here.** *(She heaves her bag onto the table and begins pulling*
30   *things from it, setting them on the table one by one. SMITH*
31   *reacts with disgust to the grime and squalor.)* **Here's my bed,**
32   *(A blanket)* **my gloves, my string collection, my lunch.**
33   *(Apple)* **Would you like a bite?**
34   SMITH: *(Recoils with disgust.)* **Good heavens, no!**
35   SIMPSON: **Very well. Let's see now . . . oh, here's some money.**

1   *(She pulls out a handful of wadded bills and hands them to*
2   *SMITH.)* **You start counting this, and I'll keep looking.**
3   **Here's my front yard,** *(A square of carpet grass)* **some**
4   **antifreeze ...**
5   **SMITH: Antifreeze?**
6   **SIMPSON: Sure, it gets cold out there. Let's see, now, here's**
7   **my rubber ducky, my Frisbee, my —**
8   **SMITH: Frisbee?**
9   **SIMPSON: Sure. It makes a great plate at the Salvation Army**
10   **kitchen. It's got sideboards, you see. Let's see now ...**
11   **SMITH: Really now, Mrs. Betty, you have only sixty-eight**
12   **dollars here. I don't think we need to keep wasting our**
13   **time —**
14   **SIMPSON: Oh, that's no problem. I have all the time in the**
15   **world. I know there's more in here. Let's see now, here's**
16   **my newspaper, my —**
17   **SMITH:** *(Looking at paper)* **Eisenhower Elected! That paper is**
18   **over forty years old.**
19   **SIMPSON: I know, I'm a slow reader. Here's my teeth, ah,**
20   **here's some more money.** *(She pulls out a huge fistful of bills*
21   *and hands them to SMITH.)* **Count this; I'll keep looking.**
22   **Hm, here are some peanuts.** *(Pops a few into her mouth.)*
23   **Pretty good with my 'backy. Want some?**
24   **SMITH: Certainly not. There is over five hundred dollars**
25   **here. I guess we have to open an account.** *(He sighs.)*
26   **SIMPSON: Is that all? I'll keep looking. Here, I'll make things**
27   **simple.** *(She turns bag upside-down and dumps the remaining*
28   *contents, including several wads of bills, on the table.)* **Help me**
29   **count this, sonny.** *(Both begin counting.)*
30   **SMITH:** *(As they finish the count)* **There is $103,276.42 here, Mrs.**
31   **Betty. Where on earth did you get that kind of money?**
32   **SIMPSON:** *(Picks up a bill and looks at it.)* **What kind of money**
33   **is it? Looks like good old American dollars to me.**
34   **SMITH: I mean, how did you ever manage to get so much**
35   **money?**

1   SIMPSON: Well, I don't know. My husband left me a little. I've
2   done a few odd jobs now and then. I find it on the streets.
3   People just give me a quarter or a dollar now and then.
4   SMITH: This is amazing. You've been accumulating this for
5   years and carrying it around in that bag? I'm sure glad
6   you decided to come to us, Mrs. Batty, I mean, Betty.
7   Would you like a cup of coffee?
8   SIMPSON: You got anything stronger?
9   SMITH: Uh, no, but I'll be happy to send out for —
10   SIMPSON: Naw, never mind. Just write up them papers, or
11   whatever it is you do, and as you suggested earlier, I'll
12   be on my way.
13   SMITH: Oh, I didn't mean you needed to be in any kind of
14   hurry. No, Ma'am. You come here as often as you wish,
15   and stay as long as you like. We're always happy to have
16   you. Just make yourself comfortable while I get the
17   papers, and we'll get this little transaction over with — I
18   mean — finished. *(SMITH gets several papers and a box of*
19   *checks from MARSHA, then he and MRS. SIMPSON sit at the*
20   *table as he begins to fill out forms. RON PENNER with KEN*
21   *and NANCY MARTIN enter right.)*
22   PENNER: Well, that about does it. May I say on behalf of the
23   bank, we really appreciate the trust you have put in us.
24   KEN: And since we trust you with that trust, we trust that
25   trust will grow, Mr. Penner. Of course, I'm interested in
26   the principle, but I'm principally interested in the
27   interest our Sally will receive.
28   NANCY: There's too much interest in Sally already.
29   PENNER: What you've done today is not likely to diminish
30   that. Well, thanks to both of you. It's been a pleasure.
31   Good-bye, now.
32   KEN and NANCY: Good-bye. *(They shake hands with PENNER*
33   *and exit left. PENNER exits right.)*
34   SMITH: That does it, Mrs. Betty. Here's your receipt and a
35   box of temporary checks. Your permanent checks will be

1 ready in about a week. **Now, if you will allow me, I'll be**
2 **glad to repack your bag.** *(He begins carefully to pick up the*
3 *strewn contents of the bag and replace them in it.)* **Say, you**
4 **might like to put some of your valuables in a safety**
5 **deposit box — your string collection, for example.**
6 SIMPSON: **Not on your debentured dividend. I'll leave my**
7 **money with you, but I'm not about to trust you or anyone**
8 **else with anything of real value.**
9 SMITH: **Very well, I just wanted to offer. Is there anything**
10 **else we can do for you?**
11 SIMPSON: **Well, maybe so. Could I have that little piece of**
12 **cardboard that came with my checks?**
13 SMITH: **Well, sure. Why do you want it?** *(Hands her the card-*
14 *board.)*
15 SIMPSON: **My shoe has a hole in it and the pavement is kind**
16 **of rough on my feet.** *(She removes her shoe and slips the*
17 *cardboard into it.)*
18 SMITH: **Mrs. Betty, with all your money, why don't you just**
19 **go to the store and buy yourself a new pair?**
20 SIMPSON: **Why? There's still plenty of good wear in these.**
21 **Waste not, want not, I always say.** *(She stands, puts her bag*
22 *strap over her shoulder.)* **I'll be on my way, now. You take**
23 **good care of my money, sonny.**
24 SMITH: **I'll certainly do that. Here, let me help you to the**
25 **door.** *(He gently escorts her to exit left.)* **Good-bye, Mrs. Betty.**
26 **It certainly has been a pleasure.**
27 SIMPSON: **Good-bye, sonny.** *(Exit MRS. SIMPSON.)*
28 SMITH: **Can you believe that bag lady made a deposit of over**
29 **one hundred thousand dollars?**
30 MARSHA: *(Innocently)* **You don't say.** *(Enter RON PENNER.)*
31 PENNER: **Marsha, here are the forms to file for the new**
32 **Martin family trust.**
33 SMITH: **A new trust, eh? How much?**
34 PENNER: **A half million dollars.**
35 SMITH: **Man, this has been some day! Feerce got a million**

1   dollar investment, you got a half million dollar trust, and

2   I got a new hundred thousand dollar depositor. What are

3   you going to do with the Martins' money?

4   PENNER: That's a good question. It seems the boss left without

5   designating anyone to handle investments. It's a little

6   hard to know just what to do.

7   SMITH: Not for me. I'm holding mine until he comes back.

8   PENNER: I would do the same if he were coming back

9   tomorrow. But it's not good banking to leave this kind

10   of money dormant for two months.

11   SMITH: It's not good banking to risk someone else's money

12   without specific authorization. If you lose that money in

13   a bad investment, you'll be on the street selling pencils

14   faster than congress raises the debt ceiling. If you want

15   my advice, put it in the vault. That's where mine is going.

16   *(Exit SMITH right.)*

17   MARSHA: What do you want me to do with the half million,

18   Ron?

19   PENNER: *(Thinks for a moment.)* Put it in the investment pool.

20   MARSHA: Are you sure?

21   PENNER: I'm sure. *(He exits right.)*

22   MARSHA: *(Excited that the three appointments went according to*

23   *plan, gives an enthusiastic thumbs up sign.)* Yes! *(Phone rings.)*

24   Who? OK, send her in. *(Enter DONNA MURDOCK left.)*

25   MURDOCK: Hello, I'm Donna Murdock with Metropolitan

26   Real Estate. The receptionist told me just to come on in.

27   MARSHA: Of course, Ms. Murdock. What can we do for you?

28   MURDOCK: I wanted to see Mr. Stonefelter, but I understand

29   he's out for two months. I have a business venture to

30   propose. Is there anyone else I could talk with?

31   MARSHA: Possibly Bill Feerce. He's head of banking

32   operations.

33   MURDOCK: That will be fine, thank you.

34   MARSHA: *(Dials phone.)* Hello, Bill; there's a Donna Murdock

35   with Metropolitan Real Estate here. Could you see her?

1   **Thanks.** *(Hangs up phone.)* **He'll be right out. Just have a**
2   **seat there at the conference table.**
3   **MURDOCK:** **Thank you.** *(She sits and begins reading a magazine.*
4   *Enter BILL FEERCE from right.)*
5   **FEERCE:** **Hello, Ms. Murdock, I'm Bill Feerce.**
6   **MURDOCK:** **Good morning, Mr. Feerce.** *(They shake hands, he*
7   *sits.)*
8   **FEERCE:** **Just call me Bill, please. What can I do for you?**
9   **MURDOCK:** **A few weeks ago, I made a tentative proposal to**
10   **Mr. Stonefelter. He seemed interested enough to talk**
11   **further when the details were firmed up. But now he's**
12   **away, and by the time he comes back it will be too late.**
13   **FEERCE:** **Why don't you explain the deal to me, Ms. Murdock?**
14   **MURDOCK:** **I was hoping you'd say that. And you can just**
15   **call me Donna.** *(She reaches into her briefcase, pulls out a plot*
16   *plan and proposal folder which she spreads on the table before*
17   *them.)* **Are you familiar with this plot of land?**
18   **FEERCE:** **Sure. It's the vacant field at the intersection of**
19   **highways 360 and 143.**
20   **MURDOCK:** **Right. And have you heard of the SCC Construc-**
21   **tion Company?**
22   **FEERCE:** **Oh, yes. They've built half the shopping malls in**
23   **the tri-state area.**
24   **MURDOCK:** **Right again. You're really a bright boy. Now,**
25   **here's the deal.** *(She points to various pages in the proposal as*
26   *she talks.)* **SCC wants to build a shopping mall on this**
27   **property and they're willing to pay a very good price for**
28   **it. They've got agreements from one hundred seventeen**
29   **stores, including three large chain department stores as**
30   **anchors. But here's the problem: One of these anchor**
31   **stores has not really signed on the dotted line yet, due**
32   **to a late decision and the normal red tape in the approval**
33   **process. And until this store actually signs on, SCC will**
34   **not sign a contract for the land purchase. Do you have any**
35   **questions so far?**

1   FEERCE: Yes. How do you know your slow-paced anchor
2   store is really on board? Isn't there a chance they'll back
3   out and the deal will fall through?
4   MURDOCK: Not at all. I have here their letter of intent and a
5   hundred thousand dollar good faith deposit.
6   FEERCE: Looks like they mean business.
7   MURDOCK: Now, here's our dilemma, Bill. Keystone
8   Components wants this same piece of land for a new
9   plant, and they're ready to buy today. I've asked the land
10   owner to hold off because I can give him a better deal.
11   But he is eager to sell and will only give me another week.
12   My problem is that it will take a month to cut through
13   all the red tape with the foot-dragging anchor store. So,
14   to keep the land available for SCC, I'm trying to put
15   together a group of investors to buy the land, hold it until
16   SCC is ready, then sell it at a handsome profit. The
17   investors could make a bundle.
18   FEERCE: How much?
19   MURDOCK: Double. The landowner is ready to sell to
20   Keystone right now for a million and a half. He'll hold it
21   a week for us if we offer two million. And I have
22   confirmation here that SCC is willing to pay four million
23   for it.
24   FEERCE: And if we become one of your investors, how much
25   do you expect us to chip in?
26   MURDOCK: I already have a million lined up from Thrifty
27   Savings and Loan and the Jameson Trust Fund. So I still
28   need another million. If you could go in for at least half
29   of that, I could quickly try to find another investor who
30   would —
31   FEERCE: My bank will put up the whole million.
32   MURDOCK: The whole million? Why, that's wonderful, Mr.
33   Feerce, I mean, Bill!
34   FEERCE: Just leave this information with me, and let my
35   staff confirm the details. You will get your check in a

1   couple of days — well ahead of your one-week deadline.

2   MURDOCK: This is just wonderful. I didn't expect you to put

3   up the entire remaining million. And time was getting

4   short to find another investor. I could just kiss you!

5   FEERCE: I can think of worse ways to seal a contract, but

6   please, not here. However, what are you doing Saturday?

7   We could go look over this land, have dinner, then take

8   in a movie.

9   MURDOCK: Oh, I'd love to.

10   FEERCE: Great. I'll pick you up at five. *(They rise and walk*

11   *toward exit left. FEERCE hands MARSHA the plot plan and*

12   *proposal.)* Marsha, please take these documents and have

13   Jenson confirm all the information in them. We're about

14   to invest a million dollars in a piece of property.

15   MARSHA: My, you sure work fast, Bill.

16   MURDOCK: He sure does!

17   FEERCE: Good-bye for now, Donna. I'll see you on Saturday.

18   *(They shake hands.)*

19   MURDOCK: Good-bye, Bill. I'll look forward to it. *(Exit DONNA*

20   *MURDOCK, left.)*

21   FEERCE: Well, if this works, I've just made the best deal of

22   my life. If not, I guess I'll soon be living in a cardboard

23   box under a bridge. *(Exit BILL FEERCE, right. Phone rings.)*

24   MARSHA: Marsha Handley speaking. Very well, send him in.

25   *(Enter MARTY BENTLEY, left.)*

26   MARTY BENTLEY: Ahoy, there! I'm Capn' Marty Bentley of

27   the good ship *Rosamunda*, the best freighter on the blue

28   Pacific. Is my ol' matey Ron Penner aboard?

29   MARSHA: Uh, yes, I believe he's in his quarters — I mean,

30   office.

31   BENTLEY: Well, blow his whistle and see if he can come

32   topside.

33   MARSHA: *(On phone)* Uh, Ron, there's a Mr. — I mean,

34   Captain Marty Bentley here to see you. You will? Very

35   well. *(Hangs up phone.)* He'll be right out, Captain; just

1   have a seat over there at the conference table.

2   **BENTLEY:**   Thankee, Ma'am. *(He sits and begins to read a*

3   *magazine. Enter RON PENNER, right.)*

4   **PENNER:**   Hello, Marty; good to see you.

5   **BENTLEY:**   And good to see you, you old landlubber. *(They*

6   *shake hands. PENNER sits at table with BENTLEY.)*

7   **PENNER:**   How're things in the freighter business?

8   **BENTLEY:**   It's tough as a temperamental typhoon for an

9   independent on the high seas these days. The big lines

10   are keepin' cargo prices flatter'n a flock of feeble

11   flounders. They tried to buy out me and the *Rosamunda*,

12   but as you know, I don't like to swim with the school. So

13   I set my sail to the course of the changin' tradewinds.

14   **PENNER:**   Ah, what a life! And just what brings you ashore?

15   **BENTLEY:**   I've had my ship sittin' at the dock for nearly a

16   week now, loaded with shipments to Singapore and

17   Taiwan. But there's still space in my hold for more, and

18   I'm not much hankerin' to shove off without gettin' it

19   filled. So I've gone out and done a little hustlin'. Finally

20   got two deals lined up, but instead of bein' just the carrier,

21   I got to be the merchant. I've got to buy the cargo and

22   resell it on delivery.

23   **PENNER:**   What are these two deals?

24   **BENTLEY:**   The first is two hundred computers with color

25   monitors and printers. And I've got a buyer in Singapore

26   eager to get his hands on them the moment they hit the

27   dock. It will take five hundred thousand dollars to buy

28   and deliver them, and they will sell for double that.

29   **PENNER:**   And the second deal?

30   **BENTLEY:**   Software. Two hundred thousand dollars worth

31   — retail. I can buy and deliver it for only a hundred thou.

32   Again, you can double your investment as easy as gettin'

33   seasick in a tugboat. Now, let me explain more about —

34   **PENNER:**   Never mind, Marty; I've heard enough. I'm willing

35   to sink five hundred thousand into your computers.

1 BENTLEY: I sure wish you wouldn't use that word.

2 PENNER: What word?

3 BENTLEY: Sink. It sort of gives me the willies. But I sure

4 like the sound of the rest of what you said.

5 PENNER: And I may know where you can get the other

6 hundred thousand for the software.

7 BENTLEY: Well, bless my barnacles! Just like that? And I

8 don't even get to make the sales pitch I worked on like

9 a fiddler crab at a clambake. Man, this is easier than

10 slidin' off a soapy deck in a nor'wester.

11 PENNER: Don't get your hopes up too much; I said I *may*

12 know where you can get it. Marsha, see if Smith can come

13 in here, please.

14 MARSHA: Sure, Ron. *(She dials.)* Hello, Wilbur, could you

15 come to the conference room for a moment? Ron needs

16 to see you. *(Hangs up phone.)* He'll be right in. *(Enter*

17 *WILBUR SMITH, right.)*

18 PENNER: Wilbur Smith, meet Captain Marty Bentley. *(They*

19 *shake hands.)*

20 BENTLEY: Mornin', Mr. Smith.

21 SMITH: Hello, uh, Captain Bentley.

22 PENNER: Marty is a merchant marine. He's got his own ship —

23 BENTLEY: The *Rosamunda*.

24 PENNER: And he makes several runs to the Orient each

25 year. I just agreed to finance a cargo of computers to

26 Singapore for five hundred thousand. Why don't you tell

27 Wilbur about the rest, Marty?

28 BENTLEY: Sure, mate. I got a load of software to go with the

29 computers, but I got to buy it here and sell it on the other

30 end. I need a hundred thousand to float the deal.

31 PENNER: Ha, ha, that's a good one, Marty. *Float* the deal?

32 BENTLEY: This deal is a good one, too. Let me explain more —

33 SMITH: There's no need to continue, Captain Bentley. I'm

34 sorry, but this sort of thing is much too risky. The

35 software might not find a ready market and you'd be

1   stuck with it.
2   BENTLEY: Got that covered, Mr. Smith. Got a confirmed
3   buyer in Singapore already on the dotted line. His signed
4   agreement came in by fax last night. Got it right here.
5   SMITH: And the software might have viruses in it.
6   BENTLEY: Oh, no; it's clean as a swabbed deck. Been tested
7   and   debugged.   And   it's   all   guaranteed — got   the
8   certification and warranties right here.
9   SMITH: And ships have a way of sinking, you know.
10   BENTLEY: *(Offended)* Not my ship! The *Rosamunda* is as
11   tight as a preacher's necktie. Besides, she's heavily
12   insured, along with all the cargo. Here's the policy.
13   SMITH: You're wasting your time, Bentley; I just can't do it.
14   BENTLEY: You're missin' out on a sure thing, Smith. You
15   could double your money in thirty days.
16   SMITH: Deals like this have a way of sounding a lot better
17   before the fact than after. I'm afraid our bank is just not
18   interested. Good day, Captain Bentley. *(SMITH rises,*
19   *shakes hands with BENTLEY, then exits right.)*
20   PENNER: Sorry about that, Marty. I thought after hearing
21   you out he might buy into it. Anyway, I'm still on board —
22   get it? *On board* — for five hundred thousand. I'll have
23   our staff inspect the papers and look over the mer-
24   chandise this afternoon. Should have your check
25   tomorrow.
26   BENTLEY: I appreciate it, Ron, and you won't be sorry. This
27   deal is solid as a lighthouse. Bon voyage, matey. *(They*
28   *shake hands and BENTLEY exits left. SMITH enters right.)*
29   SMITH: I can't believe you guys. When Stonefelter finds out
30   that you and Feerce have risked a million-and-a-half of
31   his bank's money — unauthorized, mind you, unauth-
32   orized — he'll have you out of here faster than interest
33   rates rise under Democrats. And don't say I didn't warn
34   you. *(SMITH leaves a paper on MARSHA's desk, then exits*
35   *right.)*

1 **PENNER: I guess he could be right, but it just doesn't make**
2 **sense to leave all that money dormant for two months. I**
3 **hope we haven't made a big mistake.** *(Lights dim on Scene 1)*
4
5 **Scene 2**
6
7 *(It is sixty days later. Lights come up on MARSHA at her desk,*
8 *working. Enter JOHN B. STONEFELTER.)*
9 **STONEFELTER: Helloooo, Marsha!**
10 **MARSHA:** *(Jumps and drops pencil and papers.)* **Oh! Mr. Stone-**
11 **felter, you frightened me.**
12 **STONEFELTER: Do I look that bad?** *(Hangs up coat, hat, and*
13 *umbrella.)*
14 **MARSHA: Of course not. In fact, you look great — all rested,**
15 **relaxed, and tanned. You don't look like a man who's**
16 **about to retire.**
17 **STONEFELTER: But I am about to retire, and the sooner the**
18 **better. During these last sixty days, I've relearned to**
19 **relax and enjoy life. I'm ready to spend the rest of my**
20 **days watching sunsets, smelling roses, and spoiling**
21 **grandchildren — not to mention catching up on thirty-**
22 **eight years of fishing.** *(He pantomimes casting and reeling.)*
23 **But enough about me. How did things go here while I**
24 **was gone? Did our sinister little plot work?**
25 **MARSHA: You'll have to judge that for yourself.**
26 **STONEFELTER: Come on, come on; did the money come in**
27 **as planned? What did they do with it? Is it all in the vault?**
28 **Did they invest it? Is it all lost? Tell me. Don't keep me**
29 **in suspenders.**
30 **MARSHA: I'm not saying a word. You just go into your office**
31 **and make yourself comfortable. I'll send the men in to**
32 **see you. You can judge for yourself whether the plan**
33 **worked.**
34 **STONEFELTER: Oh, all right, but hurry it up.** *(He pantomimes*
35 *a fishing cast.)* **I want out of here as soon as possible.**

1   *(STONEFELTER enters office and sits at desk.)*

2   **MARSHA:** *(On phone)* **Hello, Bill. Mr. Stonefelter is back and**

3   **wants to see you in his office right away.** *(Hangs up. Enter*

4   *BILL FEERCE from right.)*

5   **STONEFELTER:** **Come in, Bill. Have a seat.**

6   **FEERCE:** **Thank you, sir. It's good to have you back.**

7   **STONEFELTER:** **So, how did things go while I was gone?**

8   **FEERCE:** **Very well, I think. One rather interesting thing**

9   **happened the very day you left. We got a new investor**

10   **in the bank, a Mr. Henry J. Farrington.**

11   **STONEFELTER:** **You don't say. How much did he invest?**

12   **FEERCE:** **One million dollars.**

13   **STONEFELTER:** **A million? Really, now! And what did you**

14   **do with the money?**

15   **FEERCE:** *(Nervously clears throat.)* **Well, I — uh — you know**

16   **that plot of land at Highway 360 and 143?**

17   **STONEFELTER:** **Sure. A worthless chunk of dirt if I ever saw**

18   **one.**

19   **FEERCE:** **Well, maybe not, sir. You see, right after you left,**

20   **Donna Murdock with Metropolitan Real Estate —**

21   **STONEFELTER:** **That airhead? She's been trying to sell me**

22   **on her pie-in-the-sky schemes for months.**

23   **FEERCE:** **Uh, she's not really an airhead, sir. She had put**

24   **together a deal to buy and hold that plot on 360 and**

25   **offered us a chance to be a major partner in a short-term**

26   **venture.**

27   **STONEFELTER:** **Heh, heh. Wanted us to put up good money**

28   **for that scrubby gravel wasteland, eh? Well, I guess you**

29   **told her.**

30   **FEERCE:** **I did, sir. I told her we would put up a million dollars.**

31   **STONEFELTER:** *(Exploding)* **What?! You mean you blew that**

32   **million on a rocky patch of dirt with nothing on it but**

33   **grassburrs and crabgrass? Where was your head, Feerce;**

34   **where was your head? How could you have been so — so**

35   **so—**

1   FEERCE: The land sold three weeks later and I doubled our
2   money, sir.
3   STONEFELTER: — so brilliant! Well done, my boy; well done!
4   I knew that land had potential. You turned a million into
5   two million in less than sixty days. Absolutely brilliant.
6   Anything else you want to tell me?
7   FEERCE: Well, yes, there is. Donna Murdock and I were
8   married last week. She is now Mrs. Bill Feerce.
9   STONEFELTER: Congratulations, my boy! Another great
10   investment. By the way, I didn't mean it about her being
11   an airhead.
12   FEERCE: I know, sir.
13   STONEFELTER: Well, now that you have another mouth to
14   feed, and will undoubtedly have even more in the future,
15   heh, heh, it's time we thought about your career. Time
16   to move you up a notch or two on the corporate ladder.
17   FEERCE: That's great, Mr. Stonefelter. What do you have in
18   mind?
19   STONEFELTER: How would you like to run this place?
20   FEERCE: You mean, be the executive vice president?
21   STONEFELTER: Higher.
22   FEERCE: *(Raises his voice about an octave.)* You mean, be the
23   executive vice president?
24   STONEFELTER: I mean, I'm putting you in a higher position
25   than that.
26   FEERCE: The only thing higher than executive VP is the
27   president, and you can't mean that.
28   STONEFELTER: No, I don't mean president. I mean my job
29   — chairman of the board.
30   FEERCE: Me — chairman of the board? But what about you,
31   sir? What are you going to do?
32   STONEFELTER: Fish, golf, travel, play with grandkids. I'm
33   retiring, and the sooner the better. I want you in this
34   office two weeks from now, Bill. Meanwhile, don't say
35   anything to anyone about this.

1   **FEERCE:** *(Flustered)* **Oh, no, sir — I mean, yes, sir, I won't. But**
2   **are you sure? I mean —**
3   **STONEFELTER: I'm sure. You have proved to me that you**
4   **have what it takes to run this bank — courage, integrity,**
5   **loyalty, and initiative. Now, if you'll excuse me, I have**
6   **other business to attend to.** *(STONEFELTER rises and*
7   *walks FEERCE to the exit with a fatherly arm around his*
8   *shoulders.)*
9   **FEERCE: But — but — I —**
10   **STONEFELTER: We'll talk more of it later, Bill. Good**
11   **morning, and congratulations, my boy.** *(They shake hands*
12   *and FEERCE exits right.)* **Marsha, send in Ron Penner.** *(He*
13   *pantomimes casting again as she calls.)*
14   **MARSHA:** *(On phone)* **Hello, Ron; Mr. Stonefelter wants to see**
15   **you in his office right away.** *(Hangs up phone. Enter RON*
16   *PENNER, right, carrying a file folder.)*
17   **STONEFELTER: Come in, Ron. Have a seat.**
18   **PENNER: Thank you, sir. Good to have you back.**
19   **STONEFELTER: Good to be back. How have things gone in**
20   **the Trust Department?**
21   **PENNER: Quite well, I think. I have a complete report here,**
22   **which I'll be glad to go over with you.**
23   **STONEFELTER:** *(Takes folder, lays it aside.)* **Thanks, Ron. I'll**
24   **review this later. Just brief me on the high points — any**
25   **unusual events or problems?**
26   **PENNER: There was one pretty good little windfall —**
27   **happened the day you left. A Mr. and Mrs. Ken Martin**
28   **set up a half-million dollar trust for their teenage**
29   **daughter.**
30   **STONEFELTER: You don't say? And what did you do with**
31   **the money?**
32   **PENNER: Uh, well, uh, do you know a Captain Marty Bentley?**
33   **STONEFELTER: Bentley? Not that sail-by-night merchant**
34   **marine with his leaky tub of a boat?**
35   **PENNER: Uh, yes, that's the one. He came in needing**

1   financing for a shipment of computers to Singapore.

2   Wanted five hundred thousand.

3 STONEFELTER: What gall that sailor has! I've loaned him a

4   little here and there, but never thought he'd have the

5   nerve to ask a sane banker to sink a half-million into

6   his —

7 PENNER: He doesn't like that word, sir.

8 STONEFELTER: What word?

9 PENNER: Sink. It gives him the willies.

10 STONEFELTER: But in this case, it's perfectly appropriate.

11   Can you imagine anyone putting a half-million into that

12   tub of his? Ha, ha, ha. What kind of fools does he think

13   we are?

14 PENNER: The kind I am, I suppose. I backed him for the five

15   hundred thousand.

16 STONEFELTER: *(Stunned)* I can't believe this. I can just see

17   those computers scattered across the ocean floor, fish

18   and eels swimming in and out of broken screens and

19   crushed boxes. A half-million dollars vanished forever in

20   the Bermuda Triangle. Do you realize what you've done.

21   Penner?

22 PENNER: Yes, I've doubled our investment. Bentley sold the

23   computers according to contract, and we now have a

24   million dollars for a half-million investment.

25 STONEFELTER: Brilliant, Ron, brilliant! What insight,

26   what shrewd investing, what audacity and foresight.

27   You've done a fine job, my man, and I'm going to see that

28   you are well rewarded. How would you like to be

29   president?

30 PENNER: No thanks. I'm not interested in politics — just

31   banking.

32 STONEFELTER: I mean president of this bank. I'm about to

33   retire and I'm splitting my job into two. Bill Feerce will

34   become chairman of the board, and I want you to be the

35   new president.

1   PENNER: Will I get a key to the executive washroom?

2   STONEFELTER: Yes, and a lot more — corner office, company

3   car, country club membership, stock shares, and a six-

4   figure salary.

5   PENNER: I can handle that.

6   STONEFELTER: We'll talk details tomorrow. Meanwhile,

7   please keep all this to yourself.

8   PENNER: *(Rises to leave.)* I'll do that, sir. And thank you very

9   much for the promotion. I do appreciate it.

10   STONEFELTER: You're welcome, Ron. Good day, now. *(Exit*

11   *PENNER, right.)* Marsha, call in Wilbur Smith, please. *(He*

12   *pantomimes casting again.)*

13   MARSHA: *(On phone)* Hello, Wilbur, Mr. Stonefelter wants to

14   see you in his office right away, please. *(Enter WILBUR*

15   *SMITH, right.)*

16   STONEFELTER: Come in, Smith. Have a seat.

17   SMITH: Thank you, sir. Welcome back.

18   STONEFELTER: Good to be back. How did things go in your

19   department while I was gone?

20   SMITH: Very well, sir; very well indeed. Everything is pretty

21   much just as you left it.

22   STONEFELTER: Any unusual problems? Any hard-to-

23   handle circumstances or extraordinary transactions?

24   SMITH: Now that you mention it, there was one. A bag lady

25   from off the street came in. You should have seen her —

26   dirty, tattered clothes, hair like a rat's nest, stockings

27   falling to her ankles, an old, threadbare bag. But would

28   you believe she had over a hundred thousand dollars to

29   deposit?

30   STONEFELTER: Really, now. Where did she get that kind of

31   money?

32   SMITH: I have no idea, but I opened an account for her.

33   STONEFELTER: And what did you do with the hundred

34   thousand?

35   SMITH: I put it in the vault, and it's there now, all safe and

1   sound, ready for you to invest.

2   STONEFELTER: You mean it's been there in the vault for

3   two months? Didn't you think it should have been

4   invested?

5   SMITH: Yes, I thought so, sir, but I was not authorized to

6   make investments.

7   STONEFELTER: So you let a hundred thousand dollars

8   just sit in the vault for two months.

9   SMITH: You know me, sir; I play by the rules. No overstepping

10   my bounds or fiddling in areas that don't concern me,

11   unlike certain other officers I could name who have been

12   pretty free with your money. Pretty free. No sir, I stick

13   to my own job and expect everyone else to do the same.

14   And as a result, your money is all here, safe and sound,

15   and waiting for you to do with it as you will.

16   STONEFELTER: Didn't any investment opportunities come

17   your way?

18   SMITH: Well, there was one, but it was too ludicrous to

19   consider.

20   STONEFELTER: Really? What was it?

21   SMITH: A sail-by-night merchant marine with a leaky tub of

22   a boat wanted a hundred thousand to finance a shipment

23   of computer programs. A salty fellow by the name of

24   Bentley. Can you imagine him wanting us to sink that

25   kind of money into —

26   STONEFELTER: He doesn't like that word.

27   SMITH: What word?

28   STONEFELTER: Sink. It gives him the willies.

29   SMITH: Well, in this case it's perfectly appropriate. What

30   kind of fools does he think we are?

31   STONEFELTER: I could make a few guesses, but stupid

32   fools comes to mind as a likely kind for anyone who would

33   not finance Marty Bentley. He's always been a good risk

34   for us. I've loaned him money many times. He's well

35   insured and always has sound contracts on both ends of

1   the line.
2   SMITH: Well, I, uh —
3   STONEFELTER: I'm retiring soon, Smith, and I want to be
4   sure that the men who run this bank after me are men
5   of prudence and judgment, balanced with initiative and
6   courage.
7   SMITH: *(Beaming)* Well, thank you, sir. I try to reflect those
8   qualities at all times.
9   STONEFELTER: You're not hearing me, Smith. Anyone in
10   banking should know better than to leave that much
11   money dormant for that long. I hate to say it, but there
12   is no longer a place for you in this bank. We will give you
13   severance according to your contract, but I want you out
14   of here as soon as you can clean out your desk.
15   SMITH: *(Panicked)* But Mr. Stonefelter, be fair! How was I to
16   know you wanted us to do our own investing?
17   STONEFELTER: I wanted courage and initiative. But lacking
18   that, you could at least have taken the money across the
19   street to First National and earned three percent for us
20   in an ordinary savings account. But you just let it sit
21   there growing moss. Unthinkable.
22   SMITH: But Mr. Stonefelter —
23   STONEFELTER: Out, Smith, now! *(Exit SMITH. STONEFEL-*
24   *TER rises and strolls to MARSHA's cubicle.)*
25   MARSHA: Well, what do you think? Did your plan work?
26   STONEFELTER: Better than I could have hoped. Our test
27   confirmed what I already halfway knew. I am convinced
28   I am leaving my bank in the hands of capable men who
29   believe strongly in using well what is entrusted to them,
30   and, at the same time, I've cleared out the deadwood.
31   MARSHA: You know, I was just thinking; it may be that God
32   is looking at us all in the same way you were looking at
33   your three managers. He's entrusted us with all kinds of
34   treasures — families, friends, the earth, our jobs, our
35   homes, and even our own bodies. And he may not only

1   want us to simply use these things well, but use them
2   with a little courage and initiative.
3   STONEFELTER: There's no maybe about that, Marsha; no
4   maybe about it at all. I've often wondered if perhaps
5   someday God would like to do what I'm about to do.
6   MARSHA: What's that?
7   STONEFELTER: Have everything running like it's supposed
8   to so he can retire and go fishing. *(He pantomimes his casting*
9   *and reeling motion.)*
10   MARSHA: You can certainly take God fishing with you, but
11   if he ever retired, we'd all be in a heap of trouble.
12   *(STONEFELTER acts as if he has hooked a big one which is*
13   *pulling him Off-stage as lights fade to blackout.)*
14
15
16
17
18
19
20
21
22
23
24
25
26
27
28
29
30
31
32
33
34
35

ABOUT THE AUTHOR / ILLUSTRATOR

T. M. Williams' professional and avocational life has centered around his lifelong love of art, literature, music, drama, and theology.

Tom writes as a hobby and had dozens of published magazine articles and one book to his credit before he wrote his first plays to meet the needs of a church youth group.

As owner of a design and illustration studio, Tom designed or illustrated over 1,500 book covers for most of the major Christian publishers. He is currently the art director for Word Publishing. Among his many honors is the 1993 Best Book Jacket Design award from the Christian Booksellers Association. His portrait of C. S. Lewis hangs in the Wade Collection in Wheaton College's library.

Tom and his wife Faye have three married daughters and six grandchildren. They reside in Texas (which eminently qualified him to write the "Texan twang" dialect key for *Joe Bob*).

This is his third published book.

ORDER FORM

MERIWETHER PUBLISHING LTD.
P.O. BOX 7710
COLORADO SPRINGS, CO 80933
TELEPHONE: (719) 594-4422

Please send me the following books:

_____ **Divine Comedies #CC-B190**	$12.95
by T. M. Williams	
A collection of plays for church drama groups	
_____ **Don't Give Up the Script #CC-B204**	$12.95
by Robert A. Allen	
Writing original sketches for the church	
_____ **Sermons Alive #CC-B132**	$12.95
by Paul Neale Lessard	
52 dramatic sketches for worship services	
_____ **Get a Grip! #CC-B128**	$10.95
by L. G. Enscoe and Annie Enscoe	
Contemporary scenes and monologs for Christian teens	
_____ **The Best of Jeremiah People #CC-B117**	$14.95
by Jim Custer and Bob Hoose	
Humorous skits and sketches by leading Christian repertory group	
_____ **Fool of the Kingdom #CC-B202**	$12.95
by Philip D. Noble	
How to be an effective clown minister	
_____ **Teaching With Bible Games #CC-B108**	$10.95
by Ed Dunlop	
20 "kid-tested" contests for Christian education	

These and other fine Meriwether Publishing books are available at
your local Christian bookstore or direct from the publisher. Use
the handy order form on this page.

NAME: _____

ORGANIZATION NAME: _____

ADDRESS: _____

CITY: _____ STATE: _____

ZIP: _____ PHONE: _____

❑ **Check Enclosed**
❑ **Visa or MasterCard #** _____

Signature: _____   *Expiration Date:* _____
         (required for Visa/MasterCard orders)

COLORADO RESIDENTS: Please add 3% sales tax.
SHIPPING: Include $2.75 for the first book and 50¢ for each additional book ordered.

❑ *Please send me a copy of your complete catalog of books and plays.*